First World War
and Army of Occupation
War Diary
France, Belgium and Germany

3 DIVISION
9 Infantry Brigade
King's (Liverpool Regiment) 10th and 13th Battalions
and Lincolnshire Regiment 1st Battalion
4 August 1914 - 31 October 1915

WO95/1429

The Naval & Military Press Ltd
www.nmarchive.com
Published in association with The National Archives

Published by

The Naval & Military Press Ltd

Unit 10 Ridgewood Industrial Park,

Uckfield, East Sussex,

TN22 5QE England

Tel: +44 (0) 1825 749494

www.naval-military-press.com

www.nmarchive.com

This diary has been reprinted in facsimile from the original. Any imperfections are inevitably reproduced and the quality may fall short of modern type and cartographic standards.

© **Crown Copyright**
Images reproduced by permission of The National Archives, London, England, 2015.

Contents

Document type	Place/Title	Date From	Date To
Heading	3rd Division War Diary 10th Scottish Battn The Kings Liverpool Regt November To December 1914		
Heading	9th Infantry Bde. 3rd Division. 10th (Scottish) Battalion The King's Liverpool Regiment November 1914. Disembarked Havre 3rd November 1914.		
War Diary	Tunbridge Wells.	01/11/1914	01/11/1914
War Diary	Southampton	01/11/1914	01/11/1914
War Diary	Havre	03/11/1914	04/11/1914
War Diary	Train Journey	04/11/1914	04/11/1914
War Diary	Stomer	05/11/1914	05/11/1914
War Diary	Blendecques	06/11/1914	06/11/1914
War Diary	Stomer	17/11/1914	17/11/1914
War Diary	Blendecques	20/11/1914	20/11/1914
War Diary	Hazebrouck	21/11/1914	21/11/1914
War Diary	Bailleul	21/11/1914	25/11/1914
War Diary	Westoutre	25/11/1914	30/11/1914
Heading	9th Infantry Bde. 3rd Division. 10th (Scottish) Battalion. The King's Liverpool Regiment. December 1914		
War Diary	Westoutre	01/12/1914	06/12/1914
War Diary	Locre	09/12/1914	12/12/1914
War Diary	Westoutre.	15/12/1914	15/12/1914
War Diary	Locre	21/12/1914	24/12/1914
Heading	3rd Division 9th Infantry Brigade 10th Kings Liverpool Regt From 1st January To 31st December 1915 To 55 Div 166 Bde.		
Heading	9th Bde. 3rd Div. War Diary 10th (King's) Liverpool Regt. January 1915		
Miscellaneous	On His Majesty's Service.		
War Diary	Locre	31/12/1914	24/01/1915
Heading	9th Bde. 3rd Div. War Diary 10th (King's) Liverpool Regt. February 1915		
Miscellaneous	On His Majesty's Service.		
War Diary	Locre.	01/02/1915	22/02/1915
War Diary	Westoutre	28/02/1915	28/02/1915
Heading	9th Bde. 3rd Div. War Diary 10th (King's) Liverpool Regt. March 1915		
Miscellaneous	On His Majesty's Service.		
War Diary	S.E.	10/03/1915	10/03/1915
War Diary	Vlamertinghe	26/03/1915	26/03/1915
Heading	9th Bde. 3rd Div. War Diary 10th King's (Liverpool) Regt. April 1915		
Miscellaneous	On His Majesty's Service.		
War Diary		04/04/1915	04/04/1915
Heading	9th Bde. 3rd Div. War Diary 10th King's (Liverpool) Regt. May 1915		
Miscellaneous	On His Majesty's Service.		
War Diary	Dickebusch.	00/05/1915	00/05/1915
Heading	9th Bde. 3rd Div. War Diary 10th King's (Liverpool) Regt. June 1915		
Miscellaneous	On His Majesty's Service.		

Heading	3rd Division 10th Liverpool (Scottish) Vol VII 2-30.6.15.		
War Diary			
Miscellaneous	Liverpool Scottish at Bellewarde.	16/01/1929	16/01/1929
Heading	9th Bde. 3rd Div. War Diary 10th (King's) Liverpool Regt. July 1915		
Miscellaneous	On His Majesty's Service.		
War Diary		00/07/1915	00/07/1915
Heading	9th Bde. 3rd Div. War Diary 10th (King's) Liverpool Regt. August 1915		
Miscellaneous	On His Majesty's Service.		
War Diary		00/08/1915	00/08/1915
Heading	9th Bde. 3rd Div. War Diary 10th (King's) Liverpool Regt. September 1915		
Miscellaneous	On His Majesty's Service.		
War Diary		00/09/1915	00/09/1915
Heading	9th Bde. 3rd Div. War Diary 10th (King's) Liverpool Regt. October 1915		
Miscellaneous	On His Majesty's Service.		
War Diary		00/10/1915	00/10/1915
Heading	9th Bde. 3rd Div. War Diary 10th (King's) Liverpool Regt. November 1915		
Miscellaneous	On His Majesty's Service.		
War Diary		00/11/1915	00/11/1915
Heading	9th Bde. 3rd Div. War Diary 10th (King's) Liverpool Regt. December 1915		
Miscellaneous	On His Majesty's Service.		
War Diary		00/12/1915	00/12/1915
Heading	3rd Division 9th Infy Bde 13th Battalion King's Liverpool Regt Apl-Dec 1916		
Heading	9th Brigade. 3rd Division. War Diary Battalion came from 8th Brigade 4th April 1916. 13th Battalion The King's Liverpool Regiment April 1916		
War Diary	Dickebusch	01/04/1916	02/04/1916
War Diary	E. Camp Reninghelst	03/04/1916	05/04/1916
War Diary	Bailleul	06/04/1916	29/04/1916
War Diary	Locre	29/04/1916	30/04/1916
Heading	9th Brigade. 3rd Division. War Diary 13th Battalion The King's Liverpool Regiment May 1916		
War Diary	Locre	01/05/1916	04/05/1916
War Diary	Trenches	05/05/1916	10/05/1916
War Diary	Locre	11/05/1916	12/05/1916
War Diary	Trenches	13/05/1916	16/05/1916
War Diary	Locre	17/05/1916	20/05/1916
War Diary	Trenches	21/05/1916	25/05/1916
War Diary	Meteren	26/05/1916	31/05/1916
Heading	9th Brigade 3rd Division. War Diary 13th Battalion The King's Liverpool Regiment June 1916		
War Diary	Meteren	01/06/1916	30/06/1916
Heading	9th Inf. Bde. 3rd Div. War Diary 13th Battn. The King's (Liverpool Regiment). July 1916		
Miscellaneous	For Reports By O.C. 13/King's (Liverpool Regiment) On Operations Of 13/14th July and 23/24th July, see War Diary of Headquarters, 9th Infantry Brigade for July 1916		
War Diary		01/07/1916	31/07/1916

Heading	9th Brigade. 3rd Division. War Diary 13th Battalion The King's Liverpool Regiment August 1916 Attached:- Report On Operations 15th-20th August.		
War Diary	Ville Sur Ancre	01/08/1916	11/08/1916
War Diary	Sandpits	11/08/1916	31/08/1916
Miscellaneous	Report on the Operation be the 15th & 20th August 1916 in Which the 13th King's (Liverpool) Regt Were engaged	22/08/1916	22/08/1916
Heading	9th Brigade. 3rd Division War Diary 13th Battalion The King's Liverpool Regiment September 1916.		
War Diary	Marles Les Mines	01/09/1916	02/09/1916
War Diary	Maringarbe	03/09/1916	23/09/1916
War Diary	Erny St Julien	24/09/1916	30/09/1916
Heading	9th Brigade. 3rd Division. War Diary 13th Battalion The King's Liverpool Regiment October 1916		
War Diary	Erny St Julien	01/10/1916	31/10/1916
Heading	9th Brigade. 3rd Division. War Diary 13th Battalion The King's Liverpool Regiment November 1916		
War Diary	Lovencourt	01/11/1916	30/11/1916
Heading	9th Brigade. 3rd Division. War Diary 13th Battalion The King's Liverpool Regiment December 1916		
War Diary	Bus	01/12/1916	04/12/1916
War Diary	Courcelles	05/12/1916	13/12/1916
War Diary	Bus	14/12/1916	21/12/1916
War Diary	Courcelles	22/12/1916	29/12/1916
War Diary	Bus	30/12/1916	31/12/1916
Heading	3rd Division War Diary 13th King Liverpool Regt January To 31 December 1914		
War Diary	Bus	01/01/1917	07/01/1917
War Diary	Terramesnil	08/01/1917	08/01/1917
War Diary	Bonneville	09/01/1917	31/01/1917
War Diary	Ourton	01/02/1917	08/02/1917
War Diary	Magnicourt Sur Canche	09/02/1917	11/02/1917
War Diary	Houvin Houvigneul	12/02/1917	28/02/1917
War Diary	Denier	01/03/1917	17/03/1917
War Diary	Arras	18/03/1917	21/04/1917
War Diary	Duisans	22/04/1917	28/04/1917
War Diary	Arras	29/04/1917	06/05/1917
War Diary	Field	07/05/1917	21/05/1917
War Diary	Beaufort	22/05/1917	31/05/1917
War Diary	Arras	01/06/1917	07/06/1917
War Diary	Field	08/06/1917	19/06/1917
War Diary	Arras	20/06/1917	30/06/1917
War Diary	Achiet Le Petit	01/07/1917	01/07/1917
War Diary	Beugny	02/07/1917	02/07/1917
War Diary	Field	03/07/1917	22/07/1917
War Diary	Velu	23/07/1917	31/07/1917
War Diary	Demicourt	01/08/1917	07/08/1917
War Diary	Field	08/08/1917	31/08/1917
War Diary	Agnicourt	01/09/1917	21/09/1917
War Diary	Brandhoek	22/09/1917	22/09/1917
War Diary	Line	23/09/1917	30/09/1917
Miscellaneous			
War Diary		11/10/1917	31/10/1917
War Diary	Beugnatre	01/11/1917	30/11/1917
War Diary	Lagnicourt	01/12/1917	31/12/1917

Heading	3rd Division 9th Infy Bde 13th (S) Battalion King's (Liverpool) Regt. 1918 Jan-1919 Mar To 3 Northern Bde 3 Div		
War Diary	Mercatel	01/01/1918	31/01/1918
War Diary	Field	01/02/1918	28/02/1918
Heading	Minor Operation Enemy Raid S.W Of Cherisy on 13 L'Pool R, 9th Bde 3rd Div 16/2/18.		
Miscellaneous	G.S. 10/31.		
Miscellaneous	3rd Division. "G".	16/02/1916	16/02/1916
Miscellaneous	Report on enemy raid-(2nd report)	16/02/1918	16/02/1918
Map			
War Diary	Field	01/03/1918	31/03/1918
Heading	9th Bde. 3rd Div. War Diary 13th Battalion The King's Liverpool Regiment April 1918 Attached-Report on Operations 10th to 20th April 1918		
War Diary	Ivergny	01/04/1918	10/04/1918
War Diary	Field	10/04/1918	20/04/1918
War Diary	Annezin	21/04/1918	30/04/1918
Miscellaneous	13th The Kings Regt		
Miscellaneous	Account of the part taken by 13th Bn the King's Regiment in the Operation from 10th 20th April.	10/04/1918	10/04/1918
Map	Message 170 14/4/18 Regt Map Gorre 1/40000.	15/04/1918	15/04/1918
Miscellaneous	Report of action taken by P.E.K in the Operation from Apl 10th to Apl 20th.	24/04/1918	24/04/1918
War Diary	Annezin	01/05/1918	31/05/1918
War Diary	Chocques	01/06/1918	01/09/1918
War Diary	Ecoust	01/09/1918	30/09/1918
War Diary	Ribecourt	01/10/1918	31/10/1918
Miscellaneous	13th. Bn The King's Report On Operations.	11/10/1918	11/10/1918
Miscellaneous	13th. Battalion The King's		
Miscellaneous	Conclusion.	27/10/1918	27/10/1918
War Diary	Catteniers	01/11/1918	30/11/1918
War Diary	Sovet	01/12/1918	31/12/1918
War Diary	Kerpen	01/01/1919	20/02/1919
War Diary	Ehrenfeld	21/02/1919	26/02/1919
War Diary	Beuel	27/02/1919	31/03/1919
Heading	3rd Division 9th Infantry Brigade 1st Lincolnshire From 1st January to 30th June 1915		
Heading	9th Bde. 3rd Div. War Diary 1st Lincolnshires January 1915		
Miscellaneous	On His Majesty's Service.		
Heading	9th Brigade 1st Bde Lincolns Vol VI 1-31.1.15		
War Diary		01/01/1915	31/01/1915
Heading	9th Bde. 3rd Div. War Diary 1st Lincolnshires February 1915		
Miscellaneous	On His Majesty's Service.		
Heading	9th Brigade 1st Lincolns Vol VII 1-28.2.15.		
War Diary		01/02/1915	28/02/1915
Heading	9th Bde. 3rd Div. War Diary 1st Lincolnshires March 1915		
Miscellaneous	On His Majesty's Service.		
Heading	9th Brigade 1st Lincolns Vol VIII 1-31.3.15		
War Diary		01/03/1915	31/03/1915
Heading	9th Bde. 3rd Div. War Diary 1st Lincolnshires. April 1915		
Miscellaneous	On His Majesty's Service.		

War Diary		01/04/1915	30/04/1915
Heading	9th Bde. 3rd Div. War Diary 1st Lincolnshires May 1915		
Miscellaneous	On His Majesty's Service.		
War Diary		01/05/1915	31/05/1915
Heading	9th Bde. 3rd Div. War Diary 1st Lincolnshires June 1915		
Miscellaneous	On His Majesty's Service.		
War Diary		01/06/1915	30/06/1915
War Diary		19/06/1915	30/06/1915
Miscellaneous	1st Bn. Lincolnshire Regt. Operation Orders by Major H.E.R. Boxer, Commanding. 3/6/15.		
Diagram etc	Reference Zillebeke Sheet 1/10,000		
Heading	3rd Division War Diary 1st Battn Lincolnshire Regt August To December 1914		
Heading	9th Brigade 3rd Division. Disembarked Havre 14.8.14 1st Battalion Lincolnshire Regiment August 1914		
War Diary	Portsmouth	04/08/1914	13/08/1914
War Diary	Havre	14/08/1914	14/08/1914
War Diary	Harfleur Farm Rest Camp	15/08/1914	15/08/1914
War Diary	Harve	16/08/1914	16/08/1914
War Diary	Landrecies	17/08/1914	17/08/1914
War Diary	Noyelles	18/08/1914	21/08/1914
War Diary	Longueville	22/08/1914	22/08/1914
War Diary	Mons	23/08/1914	23/08/1914
War Diary	Frameries	24/08/1914	24/08/1914
War Diary	Inchey	25/08/1914	27/08/1914
War Diary	Noyan	28/08/1914	29/08/1914
War Diary	Ressons	30/08/1914	31/08/1914
Miscellaneous		11/02/1918	11/02/1918
Heading	9th Brigade. 3rd Division 1st Battalion The Lincolnshire Regiment September 1914 This diary continues until 2.10.14		
War Diary	Vauciennies	01/09/1914	21/09/1914
War Diary	Courcelles	22/09/1914	26/09/1914
War Diary	Vailly	27/09/1914	02/10/1914
Heading	9th Infantry Bde. 3rd Division 1st Battalion The Lincolnshire Regiment October 1914		
War Diary		02/10/1914	22/10/1914
War Diary	Neuve Chapelle	23/10/1914	31/10/1914
Heading	9th Infantry Bde. 3rd Division. 1st Battalion The Lincolnshire Regiment November 1914		
War Diary		01/11/1914	30/11/1914
Heading	9th Infantry Bde. 3rd Division. 1st Battalion The Lincolnshire Regiment December 1914		
War Diary		01/12/1914	31/12/1914
Heading	3rd Division 9th Infantry Brigade 1st Lincolnshires From 1 July To October 1915 To 62nd Bde 13 November 1915 21 Div 62 Bde		
Heading	9th Bde. 3rd Div. War Diary 1st Lincolnshires July 1915		
Miscellaneous	On His Majesty's Service.		
War Diary		01/07/1915	31/07/1915
Heading	9th Bde. 3rd Div. War Diary 1st Lincolnshires August 1915		
Miscellaneous	On His Majesty's Service.		

War Diary		01/08/1915	13/08/1915
War Diary	Summary		
War Diary		14/08/1915	23/08/1915
War Diary	Summary		
War Diary		24/08/1915	31/08/1915
Heading	9th Bde. 3rd Div. War Diary 1st Lincolnshires September 1915		
Miscellaneous	On His Majesty's Service.		
War Diary		01/09/1915	30/10/1915
Heading	9th Bde. 3rd Div. War Diary Battalion went to 63rd Bde., 21st Div 13.11.15. 1st Lincolnshires October 1915		
Miscellaneous	On His Majesty's Service.		
War Diary		01/10/1915	31/10/1915

2nd Division
War Diaries
10th Scottish Battn.
The Kings Liverpool Regt.
November & December
1914

9th Infantry Bde.
3rd Division.

10th (SCOTTISH) BATTALION

THE KING'S LIVERPOOL REGIMENT

NOVEMBER 1914.

Disembarked Havre 3rd November 1914.

Army Form C. 2118.

WAR DIARY
or
INTELLIGENCE SUMMARY

(Erase heading not required.) 10th (SCOTTISH) Bn. THE KING'S (L'POOL REGT.)

Instructions regarding War Diaries and Intelligence Summaries are contained in F. S. Regs, Part II. and the Staff Manual respectively. Title pages will be prepared in manuscript.

Hour, Date, Place	Summary of Events and Information	Remarks and references to Appendices
Tunbridge Wells, 1st Novr 1914	Battn entrained for Southampton, Right Half Bn at 9-30 am, left half Bn at 10-30 am. Arrived Southampton at 3 & 4 pm respectively and Embarked on s/s/ Maidan	10/8/77
Southampton. 1st Novr 1914 8 pm	Sailed per s/s/ Maidan for Havre, arrived in the Bay 7 am on the 2nd inst, steamer kept in Bay until 10 pm on the 2nd inst.	
Havre 3rd Novr 1914 8 am	Disembarked. marched to No I Rest Camp.	
Havre 4th Novr 1914 2 pm	Marched out from No I Rest Camp. Entrained & left Havre for St Omer at 6-55 pm.	
TRAIN JOURNEY	arrived Rouen midnight 4-11-14	
	left — do — 3 am 5-11-14	
	arrived Blangy 8-15 am 5-11-14	
	— do — 8-45 am 5-11-14	
	arrived EU 10-15 am 5-11-14	
	left EU 10-55 am 5-11-14	
	arrived ABBEVILLE 12-25 pm 5-11-14	
	left do 1-25 pm 5-11-14	
	arrived Calais 6-30 pm 5-11-14	
	left — do — 6-45 pm 5-11-14	
	arrived ST OMER 9-45 pm 5-11-14	
STOMER 11-30 pm 5/11/14	Left station for march to BLENDECQUES	
BLENDECQUES. 1 am 6/11/14	Arrived BLENDECQUES. Battn went into Billets.	

Army Form C. 2118.

WAR DIARY
or
INTELLIGENCE SUMMARY

(Erase heading not required.)

10th (SCOTTISH) BN. THE KING'S (L'POOL REGT.)

Instructions regarding War Diaries and Intelligence Summaries are contained in F. S. Regs., Part II. and the Staff Manual respectively. Title pages will be prepared in manuscript.

Hour, Date, Place	Summary of Events and Information	Remarks and references to Appendices
STOMER 17.11.14	The Battn lined the Route for Funeral Procession of the late Field Marshal Lord Roberts. 1 Officer & 30 men took part in Procession	
BLENDECQUES 20.11.14	LEFT by Road for BAILLEUL via Hazebrouck at which place the Battn billeted for the night	
Hazebrouck 21.11.14	LEFT at 10 am by Road for Bailleul	
Bailleul 21.11.14 4pm	Arrived Bailleul & went into Billets	
Bailleul 25/11/14	Battn left Bailleul at 8.30 am for Westoutre being inspected by the G.O.C. 2nd Army Corps General Sir H Smith Dorrien & The Prince of Wales	
Westoutre 25/11/14	arrived at 2 pm. Posted 9th Bde (1st Reserve) 3rd Div 2nd Corps	

WAR DIARY or INTELLIGENCE SUMMARY

Army Form C. 2118.

10th (SCOTTISH) BN. THE KING'S (L'POOL REGT.)

Hour, Date, Place	Summary of Events and Information	Remarks and references to Appendices

Westoutre, 27th November 1914, 4pm

9th Brigade left Westoutre at 4pm for the trenches East of Mt Kemmel, where the Brigade relieved the 5th Brigade the relief being carried out under cover of darkness and being completed by 10pm. The line to the left of the Brigade being continued by the R.S. French.

The Battn provided 150 men for the firing line [3 Platoons of no 3 Coy under Capt Twentyman] 100 men in support [Platoon no 3 & 1 Platoon no 1 Coy under Capt McLeod] 85 men [1s no 4 Coy] in Reserve [under Left Harrison]. The 1st Lincolns being on the left of the line. 5th Fusiliers being next then came the L'pool Scottish with the 4th Royal Fusiliers on the right. The Remaining Bn attn of the Brigade 1st R.S. & 1st Argyll Highlanders were in Brigade Reserve being billeted at Locre.

The Battn relieved the 2nd Batn South Wales Regt on the night of the 30th when the Brigade marched back to Westoutre arriving there at 3am 1/12/14 & going into Billets.

The trenches occupied for 3 days by portion of the Battn were without communication trenches. On the right the firing trench was within 40 yards of an advanced German trench. On the left the distance was about 200 yards.

Army Form C. 21

WAR DIARY
or
INTELLIGENCE SUMMARY

19th (SCOT (ISH) Bn. THE KING'S (L'POOL REGT).

(Erase heading not required.)

Instructions regarding War Diaries and Intelligence Summaries are contained in F. S. Regs., Part II. and the Staff Manual respectively. Title pages will be prepared in manuscript.

Hour, Date, Place	Summary of Events and Information	Remarks and references to Appendices
29th & 30th	During the period of occupation the enemy's snipers were active and it was whilst returning to the trenches on the 29th with a bomb to use against a sniper that under the parapet that Capt Twentyman was hit dying almost immediately. The Germans infantry advanced against our trench on the 2nd & 3rd nights but on each occasion the attack was beaten back by rifle fire.	Casualties 27/30 Nov Capt A Twentyman killed 29/11/14 1 Private slightly wounded no 3399 W Palin A Coy 30/11/14

10/15

9th Infantry Bde.
3rd Division.

10th (SCOTTISH) BATTALION,

THE KING'S LIVERPOOL REGIMENT.

DECEMBER, 1914

WAR DIARY
or
INTELLIGENCE SUMMARY.
(Erase heading not required.)

Army Form C. 2118.

Place	Date	Hour	Summary of Events and Information	Remarks and references to Appendices
Westoutre	1/12/14	3 am	Arrived in Billets & remained until 3 pm on the 6th December	
Westoutre	6/12/14	3 pm	9th Brigade proceeded to Kemmel to relieve the 7th Brigade. Casualties 6/9 Dec. The H.A.C. with [?] relieving the H.A.C. no 1 Company occupied the firing trench nos 2 & 4 Company being kept in support. no 3 Company under Corpl McDonell was kept in reserve until the night of the 8th Dec. when they went up to support the Lincolns who were attacking. We lost 2 German & Gentlemen. Our losses on this occasion were 2 killed and 6 wounded. The Battn was relieved on the night of the 9th Dec by the H.A.C. proceeded to Billets at LOCRE. Arrived in Billets & Dug Outs at LOCRE.	Killed 2379 Pte E.P.Breckenridge Fcoy 9/12/14 2740 – 2 Netherceft FCoy 9/12/14 Wounded No 3376 Pte B Meder A coy 7/12/14 1490 Sgt B.Ker C coy 6/12/14 3655 Pte C London E coy 6/12/14 2177 Sgt C Kittler Fcoy 9/12/14 2566 Pte McGuire Fcoy 9/12/14 2798 WDF Godan FCoy 9/12/14
LOCRE	9/12/14	9 pm		

Army Form C. 2118.

WAR DIARY or INTELLIGENCE SUMMARY

(Erase heading not required.)

10th (SCOTTISH) Bn. THE KING'S (LPOOL REGT.)

Instructions regarding War Diaries and Intelligence Summaries are contained in F. S. Regs., Part II. and the Staff Manual respectively. Title pages will be prepared in manuscript.

Hour, Date, Place	Summary of Events and Information	Remarks and references to Appendices
LOCRE. 12th Dec 1914	The 9th Brigade proceeded to KEMMEL to relieve 7th Brigade. The Battn taking over the section held by the Lincolns. No 2 Coy under Capt D Erskine & No 4 Coy under Capt Lockhart being in the first line. No 1 Coy under Capt Anderson in support and No 3 Coy under Capt McLeod in Reserve. The 5th Lancers being on our right, the French continuing the line to the left. At this point a wood held by the Germans, the Petit Bois was only 70 yards from our front line of trenches. On the morning of the 14th an attack was made on the German trenches by the 8th Brigade which simultaneously the French 3rd Division moved up at 3 am. Simultaneously by the Artillery of the 3rd, 4th & 5th gun attacked on our left. This attack was supported by the Artillery of the 3rd, 4th & 5th Divisions. The Royal Scots & Gordons who carried out this attack both lost rather heavily, but succeeded in taking several German trenches. During this engagement the Battn with the 9th Brigade were held in reserve whilst the engineers of Platoons under Lieut Turner & Lieut Gemmell, and the Machine Gun Section under Lieut Kennedy reinforced the firing line. On the 15th the 9th Brigade were withdrawn to Westoutre. Our casualties on this occasion were 1 officer & 4 men wounded.	wounded 1+4 3198 Pte Am Boyle 15/12/14 7586 - Pte McKenzie 15/12/14 Capt D McLeod 15/12/14 7696 Pte WR Davey 13/12/14 3397 - L/S Peen 13/12/14 3761 - Pte Brooking 13/12/14 7870 - F.C. Hopwood 14/12/14

Westoutre 11 Dec – 15 Dec

WAR DIARY or INTELLIGENCE SUMMARY

Army Form C. 2118.

(Erase heading not required.)

Hour, Date, Place	Summary of Events and Information	Remarks and references to Appendices
LOCRE pm 21/12/14	The 9th Brigade from being in Reserve at LOCRE went into the trenches in relief of the 7th Brigade the Battn taking over the left Sector held by the Middlesex Regt. This Section included an advance trench taken from the Germans by the Royal Irish, forming part of the Wytschaete Position whilst occupying this trench the B attn lost 5 killed & 10 wounded. These casualties occurred in Nos 2 & 3 Coys. The 5th & 7th were taken over this section on the night of the 23rd Dec. Our Battn going into Billets at Kemmel. On the evening of the 24th the 9th Brigade were relieved & returned to Billets at LOCRE	Casualties 21/4 Dec. Killed 6 3480 L/Cpl Alvarez Eary 22/12/14 7933 Pte A Cluine Eary 22/12/14 1585 — 9 Jamm F — 22/12/14 1115 L/Cpl G Thompson F 22/12/14 3487 Pte G Ward C — 22/12/14 No 7184 Pte E Rowlinson 26.12.14 E Coy died of wounds Wounded 3165 Pte A Forbes E Coy 21/12/14 ...
LOCRE 24/12/14 9am	arrived in Bivouac after the march from the night of the 24th to 9a Brigade to Reserve into Bivouac at LOCRE	

(31)

E. James Capt
Liverpool Scottish

3rd Division

9th Infantry Brigade

10th Kings Liverpool Regt.

From 1st January To 31st December

1915

To 55 DIV, 166 BDE

9th Bde.
3rd Div.

WAR DIARY

10th (KING'S) LIVERPOOL REGT.

January

1915

3.

On His Majesty's Service.

Army Form C. 2118.

WAR DIARY or INTELLIGENCE SUMMARY

10th (SCOTTISH) BN. THE KING'S (L'POOL REGT.)

(Erase heading not required.)

Instructions regarding War Diaries and Intelligence Summaries are contained in F. S. Regs., Part II. and the Staff Manual respectively. Title pages will be prepared in manuscript.

Hour, Date, Place	Summary of Events and Information	Remarks and references to Appendices
LOCRE 4pm 31.12.14	Battn left for KEMMEL being billeted there until the evening of the 4th January 1915. During this period the Battn was in Reserve. Working parties were engaged improving trenches &c. under R.E. supervision.	
LOCRE 10pm 4/1/15	Battn arrived in Bisseto, remaining until the afternoon of 8th Jany. when the 9th Brigade marched from their billets at force of 8th over the KEMMEL line of trenches from the 7th Brigade the 8th Infantry Brigade who had taken over from the French continuing the line on our left.	Casualties Killed in action Lieut Turner 10.1.15 No 3504 Pte H Wills 9.1.15 1758 6 Cpl M Mack do
LOCRE 4pm 8.1.15	The Scottish relieved the 3rd Bn Worcestershire Regt in sections F 4 & 5 and G 1. The rain had been very heavy and the trenches were in very bad condition. The fighting strength of the Battn was reduced to 35. All ranks of these 150 Rifles & machine guns were required to man the front line & support trenches. Brigades hours being 4 days in and four days out of the trenches. During this turn the usual artillery duel continued & exchange of fire between the opposing infantry. On the morning of the 10th inst Lieut Turner was shot through the head in F 4 and killed instantly. On the evening of the 12th inst the 7th Brigade was again came up in relief and the Battn was relieved by the 3rd Worcesters.	
LOCRE 10pm 12/1/15	Battn arrived in Billets	

Army Form C. 2118

WAR DIARY
INTELLIGENCE SUMMARY

(Erase heading not required.)

10TH (SCOTTISH) BN. THE KING'S (L'POOL REGT.)

Hour, Date, Place	Summary of Events and Information	Remarks and references to Appendices
16-1-15	The 9th Brigade relieved the 7th Brigade in the trenches on the evening of the 16th Jany. the Battn again taking over the Section held by the 3rd Worcesters, the Royal Fusiliers being on our right, the Lincolns on the left on the 17th Jany. Artillery fire continued on both sides throughout the greater part of the day, about 11·30 am two of our own shrapnel burst line behind & 5 wounding four of our men. During the day the enemy's shells did a great deal of damage to our front trench knocking down the parapet in several places, but luckily only wounding one man. On the 18th the weather turned very cold with frequent heavy falls of snow, at dusk the front trenches were relieved & fur coats were issued to the relieving party. On the 20th the Battn was again relieved by the 3rd Worcesters & returned to billets at LOCRE	Casualties Killed in action 2708 Pte J.S. Wallace 19·1·15 Died of Wounds 3158 Pte P.G. Boyd 21/1/15 Wounded 3351 Pte Hw Munroe 17/1/15 3367 " I.B. Neil do 2893 " P.W. Clarke do 3157 " T. Ellison do 1815 Sgt J.H. Owens do

WAR DIARY

INTELLIGENCE SUMMARY

(10th (SCOTTISH) Bn. THE KING'S (L'POOL REGT.))

Army Form C. 2118

(Erase heading not required.)

Hour, Date, Place	Summary of Events and Information	Remarks and references to Appendices
24·1·15	The Battn returned to the trenches on the night of the 24th this time being given G Section which was taken over from the R.I.R. The R.S.F. being on our right the 5th Fusiliers on the left. 150 Rifles & two machine guns were in the front line, 50 men in support (S4) the remaining coys with Bn H.Q being in two farms some 500 yards behind the firing line both farms being in full view of the German trenches and subject to shell fire, which made it necessary for the men to remain under cover during the day. On the morning of the 25th the supporting point S4 & Bn Hdqrs were shelled, a heavy shell falling within 20 yards of Bn Hdqrs at 6 p.m. Lieut Kendall who was killed in G. by a rifle bullet. On the 26th the shelling was again continued three shells hitting S4 but fortunately no casualties occurred. In the early morning of 27th Sergt Sleeper was wounded returning from Bn Hdqrs to Kennel. On the 28th the R.I.R. relieved us the Bn returning to the same billets as previously occupied at LOCRE.	**Casualties** Killed in action Lieut P.B. Kendall 25·1·15 Pte G.B. Pollerfere 26·1·15 Wounded 3195 Pte T Atherton 29·1·15 3192 ‑ J Armatong 29·1·15 1515 Sgt W H Sleeper 29·1·15

LIEUT. COLONEL
THE 10TH (SCOTTISH) BN. THE KING'S (L'POOL REGT.)

9th Bde.
3rd Div.

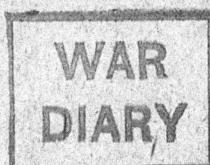

10th (KING'S) LIVERPOOL REGT.

February

1915

On His Majesty's Service.

Army Form C. 2118.

WAR DIARY
INTELLIGENCE SUMMARY
(Erase heading not required.)

Hour, Date, Place	Summary of Events and Information	Remarks and references to Appendices
1/2/15 pm LOCRE	From the night of the 1st to the evening of the 5th & by the Battn were again in the trenches this time occupying H. Section in the KEMMEL AREA, the Battalion Headquarters being at ALSTON HOUSE. During this period the support dugouts were shelled daily by the enemy. On the evening of the 5th inst the Battn was relieved by the Royal Irish R and returned to Billets in LOCRE	Casualties Killed in action 3772 Pte J.C. Frazer 4/2/15 wounded 2954 Pte J.H. Williamson 5/2/15 3795 - O.S. Barker 4/2/15 3074 - J. Hallewell 2/2/15 3190 - G. Armstrong 4/2/15 4011 - W.P. Read 4/2/15
9/2/15 pm LOCRE	On the evening of the 9th inst the Battalion returned to the trenches and took over H Section from the R.I.R. who again # relieved the Battn on the evening of the 13th. The 9th Brigade was therefore (Purtish returned to Billets at LOCRE, it being the turn of this Battn to go back to Westoutre. On the 15th Feby, the 9th Brigade received orders to move at short notice to YPRES and take the place of the 85th Infantry Brigade 28th Divn This Battn received orders to follow but on the 20th Feby the Cpool in which were transferred to the 85th Brigade who took to the place of the 9th Brigade in the 3rd Divn. [The 85th Brigade Consisted of the following Regts from INDIA. East Kent, Middlesex East Surreys, Royal Fusileers together with the H.A.C. & the Cpool invested.]	Casualties Killed in action 3517 Cann Cpl S.S. Ashmus 10/2/15 wounded 3167 Pte a. Weatherhead 10/2/15 3377 - H. McAuley 12/2/15 3653 - J. Carr 10/2/15 2720 - Cpl A. Proudfoot 11/2/15 2662 - R. Hayes 11/2/15

WAR DIARY or INTELLIGENCE SUMMARY

Army Form C. 2118.

(Erase heading not required.)

Hour, Date, Place	Summary of Events and Information	Remarks and references to Appendices
	On leaving the 9th Brigade the following Special Order was published by Brig. General W. W. Douglas C.M.G.	
	"The O.C. 9th Infy Brigade hears with great regret that the 10th (Scottish) Bn the King's (L'pool Regt) is leaving his Command. He would like it placed on record, that the Battn since it joined this Brigade has thoroughly a most trying time in the trenches, carried out its duties in a most efficient manner, and he has nothing but praise to bestow for the hard work it has done and the cheerful spirit in which that work has been conducted. He wishes Lt Col Davidson and all ranks success, and he feels sure that the Battn will always maintain its present reputation for good discipline and fine soldierly qualities.	
27/7/15	On the 2nd & 3rd Feby the 85th Bgde took over the KEMMEL trenches from the 7th Brigade	Casualties 5 Killed in action 3046. Cpl J.C.T. Hadet 24/2/15 3703 Pte W.H. Steel do 464 Pte G.H. Millar 25/2/15 1063 Pte John S.P. Hood 26/2/15 Wounded 1986 Pte W. Rogerson 6 Cambridge do Pte Brennan do
	This Battn underwent taking G section the H.A.C. who had been sent to 85th Brigade being on our right. The 7th Bgde relieved the 85th Bgde on the evening of the 7 Feby, the Battn returning to WESTOUTRE	

P. James CAPT.
ADJUTANT 10TH (SCOTTISH) Bn THE KING'S (L'POOL REGT.)

WAR DIARY
or
INTELLIGENCE SUMMARY
(Erase heading not required.)

Army Form C. 2118.

Hour, Date, Place	Summary of Events and Information	Remarks and references to Appendices
WESTOUTRE 28/7/15.	On the 28th July orders were received for the Liverpool Scottish to rejoin the 9th Infantry Brigade at YPRES. On the 2nd March the Battn marched from WESTOUTRE to VLAMERTINGHE and billeted in various farms south of that place. The 9th Brigade now formed part of 28th Divn 5th Corps. On leaving 3rd Division the G.O.C. wrote the following letter to head of we 9/R Davidson Commanding the Battn. "I wished to have liked to see the Liverpool Scottish and shew them this morrow a furewell which I shure would have proved only to be temporary before they left to rejoin the 9th Brigade. Unfortunately I could not manage it as I was obliged to inspect two Battalions and drafts at LOCRE at the same time as you were starting from WESTOUTRE. I wish to thank you for all the excellent service which you have performed during the three months you have been with the 3rd Divn. To part with so fine a Battn as yours is a grievous loss for any Division, but as I hope to have the 9th Brigade back in the Divn after they have done what is required of them where they now are, I shall look forward to having the Liverpool Scottish with me again. They have invariably done their duty in thoroughly creditable fashion and to my entire satisfaction and I feel confident that wherever they go they will maintain under your command the good reputation which they have so quickly earned in the field. With all best wishes and best of luck to you all. Sgd. A Ballard, Major General Commdg 3rd Divn.	

9th Bde.
3rd Div.

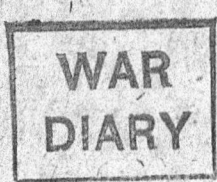

10th (KING'S) LIVERPOOL REGT.

March

1 9 1 5

On His Majesty's Service.

WAR DIARY
or
INTELLIGENCE SUMMARY
(Erase heading not required.)

Army Form C. 2118.

Hour, Date, Place	Summary of Events and Information	Remarks and references to Appendices
10th March 1915 S.E.(?)	The 9th Brigade relieved the 13th Brigade in the trenches of the ZILLEBEKE area west of YPRES on the night of the 10th March on this occasion the Bgde mustered 17 days in the trenches the boys in the front line being changed every 48 hours and returning to dug outs in immediate support or to Barracks in YPRES. Battn today were established in Dug outs some 400 yards in rear of the firing line and remained up for 12 days. On the 1st at 4:30 pm the enemy fired a succession of mines blowing up a length of trench 40 yards long on our immediate left, which was held by the Royal Fus. & which no attack followed, and during the night a new trench was made in rear. On this occasion the Officer Commanding the R.S.F. forwarded a report to Bdge in which he expressed his high appreciation of the steadiness & resource of all ranks of this Battn [Mabin Special mention of the 3/07 Pte Fleck & Wounded Shown by L/Cpl Is McKinnel and No 3427 Pte C Smith of the Maxim Gun section of No 3825 Pri L/C Bannock & L/Cpl under very trying circumstances and at a time of extreme danger] Special mention should also be made of the bravery of No 3783 X wg Aux 3783 Pioneer W to Howitt, 3718 Private Jn Wallace who at 5am on the morning Pte S g galvin of the engineering section, went out of the trenches and brought in L/Cpl of the 15th went out in front of the Engineering section who was fatally wounded and Rankine of the Engineering Section. Lieut- Gauld on hand of wire entanglements putting out wire entanglements. Lieut- Gauld on hand of our firing line. On the evening the 2nd the 15th Brigade relieved the and 1 wounded. On the evening to sluicegate Ferry in hand of 114 killed 9th Brigade & the brigade returned to billets east from the aircraft section. The 9th Brigade returned to billets this night near VLAMERTINGHE	

For CAPT.
ADJUTANT 10TH (SCOTTISH) Bn. THE KING'S (LPOOL REGT.)

Army Form C. 2118.

WAR DIARY
or
INTELLIGENCE SUMMARY

10th (SCOTTISH) BN. THE KING'S (L'POOL REGT.)

(Erase heading not required.)

Hour, Date, Place	Summary of Events and Information	Remarks and references to Appendices
26th March 1915 VLAMERTINGHE	The Battn marched from the Huts at VLAMERTINGHE to the Cavalry Barracks in YPRES taking over the Billets then occupied by the Queen Victoria Rifles (9th County of London Regt). The Brigade were holding the Right sector of the Divisional front and as then was divided for a 4 Battn holding the (Liverpool) Scottish was divided amongst the other Battns in the Brigade. A Coy was attached to the Northumberland Fusiliers, D Coy to the Lincolns and fatigue R.S.7s, while C Coy were to be retained for carrying and fatigue duties. The Royal Fusiliers being strong in numbers. The Royal Fusiliers and Lincolns held the line for the first two days the former being on the Right of the Canal and the latter on the left. B Coy went in with the Lincolns and held trench 29 on THE BLUFF known as SLAUGHTER HILL. This trench was continually shelled by the enemy. On relief A Coy held trench 28 for the N.F.s while D Coy relieved B Coy. Instead of C Coy being kept in YPRES they were put into reserve Dug-outs in rear of the BLUFF. Trenches 28 was apparently quiet except for trench mortars. During their last spell B Coy had a very bad time in 29. The enemy shelled the trench with trench mortars and the casualties were heavy.	Casualties 26th March to March 30th Officers Nil Other Ranks 9 killed 35 wounded

9th Bde.
3rd Div.

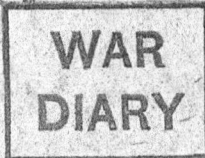

10th KING'S (Liverpool) Regt.

April

1 9 1 5

On His Majesty's Service.

WAR DIARY or INTELLIGENCE SUMMARY

10th (SCOTTISH) BN. THE KING'S (L'POOL REGT.)

Army Form C. 2118.

Hour, Date, Place	Summary of Events and Information	Remarks and references to Appendices
4th April 1915.	On the 4th of April the 85th Brigade relieved the 9th Brigade who were ordered to proceed to rejoin the III rd Division in the DICKEBUSCH area. B & D Companies relieved the W'ers of the 7th Brigade in trenches Q2 & Q3 covering ST ELOI. A & C Companies marched to DICKEBUSCH and took over huts in a wood about 3/4 of a mile in rear of the village. Transport was parked in an adjoining farm. Orderly Room established in DICKEBUSCH and Advanced Batn Headqrs at the convent in VOORMEZEELE. The Batn carried out its own relief, so that HdQrs was always forward and Lt. Col Davidson went to Hospital with influenza and Major Thin took over command. Major Anderson was left in command of two companies at DICKEBUSCH, and was well used to BHQ to deouse the C.O. On the 14th inst at about 11 p.m the enemy opened rapid fire following it with heavy shelling by whizz bangs. on our front. A platoon of A Coy went in Q2 and the remainder of A Coy in Q3. During the following the enemy fired a mine on the left of Q1 an advanced trench held by the NFs which runs from ST ELOI in front of and covering about 100 yards of Q2. On the mine blowing up Pte D McDonald (signal section) sent the S.O.S. call to "B" Battery who promptly shelled the enemy's trenches very heavily and accurately. The wires were cut immediately after.	

WAR DIARY or INTELLIGENCE SUMMARY

Army Form C. 2118

10th (SCOTTISH) BN. THE KING'S (L'POOL REGT.)

(Erase heading not required.)

Hour, Date, Place	Summary of Events and Information	Remarks and references to Appendices

All communication by telephone was now destroyed between Q2 & Q3 and between the former and H.Q. Private D.H. Thompson (Signal Section) in Q3 sent the S.O.S. Signal by lamp, getting out of the trench to do so at great personal risk as the shelling was heavy. A number of Northumberland Fusiliers who had been blown out of Q1 arrived in Q2. Capt. 2/5 L. Rae at once sent stretcher bearers out of Q1 and 15 men with spades up to Q1. All stretcher bearers and First Aid men were sent up to Q1 as quickly as possible where Capt. McKinnell organised relief work. The wounded men many of whom were buried under the debris were dug out and carried to a ruined cottage where Capt. McKinnell & Lieut. J. Guy and 2/Lt. Mc D. Guy A Coy also 2/Lt. P.A. E. Jones A Coy tendered first aid in the ruin cottage. The enemy sent bombs and grenades on the ruin but these men stuck to their work, and got all injured men dressed. The enemy were apparently unable to make any proper attack and by exceptional good fortune we suffered no casualties. The N.F.'s were reinforced and our men returned to Q2 at 5.50 A.M.

Major [Cunningham] Lieut. Col. A.S. Anable (Commanding the 1st Bn. 5th Northumberland Fusiliers) has expressed his high appreciation of the prompt action taken by the O.C. Trench Qr. (Capt. 2/5 L. Rae) on the occurrence of the mine exploding in Q1 and of the excellent work done by Capt. McKinnell only two N.C.O.'s and men and later his heard yr Stubbs and his party who at once went forward to clear the men up that position.

WAR DIARY
or
INTELLIGENCE SUMMARY

Army Form C. 2118.

10th (SCOTTISH) BN. THE KING'S (L'POOL REGT.)

(Erase heading not required.)

Hour, Date, Place	Summary of Events and Information	Remarks and references to Appendices

The Commanding Officer wishes to put on record the good work done by the men in the trenches during the night of the 14th, when the mine exploded or refused to ablow the 30 men stretcher bearers, first aid men, and signallers who were called on, responded magnificently, and their services will always be remembered in the history of the Battn.

The trenches were shelled by the enemy daily, sometimes with crumps, sometimes with Whizz bangs, and on the 16th they landed one into the left of Q close to the machine gun pit whereby 2nd Lieut V. Blackett was fatally wounded, 2nd 3716 Pte C. Blayly and 3067 Pte 2 Veitch were killed instantly, and 1667 (L.Corpl) R. Fraser machine gun section was wounded. The remainder of the month of June was devoid of any particular incident. In our immediate front but the severe fighting round YPRES was near enough to make special precautions necessary. On the occasion of the enemy using poisonous gases on the 22nd and in the north the fumes could be detected in our trenches and in VOORMEZEELE the men in the trenches complained of a smarting and watering of the eyes. YPRES was shelled for days on end with very heavy shells and the horse of them was heard clearly by all. Nearly the town have been knocked into ruins and great fires were seen every now & then.

Army Form C. 2118

WAR DIARY
or
INTELLIGENCE SUMMARY

(Erase heading not required.)

10th (SCOTTISH) BN. THE KING'S (L'POOL REGT.)

Instructions regarding War Diaries and Intelligence Summaries are contained in F. S. Regs., Part II. and the Staff Manual respectively. Title pages will be prepared in manuscript.

Hour, Date, Place	Summary of Events and Information	Remarks and references to Appendices
	During all this period the men were worked very hard. About the middle of the month we had to make dug outs in a wood between DICKEBUSCH and VOORMEZEELE called SCOTTISH WOOD and eventually the companies moved into them. Very heavy working parties were out every night and the men came to look upon their place in the trenches as a relief from the hard work of making Communication trenches to the firing line, wet duty, and much material had to be collected and carried. Throughout April the weather improved and things began to dry up a bit. There was a slight epidemic of "Flanders Flue" and a few cases of measles but on the whole the health of the Battn continued to be excellent. During the whole time Headqrs remained at the convent in VOORMEZEELE and it and SCOTTISH WOOD were gradually made more comfortable.	Casualties 4th April to 30th April 1915 Officers 1 killed 1 wounded Other Ranks 9 killed 23 wounded

Gordon Thin Major
O.C. 10TH (SCOTTISH) BN. THE KING'S (L'POOL REGT)

9th Bde.
3rd Div.

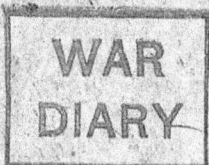

10th KING'S (Liverpool) Regt.

May

1 9 1 5

5.

On His Majesty's Service.

WAR DIARY
INTELLIGENCE SUMMARY
(Erase heading not required.)

Army Form C. 2118.

10th (SCOTTISH) BN. THE KING'S (L'POOL REGT.)

Instructions regarding War Diaries and Intelligence Summaries are contained in F.S. Regs., Part II. and the Staff Manual respectively. Title pages will be prepared in manuscript.

Hour, Date, Place	Summary of Events and Information	Remarks and references to Appendices
DICKEBUSCH May 1915	From the 1st to the 26th May the Battalion continued to hold trenches Q2 and Q3 carrying out its own reliefs from SCOTTISH WOOD. A great deal of digging and cruying was done by day and by night. On the 3rd our RE fired a small counter mine in front of Q1 blowing up successfully a German shaft. There were no developments. Every day the trenches were shelled with whizz bangs and/or humfos and the village of VOORMEZEELE came in for some practically every day. The amount of damage done was trifling. The completion of the long communication trench from the BOULEVARDS to Q3 was successfully carried out, also that from Q3 to Q2 and from Q2 to Q1 was about half done. There was also a great deal of work done in the trenches in the way of new traverses, new dug outs, new parados, improved parapet etc. While Q3 was turned into a proper fire trench. The hedge in front was thinned out and two trees were cut down, the parapet was remade, a parados was built and the work was very nearly complete when the Battn was relieved by the Queen Victoria Rifles (9th County of London).	Casualties 1st to 31st May 6 Killed 19 Wounded

Army Form C. 2118.

WAR DIARY
INTELLIGENCE SUMMARY
(Erase heading not required.)

10th (SCOTTISH) BN. THE KING'S (L'POOL REGT.)

Instructions regarding War Diaries and Intelligence Summaries are contained in F. S. Regs., Part II. and the Staff Manual respectively. Title pages will be prepared in manuscript.

Hour, Date, Place	Summary of Events and Information	Remarks and references to Appendices
	The dug outs in SCOTTISH WOOD were greatly improved and new Officers huts were built. The strain of being continually within shell range and of being within a short distance of 3 in. batteries when all the trenches made itself felt. The Officers suffered badly from a small epidemic of "Flanders Fever" with a number went to their Rest Camp. A few isolated cases of measles occurred. The reliefs were usually carried out without incident. On the night of 11th May however Regt B Coy and D Coy private H M Caskell Stretcher Bearer were killed by stray shots during the relief. The weather for the most of the time was fine and dry but about the middle of the month there were four very wet days which hindered the work greatly. On the 25th May orders came that the 13th Brigade would relieve the 9th Brigade on the 26th and the Queen Victoria Rifles relieving us. On the 26th at noon Captains Cox & Renton of that Batt were taken over the trenches and at about midnight the relief was completed. The Battalion moved to the huts in the wood behind DICKEBUSCH arriving about 2 a.m.	

WAR DIARY
INTELLIGENCE SUMMARY
(Erase heading not required.)

Army Form C. 2118.

10th (SCOTTISH) BN. THE KING'S (L'POOL REGT.)

Hour, Date, Place	Summary of Events and Information	Remarks and references to Appendices

Since taking over O₂ & O₃ on the 4th April the Commanding Officer, the Second in Command, the Adjutant, the Medical Officer & Stretcher Bearers had been continuously in VOORMEZEELE.

The night of the 27th was again spent in the DICKEBUSCH huts and at 8.30 a.m. on the 28th the Button marched off towards YPRES taking over huts from the 91st Argyll & Sutherland Highlanders just off the main POPERINGHE - YPRES road.

The following are extracts from a Special Order issued on the 26th May by Major General J.A.L. Haldane commanding 3rd Divn:—

The 3rd Divn is under orders to move into the YPRES Salient, where in the month of November it so greatly distinguished itself. At a time when practically no trenches worthy of the name existed along its front, it repulsed the attacks made upon it by the flower of the German Army including the Prussian Guard Corps.

It is once again called upon to assist in holding a portion of this important front, while the Offensive of the 1st Army and the French is in progress.

WAR DIARY

INTELLIGENCE SUMMARY

(Erase heading not required.)

Army Form C. 2118.

10th (SCOTTISH) BN. THE KING'S (L'POOL REGT.)

Hour, Date, Place	Summary of Events and Information	Remarks and references to Appendices
	At all costs the Germans must be prevented from taking YPRES. The 3rd Bn. is really now being afforded an opportunity to prove that the Treacherous methods employed by the enemy can be defeated. To do this will have a great morale effect on the British Army, and a correspondingly depressing one on the Germans. The Lincolns and ourselves were in reserve, and we shared the camp with them & the 56th Co. R.E. The remainder of the 9th Brigade had dug a line to the N.E. of Y'PRES. This place was reached about 10 a.m. on the 28th. In the evening the enemy heavily shelled with big "crumps" a wood and farm some 800 yards N.E. from the camp. On the night of the 29 & 30th practically the whole Battn. was out digging support trenches behind the Brigades line. No casualties occurred.	

Instructions regarding War Diaries and Intelligence Summaries are contained in F.S. Regs., Part II. and the Staff Manual respectively. Title pages will be prepared in manuscript.

WAR DIARY
INTELLIGENCE SUMMARY

(Erase heading not required.)

Army Form C. 2118.

10th (SCOTTISH) BN. THE KING'S (L'POOL REGT.)

Hour, Date, Place	Summary of Events and Information	Remarks and references to Appendices

On Sunday the 30th we had a good Church Parade with the Lincolns.
On our left there were a large number of French or Belgian Batteries who made a tremendous din. The enemy were not idle in the shelling line but fortunately left our camp alone. On the 31st orders came that we would be relieved by the 18th Brigade Commanded by Brigr General Arnold formerly in Command of the 1st Northumberland Fusiliers in our Brigade. At 10 p.m. the Battn marched to Camp F on the OUDERDOM - VLAMERTINGHE Road again sharing with the Lincolns.

L. Gordon Tho. Major
COMMANDING 10TH (SCOTTISH) BN. THE KING'S (L'POOL REGT.)

9th Bde.
3rd Div.

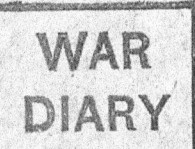

10th KING'S (Liverpool) Regt.

June

1 9 1 5

On His Majesty's Service.

107/5944

Q/
3rd Division

10th Liverpool (Scottish).

Vol VIII 2 — 30.6.15.

WAR DIARY
or
INTELLIGENCE SUMMARY
(Erase heading not required.)

Army Form C. 2118.

Hour, Date, Place	Summary of Events and Information	Remarks and references to Appendices
	On the 2nd June 1915 the 9th Brigade relieved the 83rd Brigade in trenches N of ZILLEBEKE, which had been inspected by Officers of each Battn on the previous day. Leaving E Camp on the VLAMERTINGHE-OUDERDOM Road at 6pm the Battn marched via KRUISSTRAAT, where tea was served, arriving at the trenches about midnight where we took over from the East Yorks. The trenches which were situated on the East edge of ARMAGH WOOD were well made, being very deep, and had an additional advantage in being dry. We had 470 Rifles and 4 machine guns in the fire trench, whilst a small support trench on the right was manned by 38 rifles, in addition a small garrison of 1 NCO & 19 men held a redoubt in SANCTUARY WOOD. One company of the R.S.F. in the latter wood was under the command of our C.O as Reserve. Headquarters were established in a Dug out about 30 yards behind the firing line. The 3rd & 4th June were very quiet days for the most part passed without incident, sniping was indulged in by our men on the night with some success, but unfortunately this position was open to enfilade fire	

WAR DIARY
or
INTELLIGENCE SUMMARY
(Erase heading not required.)

Army Form C. 2118.

Instructions regarding War Diaries and Intelligence Summaries are contained in F. S. Regs., Part II and the Staff Manual respectively. Title pages will be prepared in manuscript.

Hour, Date, Place	Summary of Events and Information	Remarks and references to Appendices
	from a machine gun & several casualties occurred before the traverses could be improved. On the night of the 5th the R.E. Officer in charge of mining operations blew up a small charge in an attempt to check similar operations by the enemy, the effect of his so doing was only small. Various improvements including the making of loop holes were carried out and on the night of the 16th the Brigade were relieved by the 150th Brigade, the 5th Durham Light Infantry taking over the particular section which we had occupied. The Battn marched back to VLAMERTINGHE arriving there about 4 am on the morning of the 7th. A & C Coys were billeted in A Camp & B and D Coy in D Camp. Headquarters being in a house near to the station. On Wednesday the 9th inst orders were received that the III Bn were to go back for 10 days rest & the Battn marched back to a point near to BUSSEBOOM, there encamping in a field which had been occupied by our transport for some time.	("C")

WAR DIARY
or
INTELLIGENCE SUMMARY

(Erase heading not required.)

Army Form C. 2118.

Hour, Date, Place	Summary of Events and Information	Remarks and references to Appendices
	From the 10th to the 15th June the Batn was busily engaged in training for an operation to take place on the 16th, particular attention being given to bombing. On the morning of the 12th June a composite company under Capt R.F.B. Dickinson attended a ceremonial parade near camp, when the G.O.C. III Div, General Haldane presented D C Ms to N.Cos & men of the Brigade. I wrote forward of B Coy being one of the recipients of this distinction. On the evening of the 14th June Major A.S. Anderson proceeded to RAILWAY WOOD (which is situated West of BELLEWARD farm & North of Hooge) from which point the 9th Brigade were to attack on the morning of the 16th. He took with him 2 men per company to act as markers & also 2 cyclists. At 4 pm on the afternoon of the 15th the Battn left the camping ground near Busse Boom & proceeded via YPRES to RAILWAY WOOD.	

WAR DIARY
or
INTELLIGENCE SUMMARY

(Erase heading not required.)

Army Form C. 2118.

Hour, Date, Place	Summary of Events and Information	Remarks and references to Appendices
	The attack was made on a frontage of about 100 yards, the Northumberland Royals Sots Royal & Walsers were detailed to take the first line & we in conjunction with the Lincolns were to take the 2nd line, the 7th Brigade being in Reserve. We were shelled rather heavily between 12:30 & 2:10 a.m. on the morning of the 16th & during this time several of our men were killed or wounded. Our Artillery bombardment started at 2/10 am Germans out the work of demolition so successfully that little difficulty was experienced in taking the first & second line trenches. Unfortunately however in continuing the advance we suffered many casualties owing to the difficulty experienced in obtaining signals it was impossible to keep in close ahead of the advancing infantry. Although the 3rd line German trenches were reached it was impossible to hold on to them & so the whole Brigade consolidated the 1st part of the 2nd line German trenches, Manning them until 11/30 pm on the night of the 16th	

WAR DIARY
or
INTELLIGENCE SUMMARY

(Erase heading not required.)

Army Form C. 2118.

Hour, Date, Place	Summary of Events and Information	Remarks and references to Appendices

at which hour they were relieved by the 8th Brigade.
The casualties amongst our Officers were particularly
heavy - of the 24 Officers who went up only Lieut
Wall, & Lieut J.J. Roddick & Lieut Cheverese came
back unscathed.
The work of all ranks throughout the day calls forth
the highest praise, our bombing parties doing particularly
good work.
The stretcher Bearers throughout a most trying day
did excellent work & showed great courage in attending
to so many wounded under very heavy shell fire.
The following is an extract from a special order by
Major General Haldane commanding 3rd Division published
on the 17th June.
" The Major General Commanding cannot adequately
express his admiration for the gallant manner in
which the attack was carried out yesterday.
The dash & determination of all ranks was beyond
praise, and that some actually reached the objective in
the first rush & remained there under most trying
circumstances is a proof of their superiority over the German Infantry

WAR DIARY
or
INTELLIGENCE SUMMARY

(Erase heading not required.)

Army Form C. 2118.

Hour, Date, Place	Summary of Events and Information	Remarks and references to Appendices
	that the captured ground could not all be held is disappointing, more especially as the losses incurred were heavy. But these casualties have not been in vain. The 3rd Battn carried out a fine piece of work & fought splendidly, & their commander is deeply proud of them. From the 17th to the end of the month the B attn was encamped in the same fields near Busseboom. heavy fighting was being in command, with J.G. Roddick acting Adjutant, the time being devoted to company training & Route Marching.	Leslie L. Wall LIEUT. COMMANDING 10TH (SCOTTISH) Bn THE KING'S (L'POOL REGT.)

Liverpool Scottish at
Bellewaarde.

COPY.

Tower Buildings,
22, Water Street,
LIVERPOOL.

January 16th 1929.

Ref. AM&G/BL.

Brigadier-General (Sir) J.E. Edmonds,
London.

Dear General Edmonds,

I am very much obliged to you for your letter of the 14th instant.

I know from the work which I am myself doing how difficult it is even on the limited scale of a Battalion History, to get accounts from various sources of the same action which agree with one another, and it does not require much imagination to realise how much more difficult the research work involved must be in a publication of the size and detail of the Official History of the War. I am very glad to know that in the next volume, the work of the Liverpool Scottish at Bellewaarde will be recognised. I hope you do not think I am trying to magnify their share in what was, after all, only a minor and relatively unimportant operation.

As regards casualties, our records give the number which went into action as 23 officers and 519 other ranks. Of the officers, four were killed, six missing, and eleven wounded. Of the other ranks, seventy-five were killed, one hundred and three missing, and two hundred and one wounded. All the missing officers were afterwards reported dead and, almost without exception, the same is true of the missing other ranks. It is true that our losses were exceeded by three other Battalions of the Brigade, but our numbers to begin with were very much less. Of the three officers mentioned in the War Diary as having come out unscathed, one was Captain N.G. Chavasse, the Medical Officer. Of the other two, Second Lieut. T.G. Roddick was knocked out by a shell and lay unconscious for most of the day. He was, however, able to carry on with the Battalion until the arrival of officer reinforcements. Lieut. L.G. Wall was, therefore, the only combatant officer who came through unhurt.

I should like to thank you for the facilities which you gave to Captain Philpots when he was looking up Divisional and Brigade records for me at Audit House.

Yours sincerely,

(Capt.) A.M. McGilchrist.

9th Bde.
3rd Div.

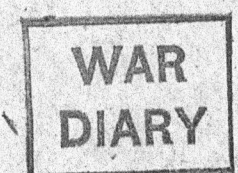

10th (KING'S) LIVERPOOL REGT.

..........July..........

1 9 1 6

On His Majesty's Service.

Army Form C. 2118.

WAR DIARY
or
INTELLIGENCE SUMMARY.
(Erase heading not required.)

Hour, Date, Place	Summary of Events and Information	Remarks and references to Appendices
JULY	During the first half of July the Battn remained encamped on field near Busseboom, training being carried out under Company arrangements. On the 2nd of the month Lieut'ys Duckworth & 2nd Lieuts K.T. Dun, J.E. Cunningham, A.J. Davidson, B. Arkle and H.B. Montgomery arrived from England. The 9th Brigade went into the trenches on the night of the 14/15th relieving the 85th Brigade, we took over trenches O3, O4 & O5 also the redoubt S8 from the East Surrey Regt, the 5th Fusiliers being on our left and the Royal Scots Fusiliers on our right. Battalion Headquarters were established with the 5th Fusiliers in Wiltshire Farm from which the fire trench was accessable by day by means of a Communication trench. Considerable work was done in improving the trenches by putting in new loopholes digging shell shelter trenches, the dug outs were also improved & knife rests were put out. On the 20th sanction was given for 40 men per day to proceed to England for special leave, this continued for 6 days which reduced the fighting strength so much that on the 31st the 5th Fusiliers took over O5 & on the 24th they also took over S8.	

WAR DIARY
INTELLIGENCE SUMMARY.
(Erase heading not required.)

Army Form C. 2118.

Hour, Date, Place	Summary of Events and Information	Remarks and references to Appendices
	Lieut-Col J.R Davidson returned from sick leave on the 91st & took over command of the Battn. the following Officers also came out with him, 2nd Lieuts R.J. Guthrie, N.B. Cockburn, J.R. Williams & W.S. Tubb, & J.B Davey. From the 23rd to the 26th One platoon of the 17th Manchesters were attached to us for instruction in trench work, this Battn. relieving us on the night of the 28/9th when we proceeded to a Farm & two dug outs at Gordon Farm. On the nights of the 29th to 31st working parties were engaged in digging a new fire support trench behind O.3 & O.A. The 9th Brigade were relieved on the night of the 1st August when the Battn. proceeded to camping ground on the OUDERDOM-VLAMERTINGHE Road. The casualties during the month were Officers 1 wounded (Lieut J.E. Cunningham) Other Ranks 2 Killed 2 Wounded	

M Davidson
LIEUT. COLONEL
¼ BNS 10TH (SCOTTISH) BN THE KING'S (L'POOL RGT.)

9th Bde.

3rd Div.

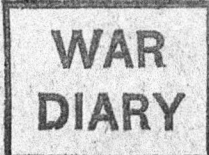

10th (KING'S) LIVERPOOL REGT.

August

1 9 1 5

2.

On His Majesty's Service.

Army Form C. 2118.

WAR DIARY
INTELLIGENCE SUMMARY.
(Erase heading not required.)

Instructions regarding War Diaries and Intelligence Summaries are contained in F.S.Regs., Part II and the Staff Manual respectively. Title pages will be prepared in manuscript.

Hour, Date, Place	Summary of Events and Information	Remarks and references to Appendices
August 1915	On the evening of the 2nd August the Battalion proceeded to Reserve Trenches, 3 Officers & 70 men being sent to POTIJZE Defences the remainder being in Dug Outs at KRUIE SALIENT where Headquarters were established, having relieved the Queens Westminster Rifles. These positions were occupied from the 2nd until the 13th August during which time new fire and communication trenches were constructed at POTIJZE Village and in the chateau grounds, whilst at the KRUIE SALIENT parties were engaged in work on the Rampart defences under R.E. Supervision. During this period the enemy's Artillery was fairly active, one man being killed and three wounded. The Batt was relieved at POTIJZE on the night of the 13th by the 8th Rifle Brigade, but nobody took over the positions at the KRUIE SALIENT. The Battn proceeded to camping ground on the OUDERDOM - VLAMERTINGHE Road and remained there for 6 days: Companies were exercised in Bomb throwing and close order drill daily. At 7.30 on the night of the 19th the Battn left camp to take over Dug outs in Wood near the White Chateau in H.23.B. which position was occupied until the end of the month. During this time the men were employed mostly at night improving communication trenches in the vicinity of ZILLEBEKE and MAPLE COPSE. The enemy shelled the neighbourhood of the Dug outs fairly often in the day time, Lieut Wall and two men being wounded.	

(73989) W4141–463. 400,000. 9/14. H.&J.Ltd. Forms/C. 2118/10.

Army Form C. 2118.

WAR DIARY
or
INTELLIGENCE SUMMARY.
(Erase heading not required.)

Instructions regarding War Diaries and Intelligence Summaries are contained in F. S. Regs., Part II. and the Staff Manual respectively. Title pages will be prepared in manuscript.

Hour, Date, Place	Summary of Events and Information	Remarks and references to Appendices
	The following Officers of the 16th Bn Liverpool Regt arrived towards the end of the month & were attached to the Battn 2nd Lieuts B. G. Thomas, C. H. Kinsman, R. M. S. Crangell, B. E. Rutherford & H. Jago.	

M. Lourden (LIEUT. COLONEL,)
COMMANDING 10TH (SCOTTISH) BN. THE KING'S (LPOOL REGT.)

9th Bde.
3rd Div.

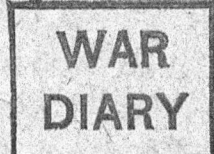

10th (KING'S) LIVERPOOL REGT.

September

1 9 1 5

On His Majesty's Service.

WAR DIARY

INTELLIGENCE SUMMARY

Army Form C. 2118.

Hour, Date, Place	Summary of Events and Information	Remarks and references to Appendices
September, 1915.	In the first two days of the month, the Battalion remained in the dugouts in Wood near the White Chateau at KRUISSTRAAT, working parties being employed at night on the communication trench at ZILLEBEKE (known as "DORMY HOUSE LANE"). At 5.45 p.m. on the 2nd, while a heavy artillery duel round the head near HOOGE, the Battalion was ordered to "stand to", but a counter-manding message arrived about an hour later. On Friday the 3rd, the Battalion relieved a company of the WORCESTER Regt in dugouts in West Bank of ZILLEBEKE LAKE. Work was continued on the DORMY HOUSE LANE dugouts, + a party was employed in SANCTUARY WOOD, building dugouts for Brigade Bomb-stores. Other parties constructed dugouts, under the orders of the Brigade Signalling Officer, and carried on revetting work on ZILLEBEKE STREET. The enemy's artillery was constantly active during this period, + several casualties were recorded. A draft of 105 men from England arrived on the 11th, + joined the companies to which they had been posted, during the following few days. On the 23rd, the Grande on Canal Bridge (Nov 12-19 inclusive) were taken over from the ROYAL SCOTS FUSILIERS. The Battalion moved the next day, to billets at the KRUISSTRAAT CHATEAU BARNS, relieving the 2nd SUFFOLKS. A British attack was made at HOOGE on the 25th, during which day the Battalion remained in Divisional Reserve. The Machine Gun Section (under Lieut. DUCKWORTH) occupying a position in SANCTUARY WOOD. In the evening, orders were received to move up immediately to SANCTUARY WOOD to relieve a company of the 1st LINCOLNS in dugouts in S.E. corner of Wood. Work was then carried on, draining + repairing a communication	

Army Form C. 2118.

WAR DIARY
or
INTELLIGENCE SUMMARY.
(Erase heading not required.)

Hour, Date, Place	Summary of Events and Information	Remarks and references to Appendices
	March from MAPLE COPSE to SANCTUARY WOOD. At dusk on the 27th the Battalion moved to dug-outs in the RAMPARTS near the LILLE GATE in YPRES, relieving two companies of the 1st LINCOLNS. The following day, while Capt. D. MACLEOD and Capt. L.F. DVN were making the guard on BRIDGE 12, both officers and two men were unfortunately killed by a single high explosive shell. During the nights, working parties were employed under the C.R.E., 56th Field Coy., repairing communication trenches at BIRR CROSS ROADS, on the MENIN ROAD. On the 30th when the British were launching a counter-attack in the salient, in SANCTUARY WOOD, three parties were detailed to carry up bombs to MAPLE COPSE. This was done under shell-fire, during which several casualties were sustained, including Sec-Lieut. H.J THOMAS, wounded, but the whole of the bombs went successfully delivered. Some of the men who carried them took part in the [struck out] bomb attack which succeeded in clearing the British trenches.	Casualties during Month Killed Wounded Total Officers 2 1 3 Other Ranks 2 24 26

9th Bde.
3rd Div.

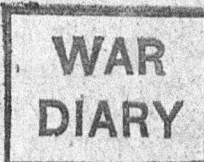

10th (KING'S) LIVERPOOL REGT.

October

1915

2.

On His Majesty's Service.

10th (Scottish) Batt. K.L.R.

WAR DIARY
or
INTELLIGENCE SUMMARY.
(Erase heading not required.)

Army Form C. 2118.

Hour, Date, Place	Summary of Events and Information	Remarks and references to Appendices
October, 1915	In RAMPARTS between the LILLE GATE & SALLY PORT in YPRES during the first part of the month. The Battalion remained in the casemates & dugouts during the first part of the month. Work was carried on (chiefly at night) — digging, revetting & perfecting communication trenches at HOOGE. On the 1st of this month, a party were employed all day in MAPLE COPSE, building a new bomb-store & detonating grenades. The enemy's artillery was fairly quiet during this period, & comparatively little shelling was experienced. On the afternoon of the 10th however, a heavy high-explosive shell struck a house opposite the H.Q. billet, in which a party of Z Coy was billeted, killing 2 men & wounding 6. On Tuesday the 12th the Battalion moved up to SANCTUARY WOOD to relieve the ROYAL SCOTS FUS. in B5, B5a, & moved dugouts. The enemy were shelling heavily the woods leading to the WOOD, but the relief was successfully completed at 10.30 p.m. A party of 10 bombers was attached to relieve a similar number of ROYAL SCOTS FUS. who had been sent to help the MIDDLESEX in B7. The tour in the trenches was of 7 days duration & during this time the defences were improved by putting out barbed wire in front of the trenches, whilst the latter was drained & revetted, the parapets & traverses being built up & strengthened. Several casualties were suffered as a result of enemy bombardments & bomb attacks.	

WAR DIARY or INTELLIGENCE SUMMARY

Army Form C. 2118.

Hour, Date, Place	Summary of Events and Information	Remarks and references to Appendices
October, 1915 (continued)	The Battalion was relieved on the evening of the 19th & proceeded to the Camp at OUDERDOM, where it rested for five days. On the 23rd, the 9th Inf Brigade moved to its new area, & the Battalion marched to GODEWAERSVELDE via RENINGHELST and BOESCHEPPE. On the remaining days of the month, parades were held under company arrangements, instruction being given in musketry, fire direction & fire control, handling & care of ammo, & section & platoon drill. When the weather was too wet for outdoor parades, lectures were given in the company billets. During the month, the following officers arrived from ENGLAND:- Capt. D. BINGHAM, Sec. Lieuts. R.T. AINSWORTH, F. DAVEY, A.H. NOBLE, H.L. WOODLAND, E.H. HOLLINS, L.B. MILL, A.A. COWAN, T.H.S. ALLEN.	Casualties Officers / Other Ranks — Killed / Wounded 5 23

J. Davidson LIEUT. COLONEL
5/12/15

9th Bde.
3rd Div.

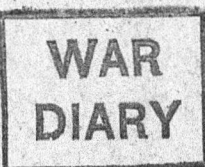

10th (KING'S) LIVERPOOL REGT.

November

1 9 1 5

2.

On His Majesty's Service.

10th (Scottish) Batt. K.L.R.

WAR DIARY or INTELLIGENCE SUMMARY

Army Form C. 2118.

Hour, Date, Place	Summary of Events and Information	Remarks and references to Appendices
November, 1915	Battalion occupied the billets at GODEWAERSVELDE, & the daily company parades were continued. On the first three days of this month, the 4th, the 9th Inf. Brigade changed its area, & the Battalion marched to billets at WINNEZEELE. The same morning, the C.O. (Lt. Col. J.R. DAVIDSON) proceeded on short leave to ENGLAND, & Capt. A.G. DAVIDSON took over the temporary command of the Battalion. During the rest at WINNEZEELE, the company parades were carried on. The training given included:- Close order & extended order drill, musketry & rapid loading, bayonet fighting, judging distance, advanced, rear, & flank guards, & smoke helmet drill. Classes for junior N.C.O.'s were held under the direction of the Regt. Sergeant Major. Concerts & football matches provided recreation for the men. On Saturday the 6th a divisional ceremonial parade was held in STEENVOORDE for the bestowal of decorations awarded by the French Government. The "CROIX DE GUERRE" was awarded to Pte. W. SHORT (V.Cy) for gallantry on 16th June. The Battalion took part in a Brigade route march on the 16th, when the Brigade was inspected on the march by the G.O.C., II nd Army.	

WAR DIARY
or
INTELLIGENCE SUMMARY.
(Erase heading not required.)

Army Form C. 2118.

Hour, Date, Place	Summary of Events and Information	Remarks and references to Appendices
November, 1915 (contd)	WINNEZEELE. On Sunday the 21st, the Battalion moved from "T" Camp and after spending the night under canvas in Reninghelst, relieved the 1st N. Staffords the following day in trenches on the left of ST. ELOI, viz: T1, T2, rT3 fire trenches, R5 & T7 support trenches, which had previously been occupied by the C.O. & the O's C. Companies. The relief was successfully completed at 8.0 p.m. Occupying the trenches to the right & left of this section were the 4 ROYAL FUSILIERS and the 1st NORTHUMBERLAND FUSILIERS respectively. The trenches taken over were found to be very wet & dirty, & in need of much attention. Throughout the tour, work was therefore carried on night & day: draining, repairing, draining & pumping. The weather was cold & wet & fresh for the first few days, & later very wet. The trenches were inspected by the G.O.C.'s III Division & 9 Inf. Brigade. On the 25th on this same day a draft of 77 men from ENGLAND reinforced the companies. The enemy in front were SAXONS, & very quiet, but from either flank snipers were at work. There was very little shelling. 29th The LONDON RIFLE BRIGADE took over the trenches on the relief was completed at 8.55 p.m. & the Battalion moved under company arrangements to Huts (known as "D" Camp) near RENINGHELST. The following day, a kit sock & foot inspection was held, & the men's clothes were dried & cleaned. M Davidson Lieut Col. 10th BATTALION OF THE PRINCESS OF WALES'S OWN (YORKSHIRE REGIMENT) 5/12/15	Casualties Officers. Other Ranks. KILLED WOUNDED KILLED WOUNDED - - - 5

9th Bde.
3rd Div.

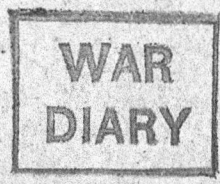

10th (KING'S) LIVERPOOL REGT.

December

1 9 1 5

On His Majesty's Service.

WAR DIARY
INTELLIGENCE SUMMARY.
(Erase heading not required.)

Army Form C. 2118.

19th (SCOTTISH) BN. THE KING'S (L'POOL REGT.)

Hour, Date, Place	Summary of Events and Information	Remarks and references to Appendices
DECEMBER 1915	The Battn rested at D CAMP, RENINGHELST, for the first few days of the month. Daily fatigue parties were furnished, including one of 10 Officer & 70 men for work at the 3rd Divn Grenade School. Other parties were employed in building Stores and in draining the Camp. On Monday the 6th the Battn moved to the Trenches to relieve the (London Rifle Brigade) in T₁, T₂, T₃ (Fire Trenches) and R₅ & T₇ (Support line). The Machine Gunners, Bombers & Snipers went up the previous day. Occupying trenches on the right & left of the Battn were the 1st R.B. & and 1st N.F. respectively. The weather was exceptionally wet, & the Trenches were in a very bad condition with mud and water. Sides were falling in, and sandbag parapets giving way; so that a great amount of work was required on all the Trenches. The rain continued throughout the week in the line, and constant work both by night and day was necessary to keep the Trenches habitable. All available men, therefore, were employed in parapetting, draining & revetting sides of Fire Trenches & C.T.s.	

WAR DIARY
INTELLIGENCE SUMMARY.
(Erase heading not required.)

Army Form C. 2118.

Hour, Date, Place	Summary of Events and Information	Remarks and references to Appendices
DECEMBER 1915	The enemy was quiet on the whole, & there was little shelling. On the afternoon of the 10th however, T. was whizz banged, with the result that in the advanced cover post one man was killed & two wounded. During the four hours representatives of the Grand Fleet spent 24 hours in T.; to carry back to their comrades an impression of life in the trenches. On the night of Monday the 13th the Battn was relieved by the London Rifle Brigade. The relief was successfully completed by 9·35 p.m. and the Battn marched back to RENINGHELST. On arrival all men had their feet washed and rubbed in the M.O.s new foot Massage Hut in D camp. For the next few days, fatigues were furnished as before, & a further party went up to the line each night in Motor Busses, being employed in the reclaiming of old trenches. About 5·30 a.m. on Sunday the 19th, a very heavy bombardment was heard from the North of YPRES. At 6 a.m. a strong smell of gas was detected & all men were immediately roused & warned (It did not prove necessary however, for helmets to be worn)	

WAR DIARY or INTELLIGENCE SUMMARY

Army Form C. 2118.

Hour, Date, Place	Summary of Events and Information	Remarks and references to Appendices
DECEMBER 1915	Five minutes later, a Brigade Order to "STAND-TO" came over the wire, & the Battn, with 1st line Transport, was ready to move by 6·30 a.m. The "Stand-to" continued until 11 a.m., but the heavy bombardment went on all day, & far into the night. On Tuesday the 21st, the Battn moved to billets in DICKEBUSCH; 90 men from X & Y Coys occupied dugouts in SPOILBANK, LANKHOF. The relief was successfully completed by 4·30 p.m. The Battn being in Brigade Reserve, all ranks were to be prepared to move on 15 minutes notice to posts allotted to Battn, if required to support any part of Brigade front. Digging fatigues for different parts of the line were sent out each night. Other parties worked on the reclaiming of Trench R2, & on the building of a Divisional Grenade store at VOORMEZEELE. The 13th K.L.R. took over the position on the 28th and the Battn moved back to the Camp at RENINGHELST. On the remaining days of the Month, parades were held under Company arrangement; Tube Helmet & Goggle drill, Musketry & rapid loading being practised. During the Month, the following Officer reinforcements arrived from ENGLAND:– 7 Lieuts: E.K. Stangroom, A.J. Bainbridge, E.R. Jasper, S.W. Kerby on.... Casualties during Month:– Killed 1 Other Rank, Wounded 6 Other Ranks.	A.W.[?] Capt for .... LIEUT. COLONEL, COMMANDING 10TH BN. THE KING'S (LPOOL REGT.) (SCOTTISH) BN THE KING'S (LPOOL REGT.)

3RD DIVISION
9TH INFY BDE

13TH BATTALION
KING'S LIVERPOOL REGT
APL - DEC 1916

From 8 BDE 3 DIV

9th Brigade.

3rd Division.

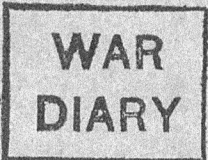
WAR DIARY

Battalion came from 8th Brigade 4th April 1916.

13th BATTALION

THE KING'S LIVERPOOL REGIMENT

APRIL 1916

April 1916.
13th Bn The King's L'pool Regt. Vol 8

WAR DIARY or INTELLIGENCE SUMMARY.

Army Form C.-2118.

Place	Date	Hour	Summary of Events and Information	Remarks and references to Appendices
DICKEBUSCH	1st-2nd		In Billets at DICKE BUSCH	
E CAMP RENINGHELST	3rd		Left Dickebusch at 9pm arrived E. Camp, RENINGHELST 9.30pm.	
	4th		In E. Camp, RENINGHELST.	
	5th		Left E. Camp at 10am & arrived Billets N. of BAILLEUL 12.30pm 5/4/16.	
BAILLEUL	6th-21st		In Billets N. of BAILLEUL & took over from 12th W. Yorks	
	21st		Left Billets at 3pm & arrived at R.E. FARM near KEMMEL at 8pm	
	25th		Left R.E FARM at 7.30pm & took over K+L trenches 6th	
	26th-29th		In K+L Trenches, Battalion Hqrs at YORKHOUSE. Relieved by 50th Division	
LOCRE	29th		Relieved about 9pm by 12th West Yorks arrived at LOCRE 1am 30/4/16	
	30th		In Billets at LOCRE	

[signature]
LIEUT. COLONEL,
COMDG. 13TH (S) BN. THE KING'S LIVERPOOL REGT.

9th Brigade.

3rd Division.

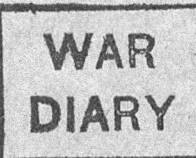

13th BATTALION

THE KING'S LIVERPOOL REGIMENT

MAY 1916

WAR DIARY
or
INTELLIGENCE SUMMARY

MAY 1916   13th BN. THE KINGS (L'POOL REGT)

Vol 9

Place	Date	Hour	Summary of Events and Information	Remarks and references to Appendices
LOCRE	1st-3rd		In Billets at LOCRE.	
	3rd	7pm	Left Billets at LOCRE at 7pm and arrived R.C. FARM & SIEGE FARM at 9pm. 2 Companies at R.C. FARM & 2 Companies at SIEGE FARM.	
	4th		Remained at R.C. FARM and SIEGE FARM, with 1 Coy from other Battalion relieved 12th West Yorks in K+L Trench. Headquarters at York House	
TRENCHES	5th-8th		Battalion in K+L Trench. Hdqrs at York House. Relieved by 12th West Yorks at 9pm & returned to R.C. FARM & SIEGE FARM. 8/5/16	
	9th-10th		At R.C. FARM & SIEGE FARM, until 8.30am 10/5/16 when Battalion left for Billets at LOCRE.	
LOCRE	11th-12th		In Billets at LOCRE, then paraded 8pm 11/5/16 when Battalion marched to relieve 12th West Yorks at K+L Trenches & York House	
TRENCHES	13th-16th		In trenches K+L. Hdqrs at York House, 9pm 16/5/16 relieved by 12th West Yorks & Battalion went to Billets at LOCRE.	
LOCRE	17th-20th		In Billets at LOCRE, marched 12th to relieve Yorks at 9pm on 20/5/16 on same piece as continual relieval	
TRENCHES	21st-24th		In trenches relieved by the Northumberland Fusiliers (50 B.D.) at 9.30pm on 24/5/16, marched to R.C. FARM & SIEGE FARM.	
	25th		At R.C. FARM & SIEGE FARM relieved by 1st Northumberland Fusiliers (50th Div) at 9pm 25/5/16 & Battalion marched to Billets near METEREN	
METEREN	26th-31st 9am		In Billets near METEREN	

9th Brigade

3rd Division.

WAR DIARY

13th BATTALION

THE KING'S LIVERPOOL REGIMENT

JUNE 1916

Army Form C. 2118.

Vol 10 June

WAR DIARY
or
INTELLIGENCE SUMMARY.
(Erase heading not required.)

13th Bn KINGS LIVERPOOL REGT.

JUNE 1916. III

Place	Date	Hour	Summary of Events and Information	Remarks and references to Appendices
METEREN	1st-4th		In Billets at METEREN	
	4th	6pm	Arrived H. Camp, RENINGHELST.	
	5th	7.45pm	Left H. Camp RENINGHELST. 2 Companies at VOORMEZEELE, 2 Companies at Scottish Wood; arrived 10.30pm.	
	6th-10th		In VOORMEZEELE and SCOTTISH WOOD.	
	10th	9pm	Relieved by 2nd Royal Scots, marched to E.I. Camp. RENING HELST.	
	11th	10pm	Marched from RENINGHELST to Billets at METEREN.	
	11th-17th		In Billets at METEREN.	
	17th	8am.	Left Billets at METEREN.	
	17th	3pm	Arrived at Billets in BAYENGHEM	
	18th-30th		In Billets at BAYENGHEM.	

[signature] Lieut. Colonel.
COMDG. 13TH (S.) BN. THE KING'S LIVERPOOL REGT.

30.6.16.

9th Inf.Bde.
3rd Div.

WAR DIARY

13th BATTN. THE KING'S (LIVERPOOL REGIMENT).

J U L Y

1 9 1 6

For Reports by O.C. 13/King's (Liverpool Regiment) on Operations of 13/14th July and 23/24th July, see War Diary of Headquarters, 9th Infantry Brigade for July 1916.

WAR DIARY or INTELLIGENCE SUMMARY

13th KINGS LIVERPOOL REGT.
9th BRIGADE
July 1916.

Army Form C. 2118.

Place	Date	Hour	Summary of Events and Information	Remarks and references to Appendices
	1-7-16	3pm	Left BAYENGHEM arrived at AUDRUICQ STATION at 6pm. Entrained for DOULLENS at 7.30pm	
	2-7-16		Arrived DOULLENS at 5am. Marched to BERNAVILLE arriving at 10am. Went into Billets	
	4-7-16	8am	Left billets at BERNAVILLE and marched to VIGNACOURT arriving 1pm (Billets)	
	5-7-16	9.30pm	Left Billets at VIGNACOURT for billets at BERTANGLES arriving 12mn.	
	6-7-16	9.30pm	Left BERTANGLES for Billets at LA HOUSSOYE arriving at 1am 7-7-16.	
	7-7-16	10pm	Left LA HOUSSOYE for billets at MORLANCOURT, arriving at 3am 8-7-16.	
	8-7-16		In Billets at MORLANCOURT	
	9-7-16	10am	Left MORLANCOURT for trenches near CARNOY; arrived 4pm. Halted en route 2 hours for dinner.	
	10-7-16		Trenches near CARNOY.	
	11-7-16	9pm	Left trenches for some trenches about 1000 yards away	
	12-7-16		In trenches	
	13-7-16	10pm	Left trenches to take part in the attack on German Front Line & BAZENTIN-LE-GRAND, attacked at 3.30 AM & took German trench & BAZENTIN-LE-GRAND.	
	14-7-16		In captured trench	
	15-7-16		In captured trench	
	16-7-16		In captured trench	
	17-7-16		In captured trench	

Continued on Sheet 2

Army Form C. 2118.

WAR DIARY
or
INTELLIGENCE SUMMARY
(Erase heading not required.)

Instructions regarding War Diaries and Intelligence Summaries are contained in F. S. Regs., Part II. and the Staff Manual respectively. Title Pages will be prepared in manuscript.

Place	Date	Hour	Summary of Events and Information	Remarks and references to Appendices
	10.7.16		In eplinere trench	
	19.7.16	2pm	Left trenches for Bivouacs about 3 miles behind the line, arrived 4 pm.	
	20.7.16		In Bivouacs	
	21.7.16		In Bivouacs	
	22.7.16	10pm	Left Bivouacs for Delville Wood to assist in the attack.	
	23.7.16	11pm	Left Delville Wood for Reserve Trenches, arriving 12mn.	
	24.7.16	11pm	Left Res. Trenches being relieved by 22nd Royal Fusiliers, & went to Bivouacs at Sand Pits.	
	25.7.16 to 27.7.16		At Sand Pits.	
	28.7.16 to 31.7.16		Left Sand Pits 5.30pm 27th for Billets at Ville-sur-Ancre. Billets at Ville-sur-Ancre.	

W. Peton Major
Comdg 13th Kings (Liverpool Regt.)

9th Brigade.

3rd Division.

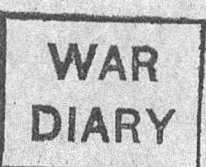

13th BATTALION

THE KING'S LIVERPOOL REGIMENT

AUGUST 1916

Attached:- REPORT ON OPERATIONS 15th-20th AUGUST

Army Form C. 2118.

WAR DIARY
or
INTELLIGENCE SUMMARY

13TH BN THE KINGS LIVERPOOL REGT
9TH BRIGADE

August 1916

Vol 12

(Erase heading not required.)

Instructions regarding War Diaries and Intelligence Summaries are contained in F.S. Regs., Part II. and the Staff Manual respectively. Title Pages will be prepared in manuscript.

Place	Date	Hour	Summary of Events and Information	Remarks and references to Appendices
VILLE-SUR-ANCRE	1-8-16 to 11-8-16		In Billets at Ville-sur-Ancre	
	11-8-16	3pm	Left Billets at Ville-sur-Ancre for Sandpits arriving 5.30pm.	
SANDPITS	11-8-16		Bn Bivouacs at Sandpits.	
	14-8-16	6pm	Left Sandpits for trenches arriving 1am 15.8.16	
	14-8-16		made attack on German trenches S. of Guillemont. Casualties heavy.	
	16-8-16	5.30pm	Remained in Trenches	
	17-8-16		Relieved and proceeded to Reserve trenches	
	18-8-16	1pm	Left Reserve trenches and marched to the Citadel arriving 10pm.	
	19-8-16	1pm	Remained at the Citadel	
	20-8-16			
	21-8-16	8am	Left the Citadel for Billets at Ville-sur-Ancre arriving 1pm	
	22-8-16	10.15am	Transport only left Ville-sur-Ancre for Candas and arrived 12 noon 23-8-16.	
	23-8-16	11.30am	Battalion left Ville-sur-Ancre and entrained at Mericourt and arrived at Candas at 10.30pm.	
	24-8-16		In Billets at Candas.	
	25-8-16	9am	Left Candas for Billets in Barly arriving 1pm	
	26-8-16	"	Left Barly for Billets at Mourcheaux arriving 12.30pm.	
	27-8-16	"	Left Mourcheaux for Billets at Hestrus arriving 1pm	
	28-8-16 29-8-16		In Billets at Hestrus.	

Army Form C. 2118.

WAR DIARY
or
INTELLIGENCE SUMMARY

August 1916 Continued   13th Bn. KINGS LIVERPOOL REGT.

(Erase heading not required.)

Place	Date	Hour	Summary of Events and Information	Remarks and references to Appendices
	30.8.16	9 am	Left HESTRUS for billets in MARLES-LES-MINES arriving 1pm.	
	31.8.16		On billets at MARLES-LES-MINES.	
	31.8.16.			

C.W. Peters Lt. Col.
Comdg. 13th Kings L'Pool Regt.

Report on the Operations
between the 15th & 20th August 1916
in which the 13th Bn Kings (Liverpool) Regt
were engaged.

On the 13th August 1916 the above
Battalion was ordered from
the SAND PITS to move up in to
the front line & to assist in
an attack on a position between
the South of the Village of GUILLEMONT
on the left & WEDGE Wood on the
right. This position was the front
assigned to the whole (9th) Brigade.
This Battalion had a section of this
front from the left of the "T" trench
(57 23 c) 57 C.S.W. to B 1. A 06. (62 C NW)
We had the Royal Fusiliers on our
~~right~~ left flank & and the Kings Own
on our right flank. The first line of
trenches was held by 2 coys of my
Batt with 2 coys in Support in
trenches behind. The 2 coys in the
front line went into these trenches on
the morning of the 14th just where they
were employed in digging & strengthening
their trenches & also in improving the
trench on the right portion of the position

(2)

their Hqrs. were at 10th the evening of the 10th inst.

The 2 Coys in Support came up with their Support trenches on the evening of the 10th inst. They had previously camped at TALUS BOISÉ.

The attack was ordered for 5.40 p.m. on the 11th inst. and my orders for attack were A & B Coys in front - 2nd lines. C & D Coys in Support, 3rd & 4 Lines & in this formation they advanced over the parapet. A Coy's line of advance was 49. (T 25 C) Map 57 D.W. B. Coy's line of advance was 40 N.E. of Trench. They had instructions to keep touch with each other & also with those on the flanks, & to advance as far as possible in a general line, & to be very careful to afford mutual support whenever required. C & D Coys (In Support) received similar orders. The attack itself was well planned, but unfortunately our Artillery fire (although intensely intense) was not evidently directed on the correct places, for as soon as the men were on the parapet

(3)

of them trenches they were met by a murderous machine gun fire from both flanks & front which it was quite impossible to get through with the result that practically no progress could be made & the casualties began extremely heavy. My men faced the position most gallantly (as the casualties show) but the task was impossible. Although the Suffolks bravely backed the first line up it was useless & impossible to advance & they had to fall back to our then (original) front line, where they remained till relieved by the West Yorks on the 17th inst, when the Batt occupied the SWAINSON and MALTZ-HORN trenches. I forgot to mention here that on the morning of the 17th inst our front line trenches were heavily shelled by our own artillery which I am sorry to say caused 40 casualties in the Batt.

We also heard messages on the

[4]

the fact that Shells were falling in
our Support trenches. We held
the Communication trench before
mentioned till relieved by the
2 Royal Scots at 2 P.M on the
18th inst. when we were moved
to TALUS BOISE and
then went into Bivouac for the
night & moved into trenches
near CARNOY on the 19th Morning
& remained till relieved the
Same evening when we moved
to The CITADEL for the night
of the 19th inst. & on the Morning
of the 21st we moved to VILLE-
SUR-ANCRE where we are at
present. The only remarks
I have to Make on the above
Operations are that I
Consider that the position
we had to attack was

(5)

was insufficiently reconnoitred
beforehand; and that
the enemy's positions were
insufficiently swept by
Artillery fire. the most
essential places to be
demolished by their fire
appear to have been left
alone: with the result that
the Infantry came in for
their Machine gun fire
when they advanced to attack.
Attacks of this description
require a long & thorough
reconnaissance beforehand
& also several days Artillery
Bombardment in order

(2)
to ensure that the front of attack has been broken up, otherwise the Infantry advance is useless. The attack on the 14th July was carefully arranged beforehand with the result that it was a great Success.

C.H. Seton Major
O.C. 13th King's Regt
22nd August 1916

9th Brigade.

3rd Division.

WAR DIARY

13th BATTALION

THE KING'S LIVERPOOL REGIMENT

SEPTEMBER 1916

Army Form C. 2118.

WAR DIARY or INTELLIGENCE SUMMARY

13th Bn. The Kings (Liverpool) Regt.

SEPTEMBER 1916

(Erase heading not required.)

Place	Date	Hour	Summary of Events and Information	Remarks and references to Appendices
MARLES-LES-MINES	1/9/16		In Billets at MARLES-LES-MINES.	
	2/9/16	6.30am	Left MARLES-LES-MINES for MARINGARBE arrived 12 noon. Transport billeted in NOEUX-LES-MINES.	
MARINGARBE	3/9/16 to 7/9/16		In Billets at MARINGARBE. Working parties every night at trenches	
	8/9/16	10 am	Proceeded to trenches near HULLUCH, took over support trenches from 7th Kings Shropshire Light Infantry. Headquarters in 10th Avenue	
	9/9/16 to 14/9/16		Occupied trenches above. Provided working parties for front line	
	15/9/16	9.30 pm	Took over Front Line trenches from 12th West Yorks	
	16/9/16 to 20/9/16		Occupied trenches above.	
	21/9/16	1 pm	Relieved by 2nd West Yorks and marched to Billets in NOEUX-LES-MINES.	
	22/9/16	8 am	Left NOEUX-LES-MINES for billets at ALLOUAGNE arriving 1pm	
	23/9/16	9 am	Left ALLOUAGNE for billets at ERNY-ST-JULIEN.	
ERNY-ST-JULIEN	24/9/16 to 30/9/16		In billets at ERNY-ST-JULIEN. Strict training.	

C.H. Peter, Lieut. Colonel

9th Brigade.

3rd Division.

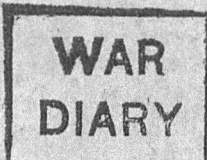

13th 3BATTALION

THE KING'S LIVERPOOL REGIMENT

OCTOBER 1 9 1 6

OCTOBER 1916. WAR DIARY or INTELLIGENCE SUMMARY.

13TH Bn THE KINGS (L'Pool) R. Army Form C. 2118.
92ND BRIGADE.

Vol 14

Place	Date	Hour	Summary of Events and Information	Remarks and references to Appendices
ERNY-ST-JULIEN	1/10/16 to 4/10/16		In Billets at ERNY-ST-JULIEN.	
	5/10/16	8.30am	Left ERNY-ST-JULIEN for billets at HESTRUS, arrived 3pm	
	6/10/16		In Billets at HESTRUS.	
	7/10/16	1.30am	Left HESTRUS 11pm for ST POL. Entrained at ST POL and detrained at PUCHEVILLERS 1pm and marched to BERTRANCOURT arriving 8.30pm	
	8/10/16	3pm	Left huts at BERTRANCOURT and went in reserve at MAILLY-LE-WOOD near MAILLY-MAILLY.	
	9/10/16 to 12/10/16		In reserve at MAILLY-LE-WOOD.	
	13/10/16	2pm	Left MAILLY-LE-WOOD for trenches, Helgis in LEGEND TRENCH.	
	14/10/16 to 18/10/16		In trenches	
	19/10/16	1pm	Left trenches for billets at LOUVENCOURT, arrived 5pm.	
	20/10/16 to 31/10/16		In Billets at LOUVENCOURT.	

CH Petere LIEUT. COLONEL.
COMDG 13TH BN THE KING'S LIVERPOOL REGT

9th Brigade.

3rd Division.

WAR DIARY

13th BATTALION

THE KING'S LIVERPOOL REGIMENT

NOVEMBER 1916

Army Form C. 2118.

1/5th Bn. The King's (L'pool Regt)
9th Brigade.

Vol 15

WAR DIARY
or
INTELLIGENCE SUMMARY.
(Erase heading not required.)

NOVEMBER 1916.

Instructions regarding War Diaries and Intelligence Summaries are contained in F.S. Regs., Part II. and the Staff Manual respectively. Title pages will be prepared in manuscript.

Place	Date	Hour	Summary of Events and Information	Remarks and references to Appendices
LOUVENCOURT.	1/11/16 to 3/11/16		In Billets at LOUVENCOURT. Battalion employed on wood clearing	
	4/11/16	7am	Commenced to relieve 1st Royal Scots Fusiliers in Left Sub Section of SERRE Sector. Guides met Companies at L of RAILWAY AVENUE = COLINCAMP-EUSTON Road at 9.30am. Relief complete at 12 noon. Trenches very muddy	
	5/11/16	9 am finished	Heavy trench bombardment and two Company Headquarters blown in but no casualties. Battalion HdQrs. obsoleted but no damage done. Front line trenches badly blown in. Practically all Battalion assisting to repair them to-day. Orders for move on 7th again received.	
	6/11/16		Commenced repairing trenches. Orders of relief received, but cancelled two hours later.	
	7/11/16		Commenced to be relieved by 12th Bn. West Yorks at 3pm. Relief complete at 5pm. Companies marched independently to billets in COURCELLES. Very wet day. Any coats issued out to men on arrival in billets.	
	8/11/16		Battalion resting. Orders received at 3pm to provide working parties 500 men on fatigue as carrying party	
	9/11/16		to R.O. 1275 re Trench feet. Issued to all Officers & senior N.C.O.'s. Fatigue party of 450 provided for carrying etc. weather improving. Orders that Battalion was being relieved next day, received.	

Army Form C. 2118.

Continued. 2 **WAR DIARY**
or
INTELLIGENCE SUMMARY.
(Erase heading not required.)

Place	Date	Hour	Summary of Events and Information	Remarks and references to Appendices
	10/1/16		Orders for relief cancelled at 9.30 a.m. Large carrying party again provided.	
	11/1/16		Remained in COURCELLES. Measures taken to get ammunition stores etc up to establishment.	
	12/1/16		Orders for move to trenches received. 12th West Yorks Hdqrs arrived at our Hdqrs at 4 p.m. Battalion marched up by Companies commencing at 10.30 p.m. to Reserve Hdqrs at JEREMIAH TRENCH. N.C.Os from each company & Specialist Section left behind in COURCELLES. at Hdqrs also 5 Officers in reserve.	
	13/1/16		Battalion remained in reserve trenches. Hdqrs where Reserve Offrs were 7 N.C.Os were billeted was shelled. Weather improving. Battalion moved up to Right sub sector.	
	14/1/16			
	15/1/16		Battalion relieved by 2nd Suffolks & 8th East Yorks. Relief not complete until 2 a.m. 16/1/16. Battalion marched to billets in BUSWOOD. Wet day.	
	16/1/16		Battalion resting all day. New clothing served out. Very wet day.	
	17/1/16		Battalion commenced training under Company arrangements. Wet day & camp became muddy.	
	18/1/16		Training under Company arrangements still continued. Performance given by Pierrot troupe 3rd Divn "MUDLARKS" in Y.M.C.A. tent for the benefit	

Army Form C. 2118.

WAR DIARY
or
INTELLIGENCE SUMMARY

(Erase heading not required.)

1/13th Kings continued 3

Place	Date	Hour	Summary of Events and Information	Remarks and references to Appendices
	19/1/16		Battalion moved to Reserve Billets in COURCELLES, commencing at 3.30 pm. Very cold day.	
	20/1/16		In Billets at COURCELLES.	
	21/1/16		In Billets at COURCELLES. Working parties provided. Skill equipment & extra jerkins issued out. Orders to move received.	
	22/1/16		Battalion commenced relieving 12th West Yorks in left sub section of SERRE Sector at 3.30 pm; relief complete 9 pm.	
	23/1/16		Battalion in trenches. 2/Knt. Seares killed. Weather fairly good.	
	24/1/16		Battalion in trenches. Weather good. 30 men whose names had been forwarded as skilled Tradesmen were sent to H.Qy.'s 134th Infy. Bgde., MAILLY, to be tested, returned same day.	
	25/1/16		Battalion in trenches. Very wet day. Trenches in rather a bad state.	
	26/1/16		Battalion in trenches. Weather very wet. Trenches now in a very bad state indeed.	
	27/1/16		Battalion relieved by 1st Gordons commencing at 6 pm. Relief complete at 11 pm, except H.Qy.'s. Battalion marched to Huts on ACHEUX ROAD.	

Army Form C. 2118.

Contained 4

WAR DIARY
or
INTELLIGENCE SUMMARY
(Erase heading not required.)

Instructions regarding War Diaries and Intelligence Summaries are contained in F. S. Regs., Part II. and the Staff Manual respectively. Title Pages will be prepared in manuscript.

Place	Date	Hour	Summary of Events and Information	Remarks and references to Appendices
	28/11/16		Battalion resting all day. Very cold day.	
	29/11/16		Battalion still in huts on ACHEUX ROAD. Working parties inspected by Brig. General in morning. Inspection by Div. General in afternoon.	
	30/11/16		Battalion providing working parties of various sorts. Weather very cold.	

W Brandon Major
Comdg. 13th Kings Regt.

1-12-16.

9th Brigade.

3rd Division.

WAR DIARY

13th BATTALION

THE KING'S LIVERPOOL REGIMENT

DECEMBER 1916

WAR DIARY

13TH Bn. THE KINGS (LIVERPOOL) REGT. Army Form C. 2118.

9th BRIGADE

INTELLIGENCE SUMMARY

DECEMBER 1916

Vol/6

Place	Date	Hour	Summary of Events and Information	Remarks and references to Appendices
BUS.	1/12/16		In Billets at Bus. Working parties provided; a proportion of men from each Company instructed in Lewis Guns by Lewis Gun Officer.	
"	2/12/16		In Billets at Bus. Working parties provided. 3 N.C.Os. proceeded to 34th Divl. Grenade School Drucelles for instruction. Classes on shoulder straps to be discontinued forthwith.	
"	3/12/16			
"	4/12/16		In Billets at Bus. Working parties provided, all money held by Battalions when going into trenches will be handed over to Divisional Treasure Chest. Relieve orders received for move to Reserve Billets.	
COURCELLES	5/12/16	10.10 am	Battalion moved to Billets at COURCELLES to relieve 1st Gordons, commencing at 10.10 am. Battn. Hdqrs. moving off first, Companies afterwards at 5 minutes interval. 8th K.O.R.L. took over our Billets in Bus. Working parties provided.	
COURCELLES	6/12/16		In Billets at COURCELLES.	
"	7/12/16		In Billets at COURCELLES. Working parties provided.	
"	8/12/16		In Billets at COURCELLES. Baths allotted to the Battalion, Company Commanders visited trenches which were to be taken over four days. Specialists moved to Ecurcheux C 4 SERRE SECTOR	
"	9/12/16	11 am 4 pm	Battalion relieved 12th West Yorks in C.4 SERRE SECTOR commencing at 11 am. Band C Companies commenced relieving at 11 am. Band D Companies at 4 pm.	

WAR DIARY
or
INTELLIGENCE SUMMARY.
(Erase heading not required.)

Army Form C. 2118.

Place	Date	Hour	Summary of Events and Information	Remarks and references to Appendices
	10/7/16		Battalion in the trenches. Detail Camp at Bus Wood. Very wet weather. Clean socks sent up at night.	
	11/7/16		Battalion in the trenches. Weather still bad.	
	12/7/16		Battalion in the trenches. Socks sent up to Battalion. Orders for relief received.	
	13/7/16		Battalion relieved by 1st Gordons commencing at 4.30pm. Relief complete about 12 midnight. Battalion returns to Billets at Bus.	
Bus	14/7/16		Battalion in Billets at Bus. New rigger in rifle looking etc.	
"	15/7/16		In Billets at Bus. 6 Officers and 6 N.C.O's instructed in rifle looking etc. all available N.C.O's instructed in Bayonet fighting by Staff Sergeant Instructor.	
"	16/7/16		Billets at Bus. Working parties provided. Baths allotted to Battalion. 4 men from each Company instructed in signalling.	
"	17/7/16		Billets at Bus. Working parties provided. 3 N.C.O's proceeded to 3rd Div. Grenade School for instruction.	
"	18/7/16		Billets at Bus. Working parties provided.	
"	19/7/16		Billets at Bus. Working parties provided. 1 Officer & 1 N.C.O. reported to 3rd Army Infantry School of Instruction. L/S.O.C 3rd Div. & 9th Bde	

Army Form C. 2118.

WAR DIARY
or
INTELLIGENCE SUMMARY.
(Erase heading not required.)

Instructions regarding War Diaries and Intelligence Summaries are contained in F. S. Regs., Part II. and the Staff Manual respectively. Title pages will be prepared in manuscript.

Place	Date	Hour	Summary of Events and Information	Remarks and references to Appendices
Bus	20/9/16		Billets at Bus. Working parties provided. Parades under Company arrangements. Orders for move received.	
"	21/9/16		Battalion relieved 1st Gordons at COURCELLES. 1 Company relieving 1 Company of 1st Gordons in the trenches, viz HITTITE trenches.	
COURCELLES	22/9/16		Billets at COURCELLES. Very wet day. Working parties provided. Draft of 13 other ranks arrived.	
"	23/9/16		Billets at COURCELLES. Working parties provided. Companies at disposal of Company Commanders. When Battn is relieved from trenches the Gordons return to companies one Coy officers from each company to report to 2/Lt Galloway R.E. for instruction.	
"	24/9/16		Billets at COURCELLES. Working parties provided. Orders to move to trenches received.	
"	25/9/16		Moved to trenches to relieve 12th West Yorks - left sub-sector. One pair of clean socks issued to men before moving off.	
"	26/9/16		Battalion in trenches. Details at BUS WOOD. News of 171 other ranks were to form Battalion. Draft sent to Training Depot at PERNOIS G.S.M.	
"	27/9/16		Battalion in trenches. Draft of 145 arrived at Detail Camp, 26 remaining at Training Depot.	

Army Form C. 2118.

WAR DIARY
or
INTELLIGENCE SUMMARY.

(Erase heading not required.)

Place	Date	Hour	Summary of Events and Information	Remarks and references to Appendices
	28/12/10		Battalion in trenches. Orders for relief received.	
	29/12/10		Battalion relieved by 10th London, & returned to Billets in Bus.	
Bus	3/12/10		Battalion in Billets, men cleaning up.	
"	3/12/10		Battalion in Billets, working parties provided, very rest day.	

J.E. Carter Major
Comdg 13th Kings (L Pool) Regt.

3rd Division

War Diaries

13th King. Liverpool Regt.

January, to 31st December

1917

Army Form C. 2118.

WAR DIARY or INTELLIGENCE SUMMARY

13th. (S) Bn. The King's (L'pool) R.
9th. Brigade.

JANUARY 1917.

Place	Date	Hour	Summary of Events and Information	Remarks and references to Appendices
BUS.	1st.		In Billets at BUS. Working parties cancelled. Officers, N.C.Os and men had "Christmas Dinner". 3rd. Division Pierrots gave an entertainment for this Battalion.	
,,	2nd.		In Billets at BUS. Working parties of about 250 strong provided.	
,,	3rd.		In Billets at BUS. Working parties provided. 1 Officer, 1 N.C.O. and 12 men proceeded to BONNEVILLE as advance billeting party. Commanding Officer inspected all Companies separately.	
,,	4th.		In Billets at BUS. Working parties provided. Commanding Officer inspected Battalion.	
,,	5th.		In Billets at BUS. Working parties provided as usual.	
,,	6th.		In Billets at BUS. Working parties provided. Appeared in Battalion Orders that Commanding Officer would inspect all Companies again to-morrow. Orders received for move to Rest Area received.	
,,	7th.		Battalion to be relieved by 16th. Lancashire Fusiliers. Battalion paraded at 9 a.m. Starting point Map lens 11 I.16.b.9.8. Halted for 2 hours at St. Leger-les-Authie for dinner. Interval of 200 yards between Companies. Arrived at TERRAMESNIL at 4.30 p.m.	
TERRAMESNIL.	8th.		Battalion rested at TERRAMESNIL. Orders for move to Rest Area at BONNEVILLE received.	
BONNEVILLE.	9th		Paraded at 10 a.m. to proceed to BONNEVILLE. Starting point Map Lens 11 20 yards N. of FME de ROSEL. Route to be followed Cross Roads 800 yards N.E. of VALHEUREUX-VALHEUREUX-BONNEVILLE. Arrived at 1.30 p.m.	
,,	10th.		In Billets at BONNEVILLE. General cleaning up.	
,,	11th.		In Billets at BONNEVILLE. Permanent fatigue party of 1 Officer and 25 men provided for work at G.H.Q. Depot. Drill etc. to be carried on in morning. Recreation in the afternoon.	
,,	12th.		In Billets at BONNEVILLE. Commanding Officer inspected the Battalion.	

Army Form C. 2118.

WAR DIARY
or
INTELLIGENCE SUMMARY.

(Erase heading not required.)

Continued. January 1917.

Instructions regarding War Diaries and Intelligence Summaries are contained in F. S. Regs., Part II. and the Staff Manual respectively. Title pages will be prepared in manuscript.

Place	Date	Hour	Summary of Events and Information	Remarks and references to Appendices
BONNEVILLE	13th.		In Billets at BONNEVILLE. Parades as usual. Lecture on Gas to all Officers; box respirators taken. This Lecture was delivered by 3rd. Divisional Gas Officer.	
,,	14th.		In Billets at BONNEVILLE. Church Parades for all Denominations. Lecture by G.O.C. 3rd. Divison to all Officers.	
,,	15th.		In Billets at BONNEVILLE. Parades continued in morning and recreation in the afternoon. N.C.Os sent to 3rd. Divisional Gas School for a course. 1 Officer, 1 N.C.O and 2x 3 men sent to 3rd. Divisional Signal School for a course. 4 Officers joined the Battalion.	5
,,	16th.		In Billets at BONNEVILLE. Parades etc. as usual.	
,,	17th.		In Billets at BONNEVILLE. Baths at FIEFFES alloted to the Battalion.	
,,	18th.		In Billets at BONNEVILLE. Parades etc. as usual. Weather very cold.	
,,	19th.		In Billets at BONNEVILLE. Parades etc. as usual.	
,,	20th.		In Billets at BONNEVILLE. Parades etc. as usual.	
,,	21st.		In Billets at BONNEVILLE. Church Parades for all Denominations. Baths at FIEFFES alloted to Battalion, for remainder of men to bath. G.O.C. 3rd. Division inspected Battalion.	
,,	22nd.		In Billets at BONNEVILLE. Lecture to all Officers at 6 p.m. by Commanding Officer.	
,,	23rd.		In Billets at BONNEVILLE. Baths at FIEFFES again alloted to the Battalion. Blankets of two Companies cleaned by the Disinfector. General Routine Orders 2040,2041,2042,2043,2044 published in Battalion Orders.	
,,	24th.		In Billets at BONNEVILLE. Lecture to all Officers and senior N.C.Os at 6 p.m. by the Commanding Officer.	
,,	25th.		In Billets at BONNEVILLE. Lecture to all Officers and senior N.C.Os at 6 p.m. by the Commanding Officer.	

Army Form C. 2118.

WAR DIARY
or
INTELLIGENCE SUMMARY.

(Erase heading not required.)

Continued January 1917.

Place	Date	Hour	Summary of Events and Information	Remarks and references to Appendices
BONNEVILLE	26th.		In Billets at BONNEVILLE. The Attack practised on 3rd. Divisional Training Ground.	
,,	27th.		In Billets at BONNEVILLE? Orders for move received.	
	28th.		The Battalion moved to DOULLENS area. Paraded at 9.30 a.m. 2 Companies billeted at RANSART. 2 Companies and Headquarters billeted at Hte.VISEE. Starting point 200 yards S.E. of S of Fienfillers.	
	29th.		The Battalion paraded at 8.30 a.m. and marched to BONNIERES arriving at 1 p.m.	
	30th.		The Battalion paraded at 8 a.m. marched to HERNICOURT arriving at 2 p.m.	
	31st.		The Battalion paraded at 8.45 a.m. and marched to OURTON arriving at 1.30 p.m.	

1/2/17.

(signature) Lieut. Colonel.
Commanding 13th. Bn. The King's (Liverpool) Regiment.

Army Form C. 2118.

WAR DIARY
or
INTELLIGENCE SUMMARY

13th. (S) Bn. The King's (Liverpool) Regt.,

9th. Brigade.

(Erase heading not required.)

FEBRUARY 1917.

Place	Date	Hour	Summary of Events and Information	Remarks and references to Appendices
OURTON.	1st.		Battalion billeted in OURTON. Men employed in cleaning billets and resting remaining in billets to rest.	
,,	2nd.		Battalion billeted in OURTON. Training commenced. 9 to 10 a.m. Physical Training, Bombing, Bayonet Fighting and Musketry. 10 to 11 a.m. Practice of small tactical schemes by Platoon and Company Commanders. 11 a.m. to 1 p.m. Practice of Attack.	
,,	3rd.		Battalion billeted in OURTON. 9 a.m. to 1 p.m. Practice of Attack. Commanding Officer gave a lecture to all officers, Warrant Officers and Non Commissioned Officers.	
,,	4th.		Battalion Headquarters, B.Company and 1 Platoon of C.Company remained billeted in OURTON. D.Company and 3 Platoons of C.Company paraded at 8 a.m. and marched to WANQUETIN to work under orders of O.C. 278 Railway Company. A.Company paraded at 8 a.m. and marched to ERIN to work under orders of O.C. Tanks Depot.	
,,	5th.		Battalion remained billeted as shewn on 4th Feb. Training of troops staying in OURTON carried on as far as possible.	
,,	6th.		Battalion remained billetd as on 4th. Feb. Troops in OURTON practiced the Attack. Baths available for troops in OURTON from 10 a.m. to 12 noon.	
,,	7th.		Battalion remained billeted as on 4th. Feb. Baths available for troops in OURTON from 8 to 10 a.m. 11 a.m. to 1 p.m. Practice of Attack. Orders for move received.	
,,	8th.		Troops in OURTON paraded at 8.30 a.m. and marched to MAGNICOURT-SUR-CANCHE arriving at 2.45 p.m. Col. Foulkes D.S.O. Commanding the Special Brigade gave a Lecture to the Commanding Officer and 3 other Officers at 4 p.m. at NOYELLEVION.	
MAGNICOURT SUR CANCHE.	9th.		Remained in billets at MAGNICOURT-SUR-CANCHE. Time spent in cleaning up etc.	
,,	10th.		Remained in billets at MAGNICOURT-SUR-CANCHE. Training continued. Orders for move received.	

Army Form C. 2118.

WAR DIARY
or
INTELLIGENCE SUMMARY.
(Erase heading not required.)

FEBRUARY 1917.

13th. K.L.R.

Place	Date	Hour	Summary of Events and Information	Remarks and references to Appendices
	11th.		Troops billetd at MAGNICOURT-SUR-CANCHE paraded at 1.30 p.m. and marched to HOUVIN-HOUVIGNEUL arriving at 2p.m. A.Company rejoined Battalion from ERIN at 3.30 p.m.	
HOUVIN HOUVIGNEUL.	12th.		Troops billeted as on Feb. 11th. Training of troops continued.at HOUVIN-HOUVIGNEUL. 9 to 10 a.m. Physical Training, Bayonet Fighting, Musketry and Handling of Arms. 10 to 11 a.m. Bombing. 11 a.m. to 1 p.m. Tactical Schemes by Platoon Commanders.	
,,	13th.		Troops remained billeted as on Feb 11th. Training of those at HOUVIN-HOUVIGNEUL continued.	
,,	14th.		Troops remained billeted as on Feb. 11th. Training of troops at HOUVIN-HOUVIGNEUL continued.	
,,	15th.		Troops remained billeted as on Feb. 11th. Training of troops at HOUVIN-HOUVIGNEUL continued.	
,,	16th.		Troops remained billeted as on Feb. 11th. Training of troops at HOUVIN-HOUVIGNEUL continued.	
,,	17th.		Troops remained billeted as on Feb. 11th. All troops at HOUVIN-HOUVIGNEUL paraded in connection with re-organization by G.H.Q.	
,,	18th.		Troops billeted as on Feb. 11th. Church Parades and inspection of billets by Commanding Officer.	
,,	19th.		B.Company and 1 Platoon of C.Company paraded at 9 a.m. and marched to WANQUETIN to relieve D.Company.	
,,	20th.		D.Company rejoined Battalion from WANQUETIN arriving at 2.30 p.m.	
,,	21st.		Troops billetd as on Feb. 20th. 2 Officers attended a Lecture given by Captain D.Lane-Ingham 3rd. Army Court Martial Officer at 2.30 p.m. at LIENCOURT.	
,,	22nd.		Troops billetd as on Feb. 20th. Training continued.	
,,	23rd.		A.Company paraded at 9 a.m. and marched to WANQUETIN to relieve C.Company.	
,,	24th.		C.Company rejoined Battalion from WANQUETIN at 2.30 p.m.	

Army Form C. 2118.

WAR DIARY
or
INTELLIGENCE SUMMARY.
(Erase heading not required.)

FEBRUARY 1917.

13th. K.L.R.

3.

Instructions regarding War Diaries and Intelligence Summaries are contained in F. S. Regs., Part II. and the Staff Manual respectively. Title pages will be prepared in manuscript.

Place	Date	Hour	Summary of Events and Information	Remarks and references to Appendices
	25th.		Troops billeted as on Feb. 24th. Church Parades and inspection of billets.	
	26th.		Troops billeted as on Feb 24th. Practice of firing with Box Respirators on. Orders for move received.	
	27th.		Troops billeted as on Feb. 24th. Training continued also men engaged in cleaning up billets preparatory to move.	
	28th.		Troops in HOUVIN-HOUVIGNEUL paraded at 10 a.m. and marched to DENIER arriving 12 noon.	

28/2/17.

[signature]
Lieut. Colonel.
Commanding 13th. Bn. The King's (Liverpool) Regiment.

Army Form C. 2118.

13th. (S) Bn. The King's (Liverpool) Regiment.

9th. Brigade.

WAR DIARY
or
INTELLIGENCE SUMMARY

(Erase heading not required.)

MARCH 1917.

Place	Date	Hour	Summary of Events and Information	Remarks and references to Appendices
DENIER.	1st.		Battalion in billets in DENIER. Parades 9 - 10.30 a.m. Rifle grenade work and Lewis Gun instruction; re-organisation. 10.30 a.m. - 1 p.m. The Attack practiced. 2 - 4 p.m. Cleaning up and re-organisation. Box Respirators tested. 4 N.C.Os instructed in Bayonet Fighting and Physical Training by Staff Sergeant Instructor; this course of instruction lasted until the 8th. March.	
"	2nd.		Parades as for 1st. March. Commanding Officer inspected all Identity Discs and Iron Rations. Commanding Officer lectured all officers at 5.30 p.m. "A" and "B" Companies rejoined the Battalion at DENIER from WANQUETIN; arriving at 2.30 p.m. Orders to the effect that copy of Battalion Fire Orders was to be posted in every billet.	
"	3rd.		Parades 9 - 11 a.m. Parades under Company Arrangements. 11 - 1 p.m. re-organisation under Commanding Officer. 2 - 4 p.m. Bombing and Lewis Gun Instruction.	
"	4th.		Church Parades. 1 Officer and 1 N.C.O. proceeded to 3rd. Divisional School for a Grenade Course.	
"	5th.		Battalion paraded at 9.30 a.m. to march to parade ground to practice the attack. 1 Company and 2 platoons of another company sent as a working party to the R.E. Notice received that the Commander in Chief would inspect the Brigade to-morrow.	
"	6th.		Parades under Company arrangements in the morning. Battalion paraded at 1 p.m. to march to the ground where the inspection was to be held. Commander in Chief expressed himself as very pleased with the turn-out of the Brigade.	
"	7th.		Parades 9 a.m. - 1 p.m. The Attack practiced. 2 - 4 p.m. Wiring and Wire cutting.	
"	8th.		Parades as on the 7th. March. 2 N.C.Os despatched to Corps School for course on Lewis Guns.	
"	9th.		Parades as on the 7th. March. 4 more N.C.Os detailed for instruction in Bayonet Fighting and Physical Training under the Staff Sergeant Instructor. G.R.Os 653 and 654 published in Battalion Orders.	
"	10th.		Battalion paraded at 9 a.m. to march to the Parade Ground; The whole Brigade practiced the Attack. Commanding Officer and 3 other officers attended a lecture at GIVENCHY le NOBLE.	

Army Form C. 2118.

WAR DIARY
or
INTELLIGENCE SUMMARY.
(Erase heading not required.)

Instructions regarding War Diaries and Intelligence Summaries are contained in F.S. Regs., Part II. and the Staff Manual respectively. Title pages will be prepared in manuscript.

Place	Date	Hour	Summary of Events and Information	Remarks and references to Appendices
DENIER.	11th.		Church Parades. 1 Officer and 1 N.C.O. despatched to 3rd. Div. School for Grenade course. 1 N.C.O. despatched to 3rd. Div. School for Lewis Gun Course.	
,,	12th.		Parades under Company arrangements, attack to be practiced. 1 Officer and 4 other ranks attended demonstration at 3rd. Div. School.	
,,	13th.		Parades 9 a.m. - 1 p.m. The Attack practiced; 2 - 4 p.m. Wiring and Wir cutting.	
,,	14th.		Parades as on 13th. March. 1 other rank despatched to Third Army School of Cookery for a course.	
,,	15th.		Parades as on the 13th. March. Orders to move received.	
,,	16th.		Battalion paraded at 8.30 a.m. to march to WANQUETIN; route followed LIENCOURT - AVESNES le COMTE - HAUTVILLE - WANQUETIN. Arrived WANQUETIN at 1 p.m. Battalion billeted. Orders to move to ARRAS received.	
,,	17th.		Battalion paraded at 4 p.m. to march to ARRAS; arrived 11 p.m. Battalion billeted in cellars etc., relieved 2nd. Royal Scots, 8th. Brigade.	
ARRAS.	18th.		Battalion billeted in ARRAS. Working parties detailed.	
,,	19th.		Similar to 18th. March.	
,,	20th.		Similar to 18th. March.	
,,	21st.		Similar to 18th. March. 1 officer wounded; 3 other ranks killed and 4 wounded.	
,,	22nd.		Similar to 18th. March. Orders received for two Companies of this Battalion to relieve 2 Coys. of the 4th. Royal Fusiliers. One Company to be in Support and One in ST SAUVEUR Defences.	
,,	23rd.		Similar to 18th. March. The two Companies relieved the 4th. Royal Fusiliers as above.	
,,	24th.		Similar to 18th. March.	

Army Form C. 2118.

WAR DIARY
or
INTELLIGENCE SUMMARY.
Continued.

(Erase heading not required.)

Place	Date	Hour	Summary of Events and Information	Remarks and references to Appendices
ARRAS.	25th.		Similar as on 18th. March.	
,,	26th.		Similar to 18th. March. Orders received for the relief of the two Companies of this Battalion by the 1st. Northumberland Fusiliers.	
,,	27th.		Relief as ordered on 26th. completed. Working parties as usual.	
,,	28th.		Working parties as usual. Other ranks 1 killed.	
,,	29th.		Working parties as usual. Other ranks 4 killed and 5 wounded.	
,,	30th.		Working parties as usual.	
,,	31st.		Working parties as usual.	

31/3/17.

W.H. Brumell (?) Lieut. Colonel.
Commanding 13th. (S) Bn. The King's (Liverpool) Regiment.

Army Form C.2118.

13th. (S) Bn. The King's (Liverpool) Regt.,
9th. Brigade.   3rd. Division.

WAR DIARY
or
INTELLIGENCE SUMMARY
(Erase heading not required.)

APRIL 1917.

Vol 20

Place	Date	Hour	Summary of Events and Information	Remarks and references to Appendices
ARRAS.	1st.		Battalion Order No 2 dated 27/3/17 reads as follows:- The Commanding Officer congratulates the undermentioned on their gallant conduct under shell fire, and will be pleased to place their names on the records of the Regiment:- 51755 Cpl Sherburn.F. 13935 Cpl Rawnsley.S. 20257 Cpl Ramsden.W. 51862 LCpl Robison.W. 20715 Pte Turner.J. 20539 Pte Salt.W. 9988 Pte Batty.F. 41666 Pte Shields.H. 51828 Heap.W. The Commanding officer also wishes to place on record the good work done by the late 2Lieut. P.F.J.Burns who was killed in action 21/3/17. Remained in billets in ARRAS.	
,,	2nd.		Remained in billets in ARRAS.	
,,	3rd.		Remained in billets in ARRAS. 2 Officers and about 35 other ranks who were not to go into the attack left ARRAS for WANQUETIN at 9.30 p.m. This party afterwards moved to St.VAAST where they were attached to the 256th. G.A. as ammunition carrying party. Orders received for the dumping of stores at WANQUETIN to be completed by night of 5th/6th April.	
,,	4th.		The battalion moved from its present billets in ARRAS and were billeted in cellars in the town.	
,,	5th.		Remained in billets taken up on the 5th.	
,,	6th.		Remained in same billets.	
,,	7th.		Remained in same billets. Orders received to move up to the Assembly Trenches about 10 p.m. on the 8th.	
,,	8th.		Battalion commenced to move up to the Assembly Trenches, by Companies at intervals; first Company left at 9.10 p.m. and the others at 10 minutes interval; Battalion Headquarters established in ICELAND TRENCH. 2/Lieut. A.Wynne was killed in ASSEMBLY TRENCHES by a shell.	

Army Form C. 2118.

WAR DIARY
or
INTELLIGENCE SUMMARY.

(Erase heading not required.)

Place	Date	Hour	Summary of Events and Information	Remarks and references to Appendices
	9th.		At 7 a.m. the Battalion attacked. The right assaulting company took HARFLEUR TRENCH without difficulty, but the left company owing to the heavy fire were at first unable to enter the trench. The fact that they did so eventually is due to the sound leadership of the officers and the undeniable spirit of the men. Difficulty was experienced in advancing through TILLOY WOOD owing to the fact that it was strongly wired, and little of the wire had been cut. Hostile snipers caused a number of casualties owing to their good shooting and good positions, which could not be readily discovered. The barrage put up by our artillery was very effective and greatly assisted the men to gain their final objective, i.e. the village of TILLOY by 8.30 a.m. 19 Officersand 449 men of the enemy were taken prisoners by this battalion; also 7 machine guns, 2 trench mortars, 1 bomb thrower, and vast quantities of M.G.ammunition in belts, S.A.A. bombs and trench mortar ammunition. The following officer were killed 2/Lieut E.G.Racine, 2/Lieut. E.B.Flenley and the following were wounded 2/Lieut. G.K.Price,2/Lieut.G.Carson,2/Lieut.A.E.Littler, 2/Lieut. L.A.Bane,2/Lieut.H.O.Foot, 2/Lieut H.G.Faragher; casualties in other ranks 170. Battalion Headquarters moved up to the captured German Third Line at 9 a.m.	
	10th.		At 8.30 a.m. Battalion Headquarters were moved up to the village of TILLOY. About 10 p.m. orders were received to be ready to move up at 15 minutes notice.	
	11th.		At 2.30 a.m. orders received to move up to occupy reserve trenches in from of BOIS de BOEUFS. Battalion Headquarters established in disused German gun-pits.	
	12th.		Remained in this position as Divisional Reserve. Captain H.V.Briscoe wounded.	
	13th.		Orders received to move forward to support attack on village of GUEMAPPE; advanced from present position at 2.30 p.m. in artillery formation; order cancelled and battalion returned to original position. At 6 p.m. battalion moved forward in support to 1st. Northumberland Fusiliers in an attack on GUEMAPPE. An intense artillery barrage was put up by the enemy and the Brigade retired a little way and commenced to dig in in a position due South of WANCOURT. 2nd Lieut. A.F.Robertson & 2/Lieut. E.M.Gardiner wounded; other ranks casualties 40.	
	14th.		Work ceased about 3 a.m. when the battalion was relieved by the K.O.S.B. of the 87th. Brigade, and marched back to their old position E. of BOIS de BOEUFS, arriving at 5 a.m. At 11 a.m.	

Army Form C. 2118.

WAR DIARY
or
INTELLIGENCE SUMMARY.

(Erase heading not required.)

Instructions regarding War Diaries and Intelligence Summaries are contained in F. S. Regs., Part II. and the Staff Manual respectively. Title pages will be prepared in manuscript.

Place	Date	Hour	Summary of Events and Information	Remarks and references to Appendices
ARRAS.	15th.		Companies commenced to march to billets in ARRAS. Commanding Officer commended Battalion on the excellent work done during the attacks.	
,,	16th.		Billets in ARRAS. The Battalion was complimented by the Brigadier and also by the Divisional General who thanked them for the exceptionally good work performed by them.	
,,	17th.		Billets in ARRAS.	
,,	18th.		Billets in ARRAS. Commanding Officer inspected all companies separately.	
,,	19th.		Billets in ARRAS. 3rd. Division Gas Corporal inspected the Box Respirators of all ranks.	
,,	20th.		Billets in ARRAS. Orders received that Brigade would move to DUISANS in the afternoon, but this was cancelled until 21st.	
,,	21st.		Battalion moved to DUISANS; first company moving off at 10.30 a.m. remainder at 200 yards interval; took over huts from H.L.I. 46th. Infantry Brigade; relief completed 1.15 p.m.	
DUISANS.	22nd.		Battalion remained in DUISANS.	
	23rd.		At 12.30 p.m. orders were received to move about 2 p.m. Headquarters and first company moved at 2.30 p.m. and remaining companies at intervals of 200 yards; took up billets vacated by 7th. King's Shropshire Light Infantry 8th. Brigade who had proceeded to the trenches.	
	24th.		Billets in ARRAS.	
	25th.		Billets in ARRAS. Parades under company arrangements.	
	26th.		Billets in ARRAS. Parades under company arrangements.	
	27th.		As on the 26th.	
	28th.		Remained in ARRAS. Baths allotted to Battalion from 7 a.m. to 10.30 a.m.	

Army Form C. 2118.

WAR DIARY
or
INTELLIGENCE SUMMARY.
(Erase heading not required)

Instructions regarding War Diaries and Intelligence Summaries are contained in F. S. Regs., Part II. and the Staff Manual respectively. Title pages will be prepared in manuscript.

Place	Date	Hour	Summary of Events and Information	Remarks and references to Appendices
ARRAS.	29th.		Remained in billets in ARRAS. Various Church Services held. The attack practiced by the battalion in the afternoon.	
	30th.		Billets in ARRAS. Baths allotted to the Battalion from 10 a.m. to 1 p.m. The attack again practiced by the battalion.	
			The undermentioned have been awarded the MILITARY MEDAL for gallantry and good work during the operations from 9th. to 14th. April:-	
			19092 Sergt. Edmondson.C. 22132 LCpl Jones.J. 52330 LCpl Oakes.R.	
			51862 LCpl Robison.W. 42965 Pte Hunter.T. 48770 Pte Simms.C.	

[signature]
Lieut. Colonel.
Commanding 15th. Bn. The King's (Liverpool) Regiment.

30/4/17.

WAR DIARY or INTELLIGENCE SUMMARY.

13th (S) Bn. The King's (L'pool) Regt.
9th Brigade 3rd Division.

Army Form C. 2118.

Place	Date	Hour	Summary of Events and Information	Remarks and references to Appendices
ARRAS.	May 1917. 1st.		The Battalion moved from Billets in ARRAS by Companies at Headquarters and the first Company moving off at 8.15 p.m. to take up positions in the front line trenches.	
	2nd		Remained in the front line trenches.	
	3rd		About 1 a.m. the Battalion moved to their assembly positions and at 3.45 a.m. the two leading Companies moved out of the front line trench. Strong Lewis Gun fire was maintained on the enemy's front line to prevent his escaping the barrage by leaving his trenches. Notwithstanding the difficulty presented by the darkness, which had not lifted, the leading Companies hugged the barrage, although assailed by heavy machine gun fire, and that task progressed to a line running N. and S. about 100 yards E. of the BOIS DES AUBEPINES. A hostile counter attack was launched at the leading Companies from the N. and N.E. It was completely beaten back, but the line was greatly depleted by M.G. and rifle fire from the northern flank and also from a North Westerly direction, which took it in the rear. A second and strong hostile counter attack which was delivered from the N. flank was met very gallantly, but the line was by this time so thin, no supports having come up that a withdrawal was necessary to prevent the troops being cut off. The withdrawal was carried out in good order in conjunction with the 4th Royal Fusiliers, back to the original front line trench. The following Officers were killed, Capt. A.E.Coates, 2/Lieut. H.B.Williams, the following Officers were wounded, Capt. J. Hunter, Capt. G.W.Byrng 2/Lieut N.M.Lee, 2/Lieut H.Harris, and the following Officers are reported missing. Lieut J.A.Phillips, 2/Lieut A.J.Innes, 2/Lieut Mc.G.Daly. 2/Lieut D.F.Wilkinson was wounded but remained at duty.	
	4th		The Battalion continued to consolidate the position held and in spite of heavy hostile fire, made good progress.	
	5th		Consolidation continued and the line held.	
	6th		Consolidation continued, and the line held.	

Army Form C. 2118.

WAR DIARY
or
INTELLIGENCE SUMMARY.
(Erase heading not required.)

Instructions regarding War Diaries and Intelligence Summaries are contained in F. S. Regs., Part II. and the Staff Manual respectively. Title pages will be prepared in manuscript.

Place	Date	Hour	Summary of Events and Information	Remarks and references to Appendices
Field	7th		Consolidation continued and the line held.	
	8th		Consolidation continued and the line held.	
	9th		Consolidation continued and the line held. 2/Lieut A.Wiles was wounded by a shell.	
	10th		Consolidation continued and the line held. Capt.E.B.Gallin was wounded in the legs by a shell.	
	11th		On the night of the 11th-12th the Battalion was relieved by the 10th Bn.Royal Welsh Fusiliers and proceeded to trenches N.of the Cambrai Road.	
	12th		Remained in trenches N.of CAMBRAI ROAD and working parties for the line were provided,	
	13th		Remained in trenches N.of CAMBRAI ROAD and provided working parties.	
	14th		Remained in trenches and provided working parties. The Commanding Officer was pleased to announce that the undermentioned Officers and men had been awarded decorations as stated. 2/Lieut E.M.Gardiner Military Cross. 2/Lieut H.B.Williams. 2/Lieut A.G.Roberts Military Cross Pte J.Hudson. D.C.M. The Corps Commander is much pleased with the work done by the Division on the defensive works about MONCHY, which has been done under great difficulty.	
	15th		At 4.50 a.m. the Battalion left the trenches and proceeded to rest billets at SIMENCOURT, where they arrived about 9.30 a.m. The day was spent in resting and re-fitting the troops.	
	16th		Remained in billets in SIMENCOURT.	
	17th		Remained in billets in Simencourt.	
	18th		At 8.50 a.m. the Battalion moved to rest billets at BEAUFORT where they arrived about 12.30 p.m.The Battn was complimented by the Divisional and Brigade Commanders for the good work done in the line.	
	19th		Remained in billets at BEAUFORT. Church Services were held.	
	20th		Remained in billets in BEAUFORT.	
	21st		Remained in billets in BEAUFORT. A programme of Training was carried out and the N.C.Os received special instruction.	

Army Form C. 2118.

WAR DIARY
or
INTELLIGENCE SUMMARY.

13th (S) Bn. The King's (Liverpool) Regt.

9th Brigade 3rd Division.

May, 1917.

(Erase heading not required.)

Instructions regarding War Diaries and Intelligence Summaries are contained in F. S. Regs., Part II. and the Staff Manual respectively. Title pages will be prepared in manuscript.

Place	Date	Hour	Summary of Events and Information	Remarks and references to Appendices
BEAUFORT.	22nd		Remained in billets at BEAUFORT, and programme of training carried out.	
	23rd		Remained in Billets at BEAUFORT, and programme of training carried out. The Armourer inspected the rifles of the Battalion. 2/Lieuts. R.W.Lewis and R.J.L.Rochfort joined the Battalion. The Commanding Officer had much pleasure in announcing that the Commander of the VI.Corps had awarded Military Medals to the undermentioned N.C.Os and men for acts of gallantry in the Field:- 14961.Cpl.J.Black. 14428 Pte. E.Hampson. 18728 Pte.J.Mulville. Major Hutchinson.D.S.O. gave a lecture on "discipline" to all combatant Officers.	
	24th		The Battalion remained in Billets at BEAUFORT.	
	25th		The G.O.C.Division inspected the Battalion on the Parade Ground BEAUFORT, whilst the Companies were at training. He expressed his appreciation of the good work the Battalion had done.	
	26th		Remained in Billets at Beaufort and carried out a programme of training.	
	27th		Remained in billets at BEAUFORT, and Church Services were held.	
	28th		From 9a.m. to 1 p.m. a programme of training was followed. In the afternoon the Regimental Sports were held, commencing at 2.30 p.m. The programme attached was followed, and the event, helped by the fine weather, passed a very interesting afternoon. The Battalion was honoured by the attendance of the G.O.C.Division and the Brigadier.	
	29th		The following Officers joined the Battalion. 2/Lieuts J.R.Ellis.J.R.Peet,A.Richards,R.W.Cowie. Remained in billets at BEAUFORT and programme of training followed. The Commanding Officer had great pleasure in announcing that the undermentioned Officers and N.C.Os and men had been mentioned in despatches for service in the Field. 2/Lieut P.F.T.Burns. 2/Lieut.A.C.Boon. 2/Lieut.A.Wiles. 52320 L/Cpl J.Littler. 37926 Pte A.Davies. 19583 L/Cpl J.W.Baker. The Commanding Officer (Lieut:Col.W.J.Cranston) was mentioned in despatches for service in the Field.	
	30th.		The Battalion remained at BEAUFORT, and carried out programme of training.	
	31st.		Battalion moved from BEAUFORT at 10.10 a.m. and proceeded to Billets at LATTRE ST QUENTIN, arriving at 11.45 a.m. The Commanding Officer is pleased to announce the following decorations:- Bar to Military Medal. 19551 L/Cpl W.Doyle. Military Medals.13239 Pte P.Synott. 48751 Pte E.Towle. 22435 L/Cpl P.Lewis. 11460 Pte.T.Fairhurst.	

WAR DIARY
or
INTELLIGENCE SUMMARY

Army Form C. 2118.

Vol 22

13th Battn. The King's (Liverpool) Regt.

June 1917.

Place	Date	Hour	Summary of Events and Information	Remarks and references to Appendices
ARRAS.	June 1st.		The Commanding Officer had great pleasure in announcing the undermentioned honours and awards:—	
			Bar to Military Medal. No 19551 L/Cpl Doyle.	
			Military Medal. 13239 Pte F.Synott. 48751.Pte F.Cowle.	
			22455 L/Cpl.P.Lewis. 11460 " Fairhurst.	
			25003 Pte A.Waite. 48696 " H.Dyche.	
			20316 " L.B.Darkin. 21260 "(L/Cpl) J.J.McConnell.	
			51826 Pte.W.Heap.	
			The Battalion moved off from LATTRE-ST-QUENTIN by road at 10.10 a.m., maintaining a distance of 100 yards between Companies.	
			On arrival at a point E.of HARBARCQ, the battalion embussed and proceeded to billets in ARRAS, where they arrived about 2.45 p.m.	
			After resting, platoons moved off at intervals of five minutes, the leading platoon moving off at 6.15 p.m., to a position in the BROWN LINE, relieving the Newfoundland Battn.	
	June 2nd.		The Battalion remained in the BROWN LINE until 9.30 p.m. when they proceeded to relieve the 1st Bn.Essex Regt.,29th Division in the right sub-sector,two companies holding the line with one in support and one in reserve. 2/Lieut. W.Cowie was wounded by a shell during the relief.	
	June 3rd.		Remained in this position,holding the line and consolidating.	
	June 4th.		Remained in this position,holding the line and consolidating.	
	June 5th.		Remained in this position,holding the line and consolidating.	
	June 6th.		The Battalion continued to consolidate the position held until 9.30 p.m., when a relief by the 4th Bn.The Royal Fusiliers commenced, and was duly completed by 2.15 p.m. a position in the BROWN LINE was then occupied.	
	June 7th.		The Battalion remained in the BROWN LINE. The day was spent in cleaning up, and working and carrying parties for the front line were provided.	

Army Form C. 2118.

Instructions regarding War Diaries and Intelligence Summaries are contained in F.S. Regs., Part II. and the Staff Manual respectively. Title Pages will be prepared in manuscript.

WAR DIARY
or
INTELLIGENCE SUMMARY
(Erase heading not required.)

13th (S) Bn. The King's (Liverpool) Regt.

June 1917.

Place	Date	Hour	Summary of Events and Information	Remarks and references to Appendices
FIELD	June 8th		The Battalion remained in the BROWN LINE, and provided working and carrying parties for the front Line.	
	June 9th		The Battalion moved to another position in the BROWN LINE - Map Reference H.34.c., taking over from the 8th Infantry Brigade.	
	June 10th		Remained in this position until 9.45 p.m. when the Battalion moved to relieve the 4th Bn. Royal Fusiliers, again taking over the right sub-sector, "C", and "D" Companies holding the Line, with "A" Company in support and holding Strong Points, and "B" Company remaining in reserve.	
	June 11th		The relief was completed by 1.30 a.m. on the morning of the 11th. The Battalion held the line and proceeded with the consolidation of the position.	
	June 12th		The reserve Company was employed for working and carrying parties.	
	June 13th		The Battalion continued to hold and consolidate the line, and carrying parties were again provided by the reserve Company.	
			The Battalion still remained in this position until about 9.30 p.m., when "A" Company moved to the reserve trench with a portion of "C" Company to make room for the 8th K.O.R.L. Regt., who had to vacate their portion of the line on account of our artillery heavily shelling the German front line in preparation for am attack by the 76th Brigade on the morning of the 14th.	
	June 14th		"A" and "C" Companies remained as indicated until 9.30 p.m., when they resumed their original position. Consolidation and depth of the trenches were improved through the day.	
	June 15th		The line was held and consolidation continued until about 10.10p.m.when a relief by the 4th Royal Fusiliers commenced. The relief was completed by 2.30 a.m. on the morning of the 16th., and the Battalion took up its position in the BROWN LINE, N. of the CAMBRAI ROAD.	
	June 16th		The Battalion was attached to the 76th Brigade as reserve, and remained in the Brown Line. The day was devoted to cleaning up.	
	June 17th		The Battalion remained in this position, and the Commanding Officer inspected Companies. Working and carrying parties were provided for the front line.	
	June 18th		Remained in BROWN LINE the Battalion again providing Working & Carrying Parties for the front line.	
	June 19th		Remained in trenches in the BROWN LINE . The day was devoted to the cleaning up of dress & equipment, and the trenches throughly cleaned. Battalion came under orders of the 9th. Bde. The relief of the battalion by the 7th. Norfolks was commenced at 9.30 p.m. and was completed by 10 P.M., when the battalion moved into billets in ARRAS, arriving at about 1 a.m. on the morning of the 20th. 2/Lieut. M.Segal was killed by a shell in the early hours of the 19th.	

Army Form C. 2118.

WAR DIARY
or
INTELLIGENCE SUMMARY
(Erase heading not required.)

13th. Battn. the King's (Liverpool) Regt.

June 1917.

Place	Date	Hour	Summary of Events and Information	Remarks and references to Appendices
ARRAS.	June 20th.	2.50 p.m.	The Battalion embussed at 1 p.m. and proceeded to rest billets at FOSSEUX. arriving at 2.50 p.m.	
	June 21st.		The remainder of the day was occupied in cleaning dress and equipment. Remained in billets at FOSSEUX, and a programme of training was followed, the battalion was re-organised. The following Officer's joined the battalion :- Capt. J.D. Atkinson 2/Lieut. E.G.Davies Lieut. F.A. Sellars " H.T. Jones 2/Lieut. H.B. Bramley " R. Ambler	
	June 22nd. 23rd.		Programme of training was followed, the Battalion remaining in billets at FOSSEUX. Remained in billets at FOSSEUX. The battalion provided a Working Party of 4 officers and 200 O.R. for work on FOSSEUX ammunition dump. Programme of training was followed, and the C.O. tested the re-organisation of "C" & "D" Coys.	
	June 24th.		Remained in billets at FOSSEUX. Church Services for all denominations were held. 4 officers and 200 O.R. were provided for Working Party on FOSSEUX ammunition dump.	
	June 25th.		Remained in billets at FOSSEUX. Programme of training was followed. The Battalion provided a Working Party of 4 Officers and 200 O.R. for work on FOSSEUX ammunition dump.	
	June 26th.		Remained in billets at FOSSEUX, and a programme of training followed. 50 O.R. were detailed for work on the Ammunition Dump.	
	June 27th.		Remained in billets at FOSSEUX. Training was carried out and 4 Officers and 200 O.R. detailed for work on the Ammunition Dump. The undermentioned officers joined for duty:- 2/Lieuts E.A.Radcliffe, F.W.Walker, J.L.Barratt.	
	June 28th		Remained in billets at FOSSEUX, and training carried out. 2 officers and 100 O.R. were detailed for duty on the FOSSEUX DUMP.	
	June 29th		Remained in billets at Fosseux and training carried out under Company arrangements. 2 Officers and 100 O.R. were detailed for working party on the FOSSEUX Dump. Warning orders for move were received. 2/Lieuts W.M.LEE AND E PEARMUND JOINED FOR DUTY.	
	June 30th		The Battalion paraded at 8.a.m. and marched to embussing point, Map Ref 51c.P10.d.23. from whence they proceeded to billets at ACHIET-LE-PETIT. where they arrived at 2.50 p.m. The Battalion was transferred from the VI to the IV Corps.	

30/6/17.

A.J.W.Howell
Major.
commanding 13th King's (Liverpool) Regt.

WAR DIARY
or
INTELLIGENCE SUMMARY

(Erase heading not required.)

13th Bn. The King's (Liverpool) Regt.

Vol 23

Army Form C. 2118.

Place	Date	Hour	Summary of Events and Information	Remarks and references to Appendices
ACHIET-LE-PETIT GRAND	1/7/17		Battalion remained in billets at ACHIET LE PETIT until 4pm when they moved off by road to BEUGNY. Tea was served on the BAPAUME-CAMBRAI Road en route and the destination reached at 9.45pm the battalion taking over camp from the 2nd R.F.	
BEUGNY	2/7/17		The Battalion rested in camp until 8.25pm when Hqrs proceeded to the front line to relieve the 1st Bedfords and Bucks Regt. "A" & "B" Coys occupying the forward posts, "C" Coy in support. "D" Coy in reserve and Bn H.Q. in Sunken Road S. of DEMICOURT. The relief was complete by 1.30 am, consolidating the positions. Patrols into Remained in the line, consolidating the positions. Patrols into the enemy lines were organised.	
FIELD.	3/7/17			
	4/7/17		Consolidation continued and patrols organised and carrying parties provided. Batt. H.Q. underwent an intermittent bombardment with light shell Casualties killed 1 OR wounded 5 ORs.	
	5/7/17		Company relief effected commencing at 10.30pm. "A" Coy proceeded to the outpost and "B" Coy to the reserve position, being relieved over and covered in by "C" and "D" Coys. All went as usual. Patrols as usual.	

Army Form C. 2118.

WAR DIARY
or
INTELLIGENCE SUMMARY
(Erase heading not required.)

Instructions regarding War Diaries and Intelligence Summaries are contained in F. S. Regs., Part II. and the Staff Manual respectively. Title Pages will be prepared in manuscript.

Place	Date	Hour	Summary of Events and Information	Remarks and references to Appendices
FIELD	6/7/17		Remained in trenches and consolidation and improvement continued. The usual patrols were organised.	
	7/7/17		Consolidation &c continued. Two Platoons of 'A' Company were engaged on the construction of Camouflage. The sentries post S. of DEMICOURT was slightly shelled during the evening. 2/Lieut. J.W. Walker was wounded by a shell. Casualties on O.R.	
	8/7/17		Killed 3, Wounded 11. At 10.30 pm the battalion relief by the H.L. Bn Royal Lancers commenced and was duly completed by 12.30am on the 9th July. The Battalion then took over the support position of the 4 R.F.s, Battn HQ being in sunken road S of DOIGNIES.	
	9/7/17		The Battalion remained in Brigade support, improving and building dugouts, and widening trenches. A party of 20 O.R. were provided for work with R.E. boring positions around DOIGNIES.	
	10/7/17		Remained in support and continued work on dugouts with R.E.	
	11/7/17		Remained in support and work continued.	
	12/7/17		Remained in support and work continued.	
	13/7/17		Remained in support and work continued.	

Army Form C. 2118.

WAR DIARY
or
INTELLIGENCE SUMMARY
(Erase heading not required.)

Instructions regarding War Diaries and Intelligence Summaries are contained in F.S. Regs, Part II. and the Staff Manual respectively. Title Pages will be prepared in manuscript.

Place	Date	Hour	Summary of Events and Information	Remarks and references to Appendices
FIELD	14/7/17		At 9.30pm the Battalion moved to relieve the 4th Bn Royal Fusiliers in the Left Sector and took over the positions as under:- Bn H.Q. SUNKEN RD So. DEMICOURT. FRONT LINE, Left Coy "B", Right Coy "A" SUPPORT "C" COY. RESERVE "D" COY AT DOIGNIES. The relief was completed at 12.15 am 15th July. The reserve company provided reconnoitering patrols from 10.30pm to 3.30 am 15/7/17.	
	15/7/17		Remained in forward positions holding and consolidating posts, and providing the usual night patrols. The patrol in front of the right front Coy encountered an enemy outpost, and after establishing direction. The patrol moved the post but the enemy were found to have evacuated the position.	
	16/7/17		Remained in forward positions continuing with consolidation and finding usual patrols who failed to come in contact with any hostile parties or posts.	
	17/7/17		An under company relief was effected commencing at 10pm and the relief was completed under protection of covering patrols by 12.30 am 18th July for report on 18th July. Heavy en. following fire.	
	19/7/17		The front trench were heavily shelled by the enemy during the day and night, especially the canal detached post. 1 Pnmt. to 7 went to Peronne was slightly wounded by a shell. Casualties on O.R. 1 killed and 6 wounded.	

Army Form C. 2118.

WAR DIARY
or
INTELLIGENCE SUMMARY

(Erase heading not required.)

Place	Date	Hour	Summary of Events and Information	Remarks and references to Appendices
FIELD	18/11/17		Remained in forward positions and proceeded with consolidation. The B. Coy HQ area was shelled during the day and with slightly more severity during the night, as were also the forward posts.	
	19/11/17		Remained in same positions and carried out further consolidation. There was continued heavy hostile shelling of R8, R9, R10 m posts from 9am. This continued throughout the day with shells and french mortars and due precaution for a rush were taken. About 11pm the bombardment became intense. The approach to the posts were barraged and R9, as a result of the increased shelling, was wrecked - the garrison remaining intact by cute stopping contrivance. The bombardment lifted at about 2.45 am on the morning of the 20th when the posts went immediately reoccupied. A barrage was put down about 200 yards N & NE of R9 post. At 2.45 am an enemy attack was made with bombs & rifle grenades on R7 post. This was presumably a feint, for at the same time a determined attack was made by a strong party, on the bombing post, post to the N of R9. This small post was garrisoned by 1 NCO and 6 men. The continuous bombardment had broken the post and the went in front out in places. The garrison however a twenty of the enemy - about 30 strong, who penetrating through the wire opened machine gun fire and attacked with bombs. A vigorous defence was conducted	

2449 Wt. W14957/Mgo 750,000 1/16 J.B.C. & A. Forms/C.2118/12.

WAR DIARY or INTELLIGENCE SUMMARY

Army Form C. 2118.

Place	Date	Hour	Summary of Events and Information	Remarks and references to Appendices
FIELD			by the garrison of the bombing posts with rifle fire and bombs and although against heavy odds succeeded in repulsing the attacking force. On the enemy retiring through the wire, the N.C.O. in charge with his garrison reduced to one combatant, rushed over to the enemy post to obtain the reinforcement of a Lewis Gun Team. Two guns from the next post opened cross fire on front of the bombing posts, but observation was hindered by the enemy's use of smoke bombs. Heavy casualties were inflicted on the enemy by the cross fire from all other posts, but two members of the Lewis gun could not be seen to remove these under covering fire. The relief of the battalion by the 4"RE was commenced at 10:45 p.m. and duly completed by 1 a.m. 23rd. On completion of relief the battalion took over reserve billets near VELU reaching camp about 11:15 a.m. After resting the remainder of the day was devoted to bathing and cleaning up. A working party of 10 officers and 400 OR was provided for	
21/7/17. 22/7/17.			work under R.E. digging C.T. S.E. of HERMIES. The Divisional band played selections from 6-7 p.m. The commanding officer wished to congratulate all ranks of the forward post on the efficient manner in which they dealt with and repulsed the enemy raid on the night of 20/21st July.	

Army Form C. 2118.

WAR DIARY
or
INTELLIGENCE SUMMARY
(Erase heading not required.)

Place	Date	Hour	Summary of Events and Information	Remarks and references to Appendices
VELU	23/7/17		The morning was devoted to cleaning up, and the afternoon to recreational training. 10 Officers & 400 OR were again provided for work. RE and 4 Officers sent for 24 hours instruction in infantry and artillery co-operation. The Commanding Officer has great pleasure in conveying to notice and causing to be placed on the records of the Battalion the gallant conduct and good work of the NCOs and men named below:— No 24360 2/Lieut G. Cornall, 14602 Pte R. Killingro, 52114 Pte Kilrush and No 26905 Pte B. Steele for gallantry in holding a post against heavy odds. No 4529 Pte S. Thorpe for carrying message ends, Lecy Shellfire. No 22732 Cpl Boardman for promptness in handling the Lewis Gun and dealing with the enemy in a critical situation. No 14314 Sergt J Hoofitt for gallantry on the night of 17 July when two posts had been nearly killed.	
	24/7/17		Remained in recent at VELU and provided usual working party and Officers for attachment to Artillery.	
	25/7/17		As above. The Corps Commander wishes to convey his congratulations on the manner in which the enemy raid on the night of 17 July had been repulsed, and which reflects great credit upon all ranks concerned.	

WAR DIARY or INTELLIGENCE SUMMARY

Army Form C. 2118.

Place	Date	Hour	Summary of Events and Information	Remarks and references to Appendices
YELU	26/7/17		Remained in Reserve. The following officers joined for duty:— 2nd Lieuts R.B. Yellow, F.I. Exley, H.E. Little and W. McKenzie. The Divisional Band played from 6 to 8 p.m.	
	27/7/17		The Battalion commenced to move off for relief of 1/5" in the left subsector at 9.0 p.m. "B" and "A" Coys taking over the forward posts with "D" Coy in support and "C" in reserve. The relief was completed by 1.30 am on the 28th and the work in hand taken over and carried on. "D" Coy found posts at the rate of 1 Platoon on the left and 2 sections on the right.	
	28/7/17		Remained in this position. Holding and consolidating the posts.	
	29/7/17		As above.	
	30/7/17		An inter Coy relief was commenced at 10.30 pm "D" Coy relieving "B" & "C" Coy relieving "A". The relief was completed 12.30 am and a working party of 1 officer & 20 OR provided for work under R.E. There was considerable artillery activity on our left during the night. A few chemical shells were reported by "A" Coy.	
	31/7/17		Remained in the forward position, holding & consolidating the position and improving the same, nothing particular came under notice. The CO is pleased to announce that 2nd Lieut P.E. B. Todd be awarded the Military Medal for gallantry in the field. W. Frankston Lieut Col Commdg 13 Kings (Liverpool) Regt	

31/7/17

Army Form C. 2118.

18TH (S)EN THE KING'S (LIVERPOOL) REGT.

WAR DIARY
or
INTELLIGENCE SUMMARY.

(Erase heading not required.)

Instructions regarding War Diaries and Intelligence Summaries are contained in F.S. Regs., Part II. and the Staff Manual respectively. Title pages will be prepared in manuscript.

AUGUST 1917.

Place	Date	Hour	Summary of Events and Information	Remarks and references to Appendices
DEMICOURT.	1st Aug.		The Battalion remained in the right sub-section, holding and continuing to consolidate the position. The usual patrols were organised and a working party of 1 Officer and 50 O.R. provided for work under the R.E.	
	2nd Aug.		Remained in the above position. The Sunken Road S. of DEMICOURT was intermittently shelled, but no casualties were sustained. The relief of the Battalion by the 4th Bn. The Royal Fusiliers commenced at 9.30 p.m. and was conducted as quickly as possible owing to a proposed bombardment of the enemy lines with gas shell. The relief was duly completed by 12.30 a.m. and the Battalion took over the VELU Camp with the exception of 1 Officer and 50 O.R. of "A" Coy who garrisonned the Catacombs at HERMIES, Posts R.R.6 and R.R.7.	
	3rd Aug.		The Battalion remained in rest at VELU and the day was devoted to cleaning up. A Working Party of 1 Officer and 50 O.R. was provided for work under the R.E. The U/m Officers proceeded on a course of entrenching under the C.R.E 3rd Division:- 2/Lieuts. F.S.Corrigan., A.R.Tetlow., E.G.Davis., E.A.Radcliffe., J.L.Barratt., C.MacKenzie., W.F.Galley., W.S.Little.	
	4th Aug		The Battalion remained at VELU, and the working party under the R.E. was again provided. The Garrison of Posts R.R.6 and R.R.7 rejoined the Battalion.	
	5th Aug.		Remained at Velu. The first portion of the day was devoted to cleaning up and kit inspections, after which Companies were inspected under the arrangements of Company Commanders. An Officers Rugby match was played against the 1st Bn.Northumberland Fusiliers.	
	6th Aug.		Remained in camp at VELU. The Corps Commander inspected the Battalion, and expressed his great satisfaction with the smartness of the Battalion after such a short time out of the line.	
	7th Aug.		Remained in Camp at VELU and a programme of training under Company Commanders carried out. At 7.45 p.m. the Battn moved off, H.Q.leading followed by platoons at 100 yards	

13TH BN THE KING'S (LIVERPOOL) REGT.

WAR DIARY or INTELLIGENCE SUMMARY

Army Form C. 2118.

AUGUST 1917.

Place	Date	Hour	Summary of Events and Information	Remarks and references to Appendices
Field.	8th August.		Interval, and proceeded to relieve the 2/5 Bn.K.O.Y.L.I. in support in the LAGNICOURT Section, H.Q., "B" and "D" Coy taking over the position in Sunken Road South of LAGNICOURT, and "A" and "C" Coys North of LAGNICOURT. Remained in support. The area N. of LAGNICOURT was lightly shelled during the day, heavier calibre being used between 7 and 9 p.m. The following working and carrying parties were provided:- 5 Officers and 100 O.R. for work under the R.E. in sector of Right Front Battalion. 2 Officers and 100 O.R. to carry wire to the front line, Right Section. 2 Officers and 100 O.R. to carry wire to the front line, Left Section. 1 Officer and 50 O.R. for work on the INTERMEDIATE LINE. The General Officer Commanding had great pleasure in announcing that the Field Marshall Commanding-In-Chief has, under authority granted by His Majesty The King, awarded the Distinguished Conduct Medal to No.24360 Private(Acting Lance Cpl) J. Cornall for gallantry in the Field.	
	9th August.		Remained in support and the usual working parties were found.	
	10th August		The Battalion remained in the support area until 9 p.m. when the relief of the 4th Bn The Royal Fusiliers in the right (LAGNICOURT) sub section was commenced. The relief was duly completed by 11 p.m. and the following positions taken up:- Battn.H.Q. Sunken Road E. of LAGNICOURT at C24.d.8.6. (Map 57c. N&W. 1/20,000). Right Front. "B" Coy. Left Front. "A" Coy. Right Support. "D" Coy. Left Support "C" Coy. All work was taken over and carried on. Owing to an enemy raid being suspected, special defensive preparations were organised.	
	11th August.		The Battalion remained in this position and provided the usual working and carrying parties.	
	12th August.		Remained in the line and the usual working and carrying parties provided.	

35TH BN THE KING'S (LIVERPOOL) REGT.

Army Form C. 2118.

WAR DIARY
or
INTELLIGENCE SUMMARY.
(Erase heading not required.)

AUGUST 1917.

Instructions regarding War Diaries and Intelligence Summaries are contained in F. S. Regs., Part II. and the Staff Manual respectively. Title pages will be prepared in manuscript.

Place	Date	Hour	Summary of Events and Information	Remarks and references to Appendices
Field.	12th August.		Remained in the Front Line and the usual working parties were provided.	
	13th August.		Remained in the Front Line and provided the usual working and carrying parties. The Corps Commander inspected the position.	
	14th August.		Remained in this position, holding and consolidating the posts.	
	15th August.		Remained in this position until 9.30 p.m. when the relief of the Battalion by the 4th Bn. The Royal Fusiliers commenced. This was duly completed by midnight, the Battalion taking over the FREMICOURT CAMP at I.29.c.	
	16th August.		Remained in Camp and the day was devoted to cleaning up.	
	17th August.		Remained in Camp and a programme of training under Company arrangements carried out.	
	18th August.		As above.	
	19th August.		Remained in Camp and Religious Services for all denominations were held.	
	20th August.		Remained in Camp and the morning was devoted to a programme of training. Regimental Sports, held by kind permission of Brig. General H.C. Potter, commenced at 2.30 p.m. and, favoured by a fine afternoon, provided great amusement. The prizes were kindly provided by the Y.M.C.A. BEUGNY and the Divisional Band was in attendance, providing selections between events.	
	21st August.		The Battalion remained in Camp at FREMICOURT and a programme of training carried out. At 7.30 p.m. Companies moved off to the relief of the 4th Bn The Royal Fusiliers in the following order, maintaining a distance of 200 yards between companies:- "D" "C" "B" "A". The relief was duly complete by 11.30 p.m. and the positions taken over in the right sub-section (LAGNICOURT) is under:-	
			Right Front. "D" Coy. Left Front. "C" Coy.	
			Right Support. "B" Coy. Left Support. "A" Coy.	
			All work was taken over and continued.	
	22nd August.		Remained in the Line, holding and consolidating the position.	
	23rd August.		Remained in the Line, providing the usual patrols, and working an carrying parties.	
	24th August.		As above.	
	25th August.		Remained in the Line. The Army Commander visited the line and expressed his appreciation of the cleanliness if the trenches and the condition of the Battalion. The usual working	

Army Form C. 2118.

WAR DIARY
or
INTELLIGENCE SUMMARY.

(Erase heading not required.)

13TH BN THE KING'S (LIVERPOOL) REGT.

AUGUST 1917.

Instructions regarding War Diaries and Intelligence Summaries are contained in F. S. Regs., Part II. and the Staff Manual respectively. Title pages will be prepared in manuscript.

Place	Date	Hour	Summary of Events and Information	Remarks and references to Appendices
Field.	26th August.		and carrying parties were provided and patrols organised.	
			Remained in the Line, holding and consolidating the position.	
	27th August.		Remained in the Line. A patrol in command of 2/Lieut.A.Richards came into contact with a large enemy party who opened fire. 2/Lieut Richards his Lewis gun into action, and replied with L.G., rifle, and rifle grenade fire. After about 20 minutes the enemy brought a cross fire to bear from the right and left front and word was passed by Mr.Richards to return to our trenches, which was received by all the patrol. When about 50 yards from our wire it was discovered that 2/Lieut Richards and 4 O.R. were missing. A search party was immediately organised and dispatched, but was unable to find any trace of the Officer or men.	
	28th August.		Remained in the Line. Further search parties were organised but failed to discover any trace of 2/Lieut Richards and party.	
			The relief of the Battalion by the 4th Bn.Royal Fusiliers commenced at 9.30 p.m., and was fully completed by 11 p.m.	
			The Battalion then took over the support position N.and S.of LAGNICOURT.	
	29th August.		Remained in the support position, and provided working and carrying parties to the Front Line.	
	30th August.		As above.	
	31st August.		Remained in the Support position, providing the usual working and carrying parties.	

31st August 1917.

commdg 13th Bn The King's (Liverpool) Regt.
Lieut.Col.

Army Form C. 2118.

WAR DIARY
or
INTELLIGENCE SUMMARY

13TH (S) BN THE KING'S (LIVERPOOL) REGT.

SEPTEMBER 1917.

Vol 25

(Erase heading not required.)

Instructions regarding War Diaries and Intelligence Summaries are contained in F. S. Regs., Part II. and the Staff Manual respectively. Title Pages will be prepared in manuscript.

Place	Date	Hour	Summary of Events and Information	Remarks and references to Appendices
AGNICOURT	1st Sept.		The Battalion remained in support to the Right sub-section (LAGNICOURT) and provided the usual working and carrying parties.	
	2nd Sept.		Remained in the above position until 8.30 p.m. when the Battalion moved forward to relieve the 4th Bn. Royal Fusiliers in the following order:- "B" "A" "D" and taking up positions as under:- "B" Coy Right Front "A" Coy Left Front "D" Coy Right Support "C" Coy Left Support All work was carried on and patrols organised. holding	
	3rd Sept.		Remained in this position and consolidating the line.	
	4th Sept.		Remained in the above position until 9 P.M. when the relief of the Battalion by the 1/12th London Regiment commenced. The relief was duly completed by 11 p.m. the Battalion taking over rest billets at FREMICOURT CAMP.	
	5th Sept.		Remained in Camp until 6.20 p.m. when the Battalion moved off in column of route to camp in LE TRANSLOY-BEAULENCOURT area at N.18.c.	
	6th Sept.		Remained in camp and the day devoted to cleaning up.	
	7th Sept.		Remained at BEAULENCOURT and a programme of training followed. The Commanding Officer had great pleasure in bringing to notice the gallant conduct of No. 11460 Private W. Fairhurst in successfully stopping two runaway horses with a G.S. Wagon on 5/9/17, thereby avoiding a serious accident.	
	8th Sept.		Remained in camp and training programme followed.	
	9th Sept.		Remained in camp and Religious Services for all denominations held. A Regimental Dinner for Officers was held in the Y.M.C.A. Tent BEAULENCOURT.	
	10th Sept.		Remained in camp at BEAULENCOURT and programme of training followed.	
	11th Sept.		Remained in camp at BEAULENCOURT and programme of training followed.	

13TH (S) Bn THE KING'S (LIVERPOOL) REGT.

Army Form C. 2118.

Instructions regarding War Diaries and Intelligence Summaries are contained in F.S. Regs., Part II and the Staff Manual respectively. Title pages will be prepared in manuscript.

WAR DIARY
or
INTELLIGENCE SUMMARY.
(Erase heading not required.)

SEPTEMBER 1917.

Place	Date	Hour	Summary of Events and Information	Remarks and references to Appendices
	12th Sept.		Remained in camp at BEAULENCOURT and programme of training followed.	
	13th Sept.		Remained in camp at BEAULENCOURT and programme of training followed.	
	14th Sept.		Remained in camp at BEAULENCOURT and programme of training followed.	
	15th Sept.		Remained in camp at BEAULENCOURT and programme of training followed.	
	16th Sept.		Remained in camp and Religious Services for all denominations held.	
	17th Sept.		Remained in camp at BEAULENCOURT with the exception of "C" Company who paraded and moved off to MIRAUMONT at 12.30 p.m. The remainder of the Battalion spent the day in cleaning up and inspection of kit.	
	18th Sept.		Battalion H.Q., "A", "B", & "D" Coys. paraded at 6.20 a.m. and marched to MIRAUMONT via BAPAUME - ACHIET LE GRAND and ACHIET LE PETIT arriving at their destination at 11 a.m. "C" Coy remained at MIRAUMONT to entrain the Brigade Transport the remainder of the Battalion entraining, after dinner had been served, and duly arrived and detrained at HOPOUTRE (BELGIUM) about 10.45 p.m. The Battalion then marched to camp in WATOU area (No. 1 area) the last Company arriving at 12 midnight.	
	19th Sept.		Remained in camp at WATOU and "C" Coy rejoined the Battalion. At 4 p.m. the Battalion moved off by road and took over ERIE CAMP (BRANDHOEK area) at 6.30 p.m.	
	20th Sept.		Remained in ERIE CAMP and the day devoted to cleaning up, kit inspections and preparation for battle.	
	21st Sept.		Remained in Camp. Parades being held under Company Arrangements.	

1/7TH (S) BN THE KING'S (LIVERPOOL) REGT

Army Form C. 2118.

WAR DIARY
or
INTELLIGENCE SUMMARY.

(Erase heading not required.)

SEPTEMBER 1917.

Instructions regarding War Diaries and Intelligence Summaries are contained in F.S. Regs., Part II. and the Staff Manual respectively. Title pages will be prepared in manuscript.

Place	Date	Hour	Summary of Events and Information	Remarks and references to Appendices
BRANDHOEK	22nd SEPT.		Remained in BRIE CAMP until 4.15 p.m. when the Battalion moved off to entraining point near BRANDHOEK duly arriving at YPRES at 7 p.m. when the Battalion proceeded to the relief of the 11th and 12th ROYAL SCOTS in the Right Support position i.e. HANNEBEKE WOOD, SANS SOUCI and POTSDAM. The relief was duly completed by 2 a.m. The Battalion details took over portion of AXE CAMP (BRANDHOEK).	
LINE	23rd SEPT		Remained in the above position which was heavily shelled throughout the day, a hostile barrage being put down from HANNEBEKE to POTSDAM in reply to our own.	
	24th SEPT		Remained in Right Support position until Midnight when the Battalion was relieved by the 8th K.O.R.L. Regt. and moved back to position in the old enemy front line which was in a battered condition.	
	25th SEPT		Remained in this position which was heavily shelled in reply to our own artillery activity. Capt. D.P.Wilkinson M.C. was wounded in the early morning.	
	26th SEPT		The 8th and 76th Brigades attacked at dawn, the Battalion being in Divisional Reserve. About 7.30 p.m. word was received that our front line was falling back owing to pressure from the enemy. The Battalion moved forward to Support position, BORRY and VAMPIRO FARMS with line running south to railway, "B" Coy taking up Support position at LOW FARM. At midnight the Battalion was ordered to occupy the RED LINE which had been next to the last objective in the days attack, with extreme difficulty after passing through barrage. The Battalion got into position about 5 a.m. on the 27th. During the move the following Officers were wounded:- Major K.Hall, 2/Lieut. M.A.Page, 2/Lieut. R.B.Bramley.	
	27th SEPT		Remained in the RED LINE. A heavy barrage came down about 6.30 p.m. and the enemy counter-attacked from HILL 40 but was repulsed by our fire. The following casualties in Officers were sustained:- KILLED 2/Lieut. J.W.Barratt. WOUNDED 2/Lieut. G.A.Glencross.	

Army Form C. 2118.

WAR DIARY or INTELLIGENCE SUMMARY

13TH (S) BN THE KING'S (LIVERPOOL) REGT.   SEPTEMBER 1917.

(Erase heading not required.)

Place	Date	Hour	Summary of Events and Information	Remarks and references to Appendices
LINE	28th SEPT.		Remained in this position. There was considerable hostile sniping during the day and M.G. Fire at night. A heavy enemy barrage was put down at 6 p.m. lasting about an hour.	
	29th SEPT.		Party of 35th Australians reconnoitred the line with a view to taking over our positions.	
	30th SEPT.		The Battalion was relieved by the 35th Battalion Australians, the relief being complete by 12.55 a.m. The Battalion took over Camp in VLAMERTINGHE AREA (No.1)	

1st October 1917.

W. [signature] Lieut:Col:
commdg 13th (S) Bn The King's (Liverpool) Regt.

Army Form C. 2118.

WAR DIARY
or
INTELLIGENCE SUMMARY.

(Erase heading not required.)

Instructions regarding War Diaries and Intelligence Summaries are contained in F. S. Regs., Part II. and the Staff Manual respectively. Title pages will be prepared in manuscript.

Place	Date	Hour	Summary of Events and Information	Remarks and references to Appendices

WAR DIARY
or
INTELLIGENCE SUMMARY.
(Erase heading not required.)

Army Form C. 2118.

1st (S) Bn. THE KING'S (LIVERPOOL) R.

OCTOBER 1917.

Instructions regarding War Diaries and Intelligence Summaries are contained in F. S. Regs., Part II and the Staff Manual respectively. Title pages will be prepared in manuscript.

Place	Date	Hour	Summary of Events and Information	Remarks and references to Appendices
	11th Oct		Remained in the line and the usual patrols and working and carrying parties provided.	
	12th Oct		Remained in the line and the usual patrols and working and carrying parties provided.	
	13th Oct		Remained in the line and the usual patrols and working and carrying parties provided.	
	14th Oct		Remained in the line and the usual patrols and working and carrying parties provided.	
	15th Oct		Remained in the line and the usual patrols and working and carrying parties provided.	
	16th Oct		The Battalion remained in the line until the evening when part of Relief by the 4th Batt. Royal Fusiliers. The Relief was all complete at 1-30 a.m. 17th October. Battalion then went over to same Reserve in VAULX VRAUCOURT.	
	17th Oct		Remained in Brigade Reserve and the day devoted to cleaning up.	
	18th Oct		Remained in Brigade Reserve and programme of training followed. Working and carrying parties provided.	
	19th Oct		Remained in Brigade Reserve and party of 7 officers and 200 O.R. provided for work on trench.	
	20th Oct		Remained in VAULX and programme of training followed under Company arrangements.	
	21st Oct		Remained in VAULX and programme of training followed under Company arrangements.	
	22nd Oct		The Battalion remained in Brigade Reserve at VAULX until 5-30 p.m. when it moved off to the Relief of the 4th Bn Royal Fusiliers in the Left Sub-section NO MAN'S section. On the completion of the Relief the battalion dispositor was "A" "B" and "C" Coys in front line with "D" Coy. in Support.
The Relief was only complete by 10 p.m. All work being taken over the carriers on.	

13TH (S) BN THE KING'S (LIVERPOOL) REGT

WAR DIARY
or
INTELLIGENCE SUMMARY

(Erase heading not required.)

Army Form C. 2118.

OCTOBER 1917

Instructions regarding War Diaries and Intelligence Summaries are contained in F.S. Regs., Part II. and the Staff Manual respectively. Title Pages will be prepared in manuscript.

Place	Date	Hour	Summary of Events and Information	Remarks and references to Appendices
	23rd Octr		Remained in the line holding and consolidating the position. The usual patrols and working parties were organised.	
	24th Octr		Remained in the line holding and consolidating the position. The usual patrols and working parties were organised.	
	25th Octr		Remained in the line holding and consolidating the position. The usual patrols and working parties were organised.	
	26th Octr		Remained in Front Line until the Relief by the 4th Bn.Royal Fusiliers commenced. The Battalion then moved into the Support (NOREUIL) position, with the exception of "C" Coy who remained in Railway Reserve	
	27th Octr		Remained in Support Position. The Commanding Officer had much pleasure in announcing that the W/M N.C.O's and men were awarded the Military Medal for gallantry in the Field and causing same to be placed in the records of the Battalion:- No. 19515 Sergeant Duffy E. "B" Coy No. 19430 Private Bradbury H. "C" Coy " 48562 Private Small R.T. "D" Coy " 48716 " Guest J.T. "B" Coy " 235140 " Dean J. "D" Coy " 31568 " Edwards R. "A" Coy " 48547 " Evans R. "A" Coy " 17729 L/Sergeant Stockdale C. "D" Coy	
	28th Octr		Remained in Support Position.	
	29th Octr		Remained in Support Position.	
	30th Octr		Remained in the Support Position until 9 p.m. when the Relief of the Battalion by the 1st Bn. R.S.F's commenced. The Relief was duly completed by 10 p.m. and the Battalion proceeded into Rest Camp in the BEUGNATRE Area.	
	31st Octr		Remained in Camp and the day devoted to cleaning up.	
31st October 1917.			W. Granton (?) Lieut.-Col. Commdg 13th Bn. The King's (Liverpool) Regiment.	

13TH (S) BN THE KING'S (LIVERPOOL) REGIMENT

Army Form C. 2118.

WAR DIARY or INTELLIGENCE SUMMARY

(Erase heading not required.)

NOVEMBER 6, 1917

Vol 27

Place	Date	Hour	Summary of Events and Information	Remarks and references to Appendices
BEUGNATRE	1st Novr		Remained in No. 7 Camp (BEUGNATRE) and a scale of training followed. Local working parties were provided.	
	2nd	"	Remained in No. 7 Camp (BEUGNATRE) and a scale of training followed. Local working parties were provided.	
	3rd	"	Remained in No. 7 Camp and a scale of training followed, and local working parties provided. A platoon of "D" Coy was selected to be trained as a Model Platoon. 2/LIEUT. J.G. HARRIS joined for duty.	
	4th	"	Remained in Camp and religious services for all denominations held. A trial run was held for competitors in Corps Cross-Country Championship, also a trial Football Match for selection of the Battalion Team. The Commanding Officer had much pleasure in announcing that the Military Medal had been awarded to No.48382 PTE.L.BOOTH for gallantry in the Field.	
	5th	"	Remained in No. 7 Camp. G.O.C. 9th Infantry Brigade presented Military Medals Ribbons to the N.C.O's and men who had been awarded same for gallantry during the ZONNEBEKE operations. The U/m Officers joined for duty:- 2/LIEUTS. D.M.WAREHAM, L.G.FOSTER, F.CHALLENER, E.A.FARRIER, G.H.WELLER, F.D.BARTLEY and J.H.CURRY.	
	6th	"	Remained in Camp and scale of parades followed. A successful raid on the enemy's Lines was carried out by "C" Coy on the night 6/7th in which three prisoners were captured. Our casualties were:- 1 O.R. KILLED and 6 O.R. WOUNDED.	
	7th	"	Remained in Camp and scale of training followed.	
	8th	"	Remained in Camp and scale of training followed.	
	9th	"	Remained in Camp and scale of training followed.	
	10th	"	Remained in Camp and scale of training followed.	

Army Form C. 2118.

WAR DIARY
or
INTELLIGENCE SUMMARY.

13TH (S) BN THE KING'S (LIVERPOOL) REGIMENT

NOVEMBER 1917

Instructions regarding War Diaries and Intelligence Summaries are contained in F. S. Regs., Part II. and the Staff Manual respectively. Title pages will be prepared in manuscript.

Place	Date	Hour	Summary of Events and Information	Remarks and references to Appendices
	11th Novr.		Remained in Camp and religious services for all denominations held.	
	12th "		Remained in Camp and a scale of training followed. LIEUT. N.C.DAWSON joined for duty.	
	13th "		Remained in Camp and a scale of training followed.	
	14th "		Remained in Camp and a scale of training followed.	
	15th "		A Brigade Field Day was held. All officers reconnoitred the positions and approaches to the Line.	
	16th "		Remained in Camp and programme of training followed. The Commanding Officer had much pleasure in announcing that the u/m had been awarded the Military Medal for gallantry in the Field:- 51810 a/CORPORAL E.CORLETT 25755 SERGEANT W.HOWARTH	
	17th "		Remained in Camp and a scale of training followed.	
	18th "		Remained in Camp and religious services for all denominations held.	
	19th "		Remained in Camp and the day devoted to cleaning up. The C.O.C. 8th Infantry Brigade presented Medals to the Battalion Football Team which won the Brigade Championship. At 10 p.m. the Battalion moved into Brigade Reserve. Battalion H.Q. being in RAILWAY RESERVE U.28.c.9.5. (Spec.Sheet U/1 to U/6 1/10,000)	
	20th "		Remained in the above position and working and carrying parties provided.	
	21st "		Remained in the above position and working and carrying parties provided.	
	22nd "		Remained in above position and working and carrying parties provided.	

Army Form C. 2118.

13th (S) BN THE KING'S (LIVERPOOL) REGIMENT

Instructions regarding War Diaries and Intelligence
Summaries are contained in F.S. Regs., Part II.
and the Staff Manual respectively. Title pages
will be prepared in manuscript.

WAR DIARY
or
INTELLIGENCE SUMMARY

NOVEMBER 1917

(Erase heading not required.)

Place	Date	Hour	Summary of Events and Information	Remarks and references to Appendices
	23rd Novr.		Remained in above position and working and carrying parties provided.	
	24th	"	Remained in above position and working and carrying parties provided. The Battalion moved from Brigade Reserve into No. 7 Camp (BEUGNATRE).	
	25th	"	Remained in Camp and day devoted to cleaning up.	
	26th	"	Remained in Camp and the attack practised. The Commanding Officer had much pleasure in announcing that 2/LIEUT.A.R.TETLOW had been awarded the Military Cross for gallantry in the Field.	
	27th	"	Remained in Camp and Coys lectured on "Open Warfare". A Scheme was carried out.	
	28th	"	Remained in Camp and Coys lectured on "Open Warfare". A Scheme was carried out.	
	29th	"	Remained in Camp. At 4 p.m. the Battalion moved off to the relief of elements of the 7th MIDDLESEX and 1st and 3rd LONDON'S in the Right Sub-section LAGNICOURT Section. The Relief was duly completed by 9 p.m. when the positions held were as under:- Right Front "B" Coy. Left Front "A" Coy. Right Support "C" Coy. Left Support "D" Coy.	
	30th	"	Remained in the above position, all work being taken over and carried on.	

30/11/17

Lieut.Col:
Comandg 13th (S) Bn. The King's (Liverpool) Regt.

13TH (S) BN THE KING'S (LIVERPOOL) REGT

Army Form C. 2118.

WAR DIARY
INTELLIGENCE SUMMARY
(Erase heading not required.)

DECEMBER 1917

Place	Date	Hour	Summary of Events and Information	Remarks and references to Appendices
LAGNICOURT DECR	1st		Remained in the Right sub-section (LAGNICOURT Section) and carrying and working parties provided. Consolidation and improvements were proceeded with and patrols organised. The vicinity of Bn. H.Q. and SKIPTON ALLEY was heavily shelled during the day.	
	2nd		Remained in the above position. Working and carrying parties provided and patrols organised.	
	3rd		Remained in above position. Working and carrying parties provided and patrols organised.	
	4th		Remained in above position. Working and carrying parties provided and patrols organised.	
	5th		Remained in above position. Working and carrying parties provided and patrols organised.	
	6th		Remained in above position. Working and carrying parties provided and patrols organised.	
	7th		Remained in above position. Working and carrying parties provided and patrols organised.	
	8th		Remained in above position. Working and carrying parties provided and patrols organised.	
	9th		Remained in the line, holding and consolidating the position until 9 p.m. November when the Battalion was relieved by the 1st Wiltshire Regt. The relief was duly completed and all work handed over. The Battalion then marched to rest billets in MORY NORTH CAMP.	
	10th		Remained in MORY NORTH CAMP and the day devoted to cleaning up, inspections of kit and arms.	
	11th		Remained in Camp until 3 p.m. when the Battalion moved off to the relief of the 1st Bn. R.S.F. in the NOREUIL SECTOR. The relief was duly complete by 10-30 p.m. and all work taken over and carried on. On completion of relief the dispositions were as follows:— FRONT LINE "A" "B" & "C" COYS. SUPPORT "D" COY. with two platoons in ILKLEY SUPPORT, and two platoons disposed of as follows:— One post at C.6.c.30.25 (Map PRONVILLE spec ed. 4d) and two blocks garrisoned in RAILWAY RESERVE.	
	12th		At 6 a.m. the enemy opened an intense barrage on our front line, supports and C.T's including Bn. H.Q., the Battalion having already "stood to" in expectation of an attack. The S.O.S. was sent up by the 12th WEST YORKS and repeated along our line. The barrage lasted for 40 minutes, and then a low flying hostile aeroplane gave the signal to lift by firing a white rocket. Immediately the barrage lifted from the front line, and the enemy infantry attacked our line. Rifle and Lewis Gun fire was directed on them and they were driven off. Our left and centre Companies did good execution by enfilade fire from rifles and L.G's catching the enemy in groups advancing to the APEX.	

13TH (S) BN THE KING'S (LIVERPOOL) REGT

Army Form C. 2118.

WAR DIARY
or
INTELLIGENCE SUMMARY
(Erase heading not required)

DECEMBER 1917

Place	Date	Hour	Summary of Events and Information	Remarks and references to Appendices
	DECR 12th (contd)		At this time our men of "A" Coy were fighting in shell holes as all their trenches were blown in. "A" Coy had during this time established two blocks in our front line at U.29.b.50.05. and U.29.b.50.15. At 7-15 a.m. a second barrage was opened on our lines as before. This lasted for 25 minutes and then lifted from front to support lines. The enemy followed up to attack but was met by very heavy rifle and machine gun fire from our lines, and the men of the left Coy (A), after all the wire in front of their trenches had been blown up, left the trench with a cheer and advanced to meet the enemy, who retired leaving many dead and wounded behind. 3 wounded were brought in prisoners and evacuated. At 8-40 a.m. everything was quiet. All men were sent into front line from SHEFFIELD SUPPORT owing to the very heavy shell fire directed on this trench. At 10-40 a.m. the enemy again barraged our trenches for half-an-hour, but no infantry action resulted. At 2-30 p.m. another barrage was put down on our lines, lasting for 15 minutes. At 4-15 p.m. enemy again barraged our lines for half-an-hour. During the intervals of times stated, enemy intermittently shelled the whole of our sector. Owing to the severe casualties suffered by "A" and "C" Coys., one platon of "D" Coy was sent up to "A" Coy to re-inforce, and one platon of "D" Coy was sent up to "C" Coy at 8-50 a.m. About 2 p.m. Brigade informed us that one Company of the 1st N.F. were being sent up to re-inforce our front, and this Coy reported at 2-30 p.m. They were disposed of as follows:- 2 platons to "A" Coy, 1 platon to "B" Coy, and 1 platoon to "C" Coy and moved into position at dusk. At 7-30 p.m. orders were received to withdraw this Company of 1st N.F. and a Company of 4th R.F. were sent to replace them. The change was effected and the N.F's relieved by 11-30 p.m. Prisoners informed us that enemy were expected to attack again on morning of 15th., but our artillery heavily bombarded enemy lines from 5-30 p.m. to 7-30 p.m. and no attack developed. During the day enemy shelled our lines all day, increasing to barrage fire at 3-15 p.m. and lasting to 4-30 p.m.	

Army Form C. 2118.

13TH (S) BN THE KING'S (LIVERPOOL) REGT   WAR DIARY   DECEMBER 1917

INTELLIGENCE SUMMARY
(Erase heading not required.)

Instructions regarding War Diaries and Intelligence Summaries are contained in F.S. Regs., Part II. and the Staff Manual respectively. Title pages will be prepared in manuscript.

Place	Date	Hour	Summary of Events and Information	Remarks and references to Appendices
	DECR 12th (contd)		At 3-30 p.m. the enemy made a bombing attack on our left, this was 15 minutes before a bombing attack was to be made by 4th R.F. and 1st N.F., but our line was held intact. 2/LIEUT.F.CHALLENER was KILLED during the hostilities and the following Officers were wounded but remained at duty:- CAPT.N.A.R.VAN GRUISEN, 2/LIEUT.A.R.TETLOW,M.C. & 2/LIEUT.W.F.GALLEY CASUALTIES in O.R. KILLED 2 WOUNDED 48.	
	13th		Remained in the line and re-consolidation proceeded with. The enemy artillery shewed all round activity throughout the day.	
	14th		Remained in the line holding and consolidating the position. The usual working and carrying parties were found and patrols organised.	
	15th		Remained in the line holding and consolidating the position. The usual working and carrying parties were found and patrols organised.	
	16th		Remained in NOREUIL SECTOR until 6 p.m. when the relief of the Battalion by the 1st N.Y. commenced. All work was handed over and the relief duly complete by 1 a.m. 17/12/17 when the Battalion marched to billets in MORY NORTH CAMP.	
	17th	11-45 a.m.	the Battalion moved off in column of route and marched to COURCELLES LE COMPTE via ERVILLERS , 200 yards being maintained between Companies. Destination was reached by 2 p.m. and the Battalion took over No. 4 Camp. The remainder of the day was spent in resting and cleaning up.	
	18th		Remained in Camp at COURCELLES and a scale of training carried out. Baths for the Battalion were arranged.	
	19th		Remained in Camp at COURCELLES and a scale of training carried out.	
	20th		Remained in Camp at COURCELLES and a scale of training carried out.	
	21st		Remained in Camp at COURCELLES and re-organisation of Companies completed.	
	22nd		Remained at COURCELLES. The following Officers and men were mentioned in Sir Douglas Haig's dispatches for good work in the Field:- LIEUT.COL.W.J.CRANSTON, LIEUT.&.Q.M. A.E.PRATT, 19609 PTE.G.E.TAYLOR & 13707 PTE J.McDONOGH.	
	23rd	8-15 a.m.	At the Battalion moved off and proceeded to MORY where Camp was taken over at	
		11-30 a.m.	During the night the whole Battalion was engaged on working and carrying parties in the line. 2/LIEUT.J.H.CURRY was wounded by a shell.	

13TH (S) BN THE KING'S (LIVERPOOL) REGT.

Army Form C.2118.

WAR DIARY
or
INTELLIGENCE SUMMARY

DECEMBER 1917

(Erase heading not required.)

Instructions regarding War Diaries and Intelligence Summaries are contained in F.S. Regs., Part II. and the Staff Manual respectively. Title pages will be prepared in manuscript.

Place	Date	Hour	Summary of Events and Information	Remarks and references to Appendices
	DECR			
	24th		Remained in Camp at MORY and parties provided.	
	25th		Remained at MORY. Work was suspended by the order of G.O.C.Division. An excellent X'mas Dinner was served to the troops, the W.O's and Sergeants having a dinner in the evening.	
	26th		Remained at MORY and the Battalion was utilised for working and carrying parties in the line.	
	27th		At 12-50 p.m. the Battalion left MORY to proceed into CORPS RESERVE at MERGATEL, arriving at their destination about 3 p.m. taking over Camp in DURHAM LINES.	
	28th		Remained in Camp and a programme of training followed.	
	29th		Remained in Camp and a programme of training followed.	
	30th		Remained at MERGATEL and religious services held.	
	31st		Remained in Camp and a programme of training carried out.	

31/12/17

signature Major
Commdg 13th (S) Bn. The King's (Liverpol) Regt.

**3RD DIVISION
9TH INFY BDE**

13TH (S) BATTALION

KING'S (LIVERPOOL) REGT.

1918

1918 JAN — 1919 MAR

TO 3 NORTHERN BDE
3 DIV

Army Form C.2118.

WAR DIARY
or
INTELLIGENCE SUMMARY   13TH (S) BN THE KING'S (LIVERPOOL) REGT.

SECRET

Vol 29

Place	Date	Hour	Summary of Events and Information	Remarks and references to Appendices
MERCATEL.	1/1/18.		Remained in camp at "DURHAM LINES" and a scale of training followed.	
	2/1/18.		Remained in Camp. Owing to heavy snowfall, field training was limited and a series of lectures were given. The afternoon was occupied by recreational exercise.	
	3/1/18.		Remained at Mercatel. Inspections of arms, kit etc being made, and a scale of training followed.	
	4/1/18.		As above.	
	5/1/18.		The battalion remained at Mercatel and wiring, bayonet fighting and field work practised.	
	6/1/18.		Religious services for all denominations held, and kit inspection made. The afternoon was devoted to recreation.	
	7/1/18.		Remained at MERCATEL and a programme of training carried out.	
	8/1/18.		As above.	
	9/1/18.		As above.	
	10/1/18.		As above. The Commanding Officer had much pleasure in announcing that the Military Medal had been awarded the following N.C.O. and men and the Bar to the Military Medal to the man named, for gallantry in the Field:- BAR TO M.M:- 19430. Pte H.Bradbury. M.M. M.M. 20920. Pte J.Liptrot. 21806.Ptd.H.T.Roberts. 11801. Pte W.Owens. 23212. Pte S.Bennison.	
	11/1/18		Remained at MERCATEL, and a programme of training followed.	
	12/1/18.		Remained as above. The Commanding Officer was pleased to announce that the undermentioned Officers had been awarded the Military Cross for gallantry in the Field: 2/LIEUT.D.M.WAREHAM.	

Army Form C. 2118.

WAR DIARY
or
INTELLIGENCE SUMMARY

(Erase heading not required.)

Instructions regarding War Diaries and Intelligence Summaries are contained in F.S. Regs., Part II. and the Staff Manual respectively. Title Pages will be prepared in manuscript.

Place	Date	Hour	Summary of Events and Information	Remarks and references to Appendices
MERCATEL.	13/1/18.		Remained at MERCATEL and a programme of training followed. The Commanding Officer had much pleasure in announcing that the u/m N.C.O. had been awarded the ~~Military Medal~~ for gallantry in the Field:- 52569 L/Cpl (a/Cpl) F.Dolman.	DCM
	14/1/18.		Remained at MERCATEL.	
	15/1/17.		The Battalion carried out a programme of field training. Working and carrying parties for the line were provided.	
	16/1/17.		As above.	
	17/1/18.		As above.	
	18/1/18.		Remained at MERCATEL, and a programme of training followed. The usual carrying and working parties were provided.	
	19/1/18		As above. The Commanding Officer had much pleasure in announcing that No 19036 C.Q.M.S. H.Donohue had been awarded the ~~Military~~ MERITORIOUS Service Medal for good work in the Field.	
	20/1/17.		Religious services for all denominations were held and the afternoon devoted to recreation. The usual working and carrying parties were found.	
	21/1/17.		Remained at MERCATEL and the usual parties provided.	
	22/1/17.		The Corps Commander inspected the Battalion at 9.30 a.m. He expressed his satisfaction with the work done by the unit, both in and out of the line, also with the cleanliness of their general turnout. The usual parties for the line were found.	
	23/1/17.		Remained in DURHAM LINES and parties provided.	

Army Form C. 2118.

WAR DIARY
or
INTELLIGENCE SUMMARY
(Erase heading not required.)

Instructions regarding War Diaries and Intelligence Summaries are contained in F. S. Regs., Part II. and the Staff Manual respectively. Title Pages will be prepared in manuscript.

Place	Date	Hour	Summary of Events and Information	Remarks and references to Appendices
MERCATEL	24/1/18.		Remained in camp and parties provided for the line.	
	25/1/18.		As above.	
	26/1/18		As above. An inter-company wiring competition was carried out after dusk, with the following result:- "B" Coy. 91. "D" Coy 90½. "A" Coy 90. "C" Coy. 81. Possible marks 100.	
	27/1/18.		Remained in camp until 3-15 p.m. when the Battalion moved to the relief of 20th Bn N.F. in Brigade Support Centre Section. The relief was duly completed by 7 p.m. and all work taken over and carried on.	
	28/1/18		Remained in Brigade Support. "D" Coy provided working and carrying parties for the line.	
	29/1/18.		Remained as above and parties provided by "B" "C" and "D" Coys.	
	30/1/18.		At 9 a.m the battalion moved to the relief of the 1st Bn N.F. in the left sector, the relief being duly complete by 2·0p.m. All work was taken over and consolidation proceeded with. The front line was held by "B" "C" and "D" coys with "A" Coy in support.	
	31/1/17.		Remained in the above position and consolidation proceeded with.	

31/1/17.

[signature]
Lieut:Col:
commdg 13th Bn The King's (Liverpool) Regt.

Army Form. 2118.

WAR DIARY
or
INTELLIGENCE SUMMARY
13TH BN THE KING'S (LIVERPOOL) REGT.

(Erase heading not required.)

Place	Date	Hour	Summary of Events and Information	Remarks and references to Appendices
FIELD.	February 1918.			
	1		The Battalion remained in the Left Sub-Section, holding and consolidating the position. Patrols were organised and working and carrying parties provided.	
	2.		Remained in the above position and work continued.	
	3.		At 9 a.m. the relief of the Battalion By 1st Bn .N.F. commenced and was duly complete by noon. The Battalion then moved into Brigade Reserve in the Hindenburg Line, from whence working and carrying parties for the front line were provided.	
	4.		Remained in Brigade and working and carrying parties provided.	
	5.		As above	
	6.		As above.	
	7.		The Battalion moved to the relief of the 1st Bn Northumberland Fusiliers, commencing at 9 a.m, taking over the Left Sub-Section. The relief was duly complete by mid day, the position of Companies than being as under:- Right Front. "B" Coy. Centre. "C" Coy. Left Front. "A" Coy. "D" Coy. 2 Platoons Mallard Trench and 2 Platoons Cuckoo Court. All work was taken over and carried on, and the usual patrols organised.	
	8.		Remained in the above position. At about 6-15 a.m. a heavy hostile barrage was placed on our front defences. All precautions against attack were at once taken, and after about forty five minutes the enemy artillery ceased and the situation became normal. The necessary repairs to our line were at once taken in hand.	
	9		Remained in the front line, patrols and working parties organised, and consolidation continued.	
	10		As Above.	

Army Form 2118.

WAR DIARY
or
INTELLIGENCE SUMMARY
(Erase heading not required.)

Instructions regarding War Diaries and Intelligence Summaries are contained in F. S. Regs., Part II. and the Staff Manual respectively. Title pages will be prepared in manuscript.

Place	Date	Hour	Summary of Events and Information	Remarks and references to Appendices
Field	11		Remained as above. The Commanding Officer had much pleasure in announcing that the following soldiers had been awarded the Belgian Croix de Guerre for service in the Field. 15899 PTE J.J.NAVIEN. 8266. PTE. E.MUNSEY. 12661. PTE A.ALLEN.	
	12.		The relief of the Battalion by 4th Bn The Royal Fusiliers was commenced at 9 a.m. and duly completed by noon. The Battalion then took over positions as follows:- "A" and "D" Coys in the HINDENBURG LINE. "C" Coy in EGRET LOOP, and "B" Coy in EGRET TRENCH. Working and carrying parties were provided for the front line.	
	13.		Remained in the above position and working and carrying parties provided.	
	14.		As above.	
	15.		At 8.50 a.m. the Battalion moved to the relief of 1st.Bn.N.F. in the Right Sub-Section. The relief was duly complete by 2p.m. the positions then held being:- Right Front "D" Coy Left Front "A" Coy Right Support "C" Coy. Left Support "B" Coy. All trench stores were taken over and work continued. Patrols were organised and working parties provided.	
	16.		Remained in this position. At 5.55 a.m. the enemy put down a heavy barrage of T.M's and 5.9 and 4.2 shells on our front and support lines, including gas shell. The front line was bombarded from U1.a.9.8. to O.31.b.8.2. SWIFT SUPPORT and the following C.T's were also barraged:- PIONEER ALLEY,FIRST AVENUE AND WOOD TRENCH. FIRST AVENUE was bombarded as far back as Batta.H.Q. (N.36.b.4.2.)and BROWN SUPPORT was also shelled. The enemy about 100 strong attacked from U.1.b.4.8. to O.31.d.6.5. at about 5.50 a.m. He was met by Lewis Gun and rifle fire from all posts but succeeded in entering our line at U.1.b.5.7.,and on each flank of post at O.31.b.7.3. He commenced to bomb outwards from these points. Garrison of posts 7a (O.31.d.7.3.) bombed southwards and drove enemy out,and established a block at the junction of FIRST AVENUE and the front line. The party of the	

WAR DIARY
or
INTELLIGENCE SUMMARY.
(Erase heading not required.)

Army Form C. 2118.

Place	Date	Hour	Summary of Events and Information	Remarks and references to Appendices
	16	(contd)	enemy which penetrated to the North of the post succeeded in bombing No 8 (L.G.) post O.31.d.6.4. The garrison moved North and established a block at trench junction O.31.d.6.5. A counter attack was immediately launched from the support line and the enemy driven out at all points. At 6.10 a.m. three red lights were sent up from the enemy line and a bugle sounded. Hostile fire then ceased. Three enemy dead remained in our trench, and identifications were made. 2/Lieut J.G.Harris was wounded during the operations. Map Reference to above HENINEL & GUEMAPPE 1/10,000. The remainder of the day was normal and the usual patrols etc were organised, and trench repair executed.	
	17		Remained in the front line and the usual work carried out.	
	18.		As above.	
	19		As above.	
	20		Remained in the above position and consolidation continued.	
	21		At 9 a.m. the relief of the Battalion by 4th Bn The Royal Fusiliers commenced and was duly complete by 1P.m. The Battalion then moved to positions in BRIGADE SUPPORT dispositions being as follows:- Battn.H.Q., "D" "B" and "C" Coys in SHAFT TRENCH. "A" Coy in EGRET TRENCH and LOOP. Working and carrying parties for the front line were provided after dusk.	

Army Form C. 2118.

WAR DIARY
INTELLIGENCE SUMMARY.

15th Bn The King's (Liverpool) Regt.

(Erase heading not required.)

Instructions regarding War Diaries and Intelligence Summaries are contained in F. S. Regs., Part II. and the Staff Manual respectively. Title pages will be prepared in manuscript.

Place	Date	Hour	Summary of Events and Information	Remarks and references to Appendices
FIELD.	22		Remained in Brigade Support and working and carrying parties for the time provided.	
	23		As above.	
	24.		The Battalion moved to the relief of the 1st Bn Northumberland Fusiliers in the Left Sub-Section at 9.0 a.m. The relief was duly completed by 12.15 p.m., and all trench stores taken over and work continued. Reconnoitring patrols and Working and carrying parties were provided. The Commanding officer was pleased to announce that the u/m were awarded th MILITARY MEDAL for gallantry in the Field:- No 14440 Sgt.R.Armitage. 14825 L/Cpl Gerrard. 235165 Pte HOLDEN.	
	25		Remained in the Left Sub-Section and the usual patrols etc provided.	
	26		As above.	
	27.		As above.	
	28		as above.	

28/2/19.

[signature]
Lieut:Col:
commdg 15th Bn The King's (Liverpool) Regt.

SECRET

FILE No. **G.12.**

Sub-Nos. 192-

SUBJECT. **Minor Operations.**

Sub-head. **Enemy Raid S.W. of Cherisy on 13 L'pool R., 9th Bde; 3rd Divn.**

16/2/18.

(VI Corps).

Referred to	Date.	Referred to	Date.

V. Corps.

SECRET.

G.S.10/31.

1. I forward copies of a report by the Brigade and Battalion Commander concerned on the raid made by the enemy on the morning of the 16th February 1918, S.W. of CHERISY.

2. For the past few days the enemy had shown considerable Trench Mortar activity on the front line in the raided area. The opposing front lines are about 100 yards apart at this point, and are more adjacent than at any other point in the Divisional front. From personal inspection, and daily reports, I found that the hostile T.M. work was systematic and devoted almost entirely to our front line wire and to the junctions of the C.T's with the front line.

3. The hostile T.M's were very actively engaged by our Artillery and Trench Mortars, and their fire checked but only to re-open after a prolonged interval. Special wiring parties were detailed nightly to put out fresh wire and good results were obtained under difficult conditions. It is to be noted that the wire for the most part on the front now held by the 9th Inf. Bde. has in the past been put out too close to our own parapet and is not strong. The proximity of the enemy trenches has doubtless been the cause of this, but since taking over the line, one complete fence of double apron wire has been put out in front of the existing wire, and that fence is being strengthened nightly.

4. In view of a probable raid the following measures were taken to meet it:-

8 Field Guns - 18/pdrs - were taken off their ordinary S.O.S. lines and placed on the suspected area.

6 Vickers Guns were arranged to sweep No Man's Land in enfilade in the suspected area.

All available Trench Mortars were in readiness to come into action at once.

The posts in the front line were self contained - adequate frontal and flanking Lewis Gun fire was arranged.

Chevaux-de-Frise were made to block the trench between Posts, and Platoons were close at hand in the support line to counter-attack over the top when the hostile barrage lifted off the front line on to the support line on the box pattern which appeared to be indicated.

I am satisfied that every arrangement was made to deal with the expected raid.

5. The course of the raid is described in the attached reports.

6. I visited the trenches after the raid and personally examined each Post. The trenches were remarkably little damaged - the ground in front of the parapet had been converted into a crater area - much of the wire still formed an obstacle and testified to the repair and construction work of the past few nights, but in places gaps had been cut. 2/Lieut. HARRIS informs me that in a great part of the line the enemy was stopped by the new wire which had been erected during the night and which came as a surprise to them. The ground round the C.T's had been heavily shelled especially at the head of FIRST AVENUE. A few shells had hit the C.T's but the front line was in good order throughout and there was no obstacle to free passage anywhere - the trenches there are good, deep and well fire-stepped. There were signs of bombing all along the trench.

7. I examined the men closely, and I agree with the G.O.C. 9th Inf. Bde. that some of the older men fought well, and were ably and gallantly led by 2/Lieut HARRIS. That Officer reports that the men around him about 20 in number fought very well and inflicted many casualties on the enemy. There is no doubt left in my mind that when the enemy threw their bombs and attacked that some of the garrison left their posts and climbed over the parados or made their way down the C.T's. and scattered and that their action allowed the enemy to enter the trench and bomb on both flanks of men holding on. This retirement applies to the men on the right principally. 2/Lieut HARRIS was not there and cannot say exactly what happened, but reports that very little rifle or Lewis Gun

3rd Division. "G".

Herewith report of O.C., 13th King's on the hostile raid about 5-45 a.m. to-day.

From the enemy's Trench Mortar activity the raid was not unexpected and efforts had been made to repair nightly the damage done to our wire during the day, but work was greatly hindered by enemy Machine Guns. CHEVAUX-DE-FRISE being made to block the front line trench on the flanks of Posts and a number of wire gates were in position. The Company of Pioneers were taken off wiring the Support Line and put onto the wiring of the front raided, and had greatly strengthened it on the night of the raid. Eight Field Guns were taken off their normal S.O.S. Lines and covered the Salient attacked, and every Post in this portion of the Line were warned to expect a raid at any time, either by day or night.

From enquiries I have made on the spot the following appears to have been the course of events:-

The dawn patrols on this Company front had gone out from No.7.Post and returned by No.1.Post reporting "All Correct" only a few minutes before the firing commenced.

At about 5-40 a.m. all the troops were "Standing To" as usual, when a very heavy Artillery and Trench Mortar barrage opened on the front and Support trenches and Communication Trenches.

This drove some of the men off their fire-steps and one Post at the Head of WOOD TRENCH undoubtedly retired down it. Under cover of this bombardment the enemy crept forward to our wire "about 100 yards from his own" and, on the sound of a trumpet they rose to a man and commenced bombing the front line trench.

The wire, unfortunately, along practically the whole of our front has been put within easy bombing range of the trench. Under cover of this rain of bombs, which caused great confusion in the trench, gaps were probably cut where necessary and the enemy rushed in. The flanks of the attack rested between 4 and 5 Posts on our right and between 7a and 8 Posts on our left (about 300 yards). In the melee which ensued a number of men climbed out of the trench over the parados where some of them continued to fight. On the left some of the enemy appear to have got on the parados but were driven into the trench again by fire from Posts 9, 9a, etc.. The Lewis Guns kept firing for some time, as testified by the empty cases I saw. The enemy were eventually ejected and suffered some loss retiring.

S.O.S. Rockets were said to have been fired by O.C., Company in the front line and a Sergeant from the Support line, but were not seen further back and as a consequence no barrage was put down.

All telephone wires were cut immediately.

There was a slight mist and considerable smoke. The Battalion had not been in 24 hours and was new to the Section. Some of the older men fought well, but some of the younger hands undoubtedly lost their heads and did not. It is the rule in the Battalion to mix up young and old soldiers in Sections and place an old and young soldier on double sentry. The damage to trenches was not serious.

(sd) H.CECIL POTTER.
Brigadier General.
Commanding 9th Infantry Brigade.

16/2/18.

9th Inf. Bde.   K.Z.35.

Report on enemy raid - (2nd report).   16/2/1918.

1. The enemy entered our front trench at the point stated in my previous report.

2. 2/Lieut.J.G.HARRIS who was in command of the right front Coy. reports -
When visiting his Coy. at about 5-40 a.m. his front line was bombarded by T.M's and at the same time his support line was barraged with 5.9" and 4.2". After about 5 minutes the bombardment of the front line ceased. A horn was sounded in NO MAN'S LAND and suddenly a strong party of the enemy appeared in front of our wire and barraged our front line with bombs. Meanwhile parties of the enemy passed through gaps in the wire and entered the trench. L.G's and Rifles engaged the enemy to the front and some men dealt with the bombing parties moving down the trenches.

3. As No.7. Post was being bombed from 3 sides 2/Lieut HARRIS with all on wounded men took up a position behind the parados and engaged the enemy from this position.
2/Lieut CARSON who was with a L.G.Team at No.6.Post took up a position in a shell hole and kept up continuous fire to his front.

4. 2/Lieut HARRIS at once organised two bombing parties. One was commanded by himself and entered the trench at the junction of FIRST AVENUE and the front line. The other commanded by Sergt.(A/C.S.M.) ARMITAGE entered trench at junction of WOOD TRENCH and the front line. They experienced great difficulty in clearing the enemy out between these two points owing to the number of our wounded lying in the trenches. 2/Lieut HARRIS was wounded during this fighting. This part of the line was eventually cleared.

5. The garrison of 4 and 5 Posts succeeded in clearing the enemy from the trench between these two Posts.

6. No.7a.Post being bombed from 3 sides bombed the enemy South past FIRST AVENUE. Here they formed a block.

7. No.8. Post were all killed or wounded except one man who joined 8a.Post.

8. No.8a.Post bombed South towards FIRST AVENUE. Two enemy dead were found in vicinity of No.8.Post.

9. During the fighting an enemy Bugler sounded the "No Parade Call".

10. At 6-10 a.m. 3 Red Very Lights were fired in rapid succession, whistles were sounded and a bugle call sounded, whereupon the whole of the firing ceased.

11. Posts were at once re-established.

12. During the fighting the L.G's of No.4 and No.8a Posts directed enfilade fire in front of portion of our line which was attacked and claim to have inflicted heavy casualties on the enemy. One German body was left in our wire and many men were seen to be limping back.

13. One of our own wounded was dragged out of the trench and left in a shell hole near our wire. He was brought in by our stretcher bearers. A man has been seen raising his arm from a shell hole near the enemy's wire. Patrols have been detailed to search the area for any wounded.

14. Our observers report that about a dozen stretcher cases and about the same number of walking cases have left a dressing station in rear of the German lines this morning. They report that on shells falling in the vicinity they dropped the stretchers and took cover in a trench. The stretchers therefore probably carried out wounded or their dead.

15. Of the missing 5 have been serving with the Battalion for some months. The other three have joined the Battalion in the trenches since we came into this Sector. The Sergt. who has been with the Battalion in FRANCE since September 1915 was known to be a stout fighter.

16. The following is a list of the Posts showing casualties:-

Posts.	Casualties.	Remaining.
5	5	4
6	2	5
7	18	12
7a	3	5
8	6	1

No.7 Post had two L.G's and No.8.Post was an L.G.Post. All these guns are missing.

17. The following shows Number of new men who have joined Coys. in the trenches:- "A" Coy. 54., "B" Coy. 57., "C" Coy. 68., "D" Coy.89.

(sd)F.L.LAWRENCE. Lt.Col.
16/2/18.   Commanding 13th The King's Regiment.

(2)

gunfire came from that direction.

These men failed to do their duty in a most regrettable manner. I have spoken to them in the trenches, and I intend to take an early opportunity of again bringing their duty home to them. Had they done their duty the raid should and would have been defeated, and prisoners probably taken by us. 2/Lieut HARRIS saw only one man - wounded - being dragged away as a prisoner.

The 13th King's Liverpool Regiment has recently done particularly well as a Battalion and in the enemy's attack at BULLECOURT entirely repulsed the attack launched against its front. It has recently received large numbers of reinforcements under the re-organisation scheme, and these men are not yet assimilated in the Battalion. I anticipate that the men concerned will shortly make good their short-comings on this occassion. The Company attacked had 69 new reinforcements amongst them.

8. I have examined the S.O.S. question and I am not satisfied that it was properly put up. I could find no-one who had seen it, and I am of opinion that if it had been properly put up and repeated as ordered it must have been seen. 2/Lieut HARRIS is certain that he put up the Signal once - he knows that the Sergt. who had the other Signals failed as he dropped the cartridges. Guns, Machine Guns, Trench Mortars, and Infantry were all Standing to Arms - all were expecting a raid, and all guns, Trench Mortars and Machine Guns were actually ready to fire immediately the S.O.S. went up and we were surprised not to see it. The hostile barrage was heavy and concentrated - it was seen from our Artillery O.P., who spoke on the telephone to the Battalion H.Q. about it. The Battalion H.Q. cannot see the front line, but have a Post from which the S.O.S. can be seen. Seeing the heavy barrage the Artillery should have opened with a steady rate of fire without awaiting the S.O.S. - had they done so the Trench Mortars and M.G's would have also opened. I can not understand their failure to open fire on this occasion, and I have informed my C.R.A. accordingly and he agrees entirely with my opinion. Steps have been taken to remedy this for the future.

The Battalion Commander should, knowing that the wires were cut to his front companies and that a heavy barrage was evidently being placed on his line, have communicated with the Artillery and his Brigade. It was his first experience in Command of his Battalion in more active operations - and his first morning in the trenches in his present area. He had been informed on taking over that the enemy had made a practice of putting down a barrage at dawn, and he accordingly decided to await the S.O.S. Signal. The whole raid was quickly over, and the opportunity of getting the guns into action was lost. I have directed the G.O.C. Brigade to point out his mistake to him, as it was the obvious course to order counter-measures even if an S.O.S. was not required.

9. I found the men perfectly steady in the trenches when I visited them, and they showed no signs of anything unusual having occurred.

2/Lieut HARRIS the Company Commander, obtained his Commission from the Welsh Guards and he considers that the men immediately with him were most praiseworthy. He says the enemy appeared to be a picked Storm Troops, they were all tall big men and worked together in line on the bugle sounding. The corpses that I saw were all of those of fine big looking men.

C.J. Deverell
Major General.
Commanding 3rd Division.

February 17th 1918.

3rd Army.

Forwarded.

17/2/18

Comdg. VI. Corps

Army Form C.2118.

WAR DIARY
INTELLIGENCE SUMMARY. 13TH BN THE KING'S (LIVERPOOL) REGT

(Erase heading not required.)

Vol 31

Place	Date	Hour	Summary of Events and Information	Remarks and references to Appendices
Field	MARCH. 1/		At 9.30 a.m. the relief of the Battalion by the 4th Bn Royal Fusiliers commenced, and was duly completed by 10 p.m. The Battalion moved to reserve billets in DURHAM LINES, the last company arriving at 1-15 a.m. 2nd March.	
	2.		Remained in DURHAM LINES and the day devoted to cleaning up, kit inspections and inspection of feet.	
	3.		Remained in DURHAM LINES. At 4.30 p.m. the Battalion marched off for working parties engaged in trench digging and wiring, two companies being detailed for each task. The party returned at 2.30 a.m. 4th March.	
	4.		At 12.30 p.m. the Battalion moved to the relief of the 4th Bn Royal Fusiliers in Brigade Support (SHAFT TRENCH, HINDENBURG LINE), advance parties leaving DURHAM LINES at 11 a.m. "C" Coy garrisoned Post C.10 and the H.Q. Lewis Gunners relieved the anti-aircraft L.G. Post on Bn H.Q. Both these reliefs were complete by 11 a.m. The main relief was duly completed and all trench stores taken over by 3 p.m.	
	5.		Remained in Brigade Support. Work was continued, blocks being made, and carrying and wiring parties provided.	
	6		Remained in Brigade Support and working and carrying parties provided.	

Army Form C. 2118.

SHEET 2.

WAR DIARY

INTELLIGENCE SUMMARY. 13TH BN THE KING'S (LIVERPOOL) REGT

(Erase heading not required.)

Instructions regarding War Diaries and Intelligence Summaries are contained in F. S. Regs., Part II and the Staff Manual respectively. Title pages will be prepared in manuscript.

Place	Date	Hour	Summary of Events and Information	Remarks and references to Appendices
FIELD	MARCH 7		Remained in Brigade Support and carrying and working parties provided.	
	8		As above.	
	9		Remained in Brigade Support, supplying parties for work under R.E., and forward carrying parties.	
	10		As above.	
	11		At 9-30 a.m. the relief of the 4th Bn. ROYAL FUSILIERS in the front line commenced, ten minutes interval being maintained between platoons. The relief was duly completed by 12-30 p.m. and work taken over and carried on.	
	12		The Battalion remained in the front line and work on the defences proceeded with.	
	13		Remained as above. At about 12-30 a.m. 14th March our artillery of all calibre opened out upon the enemy's positions, continuing in bursts of ten minutes intense and ten minutes slow rate of fire. This continued at intervals of about 1½ hours until about 6-30 a.m. The hostile artillery made only slight reply.	
	14		Remained as above.	
	15		Remained as above.	
	16		Remained as above.	
	17		The 1st Bn. N.F. commenced to relieve the Battalion at 8-30 a.m. 17th March, and the relief	

SHEET 3

Army Form C. 2118.

WAR DIARY
or
~~INTELLIGENCE~~ SUMMARY 1/THE KING'S (LIVERPOOL) REGT.

(Erase heading not required.)

Instructions regarding War Diaries and Intelligence Summaries are contained in F. S. Regs., Part II. and the Staff Manual respectively. Title pages will be prepared in manuscript.

Place	Date	Hour	Summary of Events and Information	Remarks and references to Appendices
FIELD.	MARCH 17		was duly complete by 12.30 p.m., the battalion taking over positions in BRIGADE RESERVE in SHAFT TRENCH.	
	18		Remained in SHAFT TRENCH and working and carrying parties provided.	
	19		As above.	
	20		As above.	
	21		On 21st March the Battalion was in Brigade Reserve which had been moved close to the line in view of an expected hostile attack. The Battalion was accommodated in SHAFT TRENCH in the HINDENBURG TUNNEL and for the three previous days in reserve, after coming from the front line, had been working hard on the defences of the 2nd System. At dawn on the 21st March the enemy suddenly put down an intense barrage of H.E. and gas shell on the whole of the Brigade Sector. At this time the Battalion was in its battle positions with two companies garrisoning the reserve line 2nd System, "C" Coy SOUTH of SHAFT TRENCH (with two platoons in HIND AVENUE, forming a defensive flank on the right) and "D" Coy NORTH of SHAFT TRENCH (EARLS COURT and CROW TRENCH). Battalion H.Q. and the two remaining Companies in SHAFT TRENCH. The bombardment of the whole of the Battalion area was intense - many gas shells were used and box respirators were worn for several hours. Throughout the day the bombardment continued intermittently, but on the Brigade Front the attack had been held, and the Battalion was not called upon to move. During the night, rations and water were carried up to the 1st Bn. NORTHUMBERLAND FUSILIERS, who were holding the Front Line.	
	22		At dawn the enemy again put down a heavy barrage but gas shells were not used as much as on the previous morning. We were informed that during the previous night a fresh Brigade had been pushed up on our right flank between ourselves and the Division on our right who had been pressed back in places on the 21st - touch was not immediately obtained with this Brigade as its position was in advance of our portion of the reserve line. During the day the right flank of the Brigade became threatened, the enemy having gained a footing on the high ground NORTH of CROISILLES on which he could be clearly seen massing troops. "C" Coy was	

WAR DIARY or INTELLIGENCE SUMMARY

SHEET 4

13TH BN THE KING'S (LIVERPOOL) REGT

Army Form C. 2118.

Place	Date	Hour	Summary of Events and Information	Remarks and references to Appendices
FIELD	MARCH 22		Immediately ordered to occupy HIND AVENUE from FULDNER LANE to FOOLEY LANE and "D" Coy was moved from SHAFT TRENCH to occupy HIND AVENUE from FOOLEY LANE to the RESERVE LINE with two platoons the remaining two platoons garrisoning the RESERVE LINE. "C" and "D" Coys now formed a defensive flank facing SOUTH and protected the Brigade's right flank. Patrols got into touch with the elements of the Brigade on our right, but they seemed to be holding no organised line, and were in scattered parties. During the afternoon the enemy was seen advancing NORTH FROM THE high ground NORTH OF CROISILLES and at the same time was attacking the Brigade front from the direction of FONTAINE. The enemy was advancing NORTH in large numbers, and the troops of the Brigade on our right fell back. Some of these were collected and garrisoned HIND AVENUE. HIND AVENUE had now become the front line of resistance. On the left - the EASTERN flank - we were in touch with troops of our own Brigade in FULDNER LANE (the reserve line of the 1st System). On the right we were exposed as we only held HIND AVENUE as far as the RESERVE LINE. Late in the afternoon the enemy had reached the wire - the wide belts of wire which the Germans had erected to protect the HINDENBURG LINE and on which he was now making a frontal attack. As soon as he came within range a heavy fire from Rifles and Lewis Guns was opened - the two platoons of "D" Coy in the RESERVE LINE were moved in to reinforce the FRONT LINE which was now held by two of our Coys plus elements amounting to about two Coys of the Right Brigade who had fallen back on to us. The enemy made repeated attempts to penetrate the gaps in our line but was held up at all points and was kept at the far side of the wire when night came. This penetration to the SOUTH had however severely threatened our flank and rear. About 10 p.m. the Germans made a heavy bombing attack at the junction of HIND AVENUE and FULDNER LANE but were immediately driven out by the initiative of "C" Coy who were holding that part of the line. During the evening the enemy again made a heavy frontal attack against the Brigade, and "E" Coy were moved forward from EARLS COURT to occupy the front line of the 2nd System - GREY STREET. The Battalion was now reinforced by two Coys K.R.R.C., one of which occupied EARLS COURT vacated by "E" Coy; the other occupied HIND AVENUE extending the line to the N.W. on our right flank. Shortly before midnight, orders were received that the Brigade would withdraw during the night in order to conform with the line. 13th The King's Regt were to cover the withdrawal, and to form the right flank guard of the Division. At midnight the withdrawal commenced - the two front Battalions of the Brigade withdrawing through our lines. The Battalion in turn withdrew, covered by bombing blocks which were established in the trenches.	

SHEET 5

Army Form C. 2118.

WAR DIARY
INTELLIGENCE SUMMARY: 13TH BN THE KING'S (LIVERPOOL) REGT

Place	Date	Hour	Summary of Events and Information	Remarks and references to Appendices
	MARCH			
FIELD	22		The withdrawal from the Trench System was complete at 4-15 a.m. 23rd March and the Commanding Officer gave the final order for the electric light plant in the tunnel to be blown up. Five Lewis Guns were placed in a semi-circular position on the EAST side of the track to HENIN, along which the Brigade had to move. Before dawn the whole Brigade had passed through the GUARDS, who were occupying a position near HENIN.	
	23		The Battalion rested in Camp and officers and N.C.O's reconnoitred the GREEN LINE NORTH of BOISLEUX ST.MARC.	
	24		At 5 a.m. the Battalion marched to its battle positions in the GREEN LINE and worked for two hours on the defences, deepening the steps and constructing fire steps. On our right the WELSH GUARDS were garrisoning the trench running WEST of BOISLEUX ST.MARC. About mid-day the Battalion was ordered to be prepared to move. At 3 p.m. the order came to occupy our battle positions in the GREEN LINE - this was immediately carried out. There was no activity in our sector. During the afternoon orders were received to relieve 2nd Bn. THE ROYAL SCOTS in the 3rd System near HENIN. The Battalion moved forward from the GREEN LINE at 7-30 P.M. and carried out the relief. After relief the Battalion was disposed as follows:- "B" Coy on the Right and "A" Coy on the Left. "C" and "D" Coys were in SUPPORT. BN. H.Q. at the NEUVILLE VITASSE - HENIN ROAD.	
	25 & 26		The next two days passed quietly except for occasional sniping and intermittently shelling. By day much enemy movement was observed on HENIN HILL and by night our patrols occasionally came into touch with a few of the enemy but he was not found to be in any numbers within 300 yards or 400 yards from our line.	
	27		Our positions were heavily shelled throughout the day, more particularly the RESERVE LINE and the vicinity of the Road by BN. H.Q. At dusk the shelling decreased. At mid-night 27/28 March "C" and "D" Coys relieved "B" and "A" Coys respectively in the front line - "A" and "B" coming back into the Support positions.	
	28		At 4-30 a.m. the enemy put down an intense barrage on the whole of our sector. The Trench Mortar barrage on the front line was more intense than anything previously experienced. The RESERVE LINE was barraged with field guns and heavies. Under cover of this barrage the enemy launched a terrific attack with masses of troops. In spite of the intensity of the bombardment the front line stood firm and poured a devastating fire into the enemy whose attack was beaten off with colossal casualties to the attackers.	

WAR DIARY
or
INTELLIGENCE SUMMARY. 13TH BN THE KING'S (LIVERPOOL) REGT.

SHEET 6.

Place	Date	Hour	Summary of Events and Information	Remarks and references to Appendices
FIELD	MARCH 28		The value of this steadfastness against tremendous odds cannot be estimated - it gave the enemy his first check at a point where he was to be subsequently checked throughout the day. The enemy came back again in a second attack with even greater numbers. The Battalion on our right were pressed back and the enemy poured in behind "C" and "D" companies from the right flank. What happened on the left flank is not known. All that is known is that these two companies, attacked on all sides, mounted the parapet and fought to a finish on the ground on which they stood. Under cover of the barrage the enemy came on up the hill to the reserve lines. Owing to the nature of the ground, he could not be observed along most of the battalion front until nearly on our wire. The barrage lifted, and in dense waves the Germans swept on to our lines. It was the beginning of a fierce battle which lasted until 2 p.m. The courage, coolness and endurance of the Garrison were beyond praise. Every rifle and Lewis Gun brought a tremendous volume of fire to bear on the approaching masses. Inspite of his losses the enemy continued to push on until the thin line remaining could go no further, and turned down the slope. Our men mounted the parapet to keep him under fire as long as they could keep him in sight. The first attack on the first line had been beaten off, and our line was everywhere intact. On the right we were in touch with the 7th Bn K.S.L.I. and on the left with the 1st Bn NORTHUMBERLAND FUSILIERS. Our Bn H.Q. on the road(N.26.c.0.8) was also the Bn H.Q. of the 1st Bn NORTHUMBERLAND FUSILIERS, and their H.Q. also garrisoned the trench in this vicinity. The road - through which a trench had been dug the night before - was held by a L.G. and a Rifle Grenade Post. All communication by wire was lost from the commencement of the action. Communication was however kept by lamp with the Brigade, and by this means some field guns were brought to cover our front on the EASTERN side of the HENIN ROAD. The enemy now resumed his barrage on our position by firing green lights. An intense barrage came down for 10 or 15 minutes. As soon as it lifted the enemy immediately came on to another attack. This also was repulsed with heavy loss to the enemy. Our flanks were still intact, but it was known that further to the left the enemy was making progress and our Left flank was becoming exposed. Twice again the enemy fell back, each time bringing down the barrage on our position with green lights, and pushing on his attack as soon as it lifted. About mid-day the enemy's fourth attack penetrated on our right. A block was immediately made and maintained about 150 yards from the Road on	

Army Form C. 2118.

WAR DIARY
or
INTELLIGENCE SUMMARY. 13TH BN THE KING'S (LIVERPOOL) REGT.

SHEET 7.

(Erase heading not required.)

Place	Date	Hour	Summary of Events and Information	Remarks and references to Appendices
FIELD	MARCH 28		the SOUTHERN side approximately N.25.d.7.4. A defensive flank was put out about N.25. Central and a few men lined the banks of the NEUVILLE VITASSE ROAD to guard our rear as far as possible. During the morning one company of the 4th Bn ROYAL FUSILIERS had come up to reinforce, and was distributed with two platoons on the S.W. side of the HENIN ROAD, and two platoons, and two platoons near the ST.MARTIN-sur-COJEUL ROAD in N.26.a. From mid-day onwards only about 500 or 600 yards of the reserve line remained in our hands, the troops on both flanks having fallen back some hundreds of yards. It was evident that when the next hostile attack came the position would inevitably be surrounded and would hold out no longer. However it was decided to hold on, though the Brigade message informed us that no reinforcements were available. At 2 p.m. a message from Brigade instructed us to rendezvous in N.24.Central if withdrawal became necessary. Withdrawal to support of the 4th Bn ROYAL FUSILIERS in the GREEN LINE was then decided upon and orders were issued for an immediate withdrawal. It commenced at 3.30 p.m., the movement from the front line being covered by small posts and blocks and the defensive flank on the right remaining in position until all the garrison of the Reserve Line had moved off to the S.W. of NEUVILLE VITASSE ROAD by the SUGAR FACTORY. The enemy moving forward for another attack, severely harassed the withdrawal, and it was only by great gallantry and initiative by individuals that the enemy was warded off until the line was clear. By 5 p.m. all troops had passed through the GREEN LINE with all wounded evacuated, and without anyone being cut off. The Battalion re-organised under cover of the ridge in N.24.Central, and at dusk moved back into Brigade Reserve, and occupied trenches in M.22.c.	
	29		Remained in Brigade Reserve - situation quiet. At 11 p.m. the Battalion was relieved by I Company 22nd Canadian Battalion, and marched back to MONCHIET	
	30		At 1.30 p.m. the Battalion moved byroad to IVERGNY where they arrived at 6.45 p.m.	
	31		The Battalion remained in billets at IVERGNY and the day was devoted to resting, re-organisation, and the completion of kits.	

NOTE:- Map ref to the above operations. Sheet 51.b.S.W. 1/20,000.

4/4/18.

Ҩ Lawrence Lieut:Col:
commdg 13th Bn The King's (Liverpool) Regt.

9th Bde.
3rd Div.

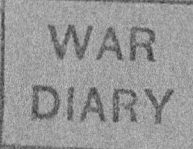

13th BATTALION

THE KING'S LIVERPOOL REGIMENT

APRIL 1 9 1 8

ATTached - Report on Operations
          10th to 20th April 1918

Army Form C. 2118.

WAR DIARY
or
INTELLIGENCE SUMMARY. 13TH BN THE KING'S (LIVERPOOL) REGT. April/18

(Erase heading not required.)

Instructions regarding War Diaries and Intelligence Summaries are contained in F. S. Regs., Part II. and the Staff Manual respectively. Title pages will be prepared in manuscript.

Place	Date	Hour	Summary of Events and Information	Remarks and references to Appendices
IVERGNY.	1		The Battalion embussed for HOUDAIN at 8 a.m., arriving at their destination at about 1.30 p.m. and took over billets.	
	2		Remained in billets in HOUDAIN and the day devoted to kit inspections and cleaning up.	
	3		Remained in HOUDAIN. A draft of 431 O.R. joined the Battalion.	
	4		The Battalion commenced a programme of training and the Commanding Officer and Officers reconnoitred the Reserve Lines.	
	5		Training continued. The C.O. and officers reconnoitring further reserve positions.	
	6		The C.O. and Officers again reconnoitred. The Battalion marched to COUPIGNY where camp was taken over.	
	7		Remained in camp at COUPIGNY. Training was continued and "C" and "D" Coys dug a new Army line near HOUCHIN.	
	8		"A" and "B" Coys continued the work commenced on the Army line. Training was carried out by the remaining two Coys, and the 2nd C.O. and Officers reconnoitred the reserve positions.	
	9		At about midday the order to "stand to" was received and working parties cancelled. At 8 p.m. the battalion was ordered to march off at once to a point between COUPIGNY and BETHUNE, where they embussed at 9 p.m. and were conveyed to BETHUNE. From thence they marched to GORRE Chateau and were placed under the orders of the G.O.C. 165th Infy Bde, who placed them in Brigade Reserve.	
	10		Early in the morning, "D" Coy under Lieut J.R.Ellis was sent to replace a company of the 165th Brigade in a position lining a stream N.W. of GORRE WOOD in X.27.a. In the evening, CAPT R.J.BARRETT with "C" Coy was ordered to report to O.C. 5th King's at FESTUBERT KEEP. This he did and was instructed temporarily to put 2 platoons in FESTUBERT KEEP, and the remainder of his company under 2/LIEUT F.D.BARTLEY D.C.M. was	

Army Form C. 2118.

WAR DIARY
or
INTELLIGENCE SUMMARY.   13TH BN THE KING'S (LIVERPOOL) REGT.
(Erase heading not required.)

Place	Date	Hour	Summary of Events and Information	Remarks and references to Appendices
FIELD	10 (contd)		placed in shell hole position in S.25 a. to form a defensive flank to the battalion.	
			At about 10.30 p.m. CAPT BARRETT received orders to send one platoon of the two from FESTUBERT KEEP to strengthen the garrison of FESTUBERT CENTRAL at about S.25.d.8.3 (which was the front line at that point).	
			At about 7 p.m., CAPT N.A.R. van GRUISEN with "B" Coy was ordered to take up the following positions:- Two platoons in TUNING FORK SWITCH and two platoons in TUNING FORK LOCALITY.	
	11		At dawn, CAPT G.T. HICK with "A" Coy was ordered to take his company and dig a position running N.W. - S.E. in X.27.c.behind an existing belt of wire. By night he had completed 250 yards of continuous trench and the remainder of the line was held with small posts and rifle pits.	
			About noon on the 11th inst the enemy artillery became very active in and about FESTUBERT and at 4 p.m. the garrison of FESTUBERT KEEP EAST (S.26.c.7.3. and of CAILLOUX KEEP NORTH and SOUTH (near BREWERY CORNER) were driven back.	
			CAPT BARRETT was ordered by O.C. 5th KING's to retake FESTUBERT EAST with his platoon in FESTUBERT KEEP.	
			This counter attack was entirely successful and "C" Coy continued to hold this position until relieved on night 13/14th April.	
			2/LIEUT F.D. BARTLEY D.C.M. also received orders that when the barrage lifted he was to retake CAILLOUX KEEP. This was also done and the position held until the company was relieved on night 13/14th April.	
			In the afternoon two platoons of "B" Coy in TUNING FORK LOCALITY were placed under the orders of O.C. 5th King's, and were ordered to take up positions in shell holes Immediately on the left of BREWERY CORNER (S.25.b.6.8. where they remained until relieved. Capt G.T.HICK with "A" Coy was ordered to relieve elements of 5th King's in FESTUBERT AREA and came under orders of OC 10th Liverpool Scottish.	
	12		LIEUT.COL: T.B.LAWRENCE M.C. D.C.M. took over command of the TUNING FORK AREA from O.C. 6th King's.	

Army Form C. 2118.

WAR DIARY
or
INTELLIGENCE SUMMARY.

Instructions regarding War Diaries and Intelligence Summaries are contained in F. S. Regs., Part II. and the Staff Manual respectively. Title pages will be prepared in manuscript.

Place	Date	Hour	Summary of Events and Information	Remarks and references to Appendices
FIELD	12 (contd)		One platoon of "A" Coy under 2/LIEUT W.F.GALLEY was sent to strengthen the garrison at FESTUBERT EAST.	
			The platoon of "C" Coy in FESTUBERT CENTRAL was moved to hold a flank position near the cottages at about A.1.b.7.4.	
			During the afternoon orders were received from G.O.C. 165th Bde that ROUTE A KEEP was to be retaken by one company 13th King's and one company LIVERPOOL SCOTTISH LIEUT J.R.ELLIS of "D" Coy, and CAPT MC.SWINEY 10th Scottish received full instructions and personal explanations from LIEUT:COL:LAWRENCE and reconnoitred the position in daylight. ZERO HOUR was fixed for 12 midnight.	
			The night was very dark, and great difficulty was experienced in getting through the wire and over the many ditches between Batta H.Q. and the point of assembly.	
			The barrage came down punctually and consisted of 3 Trench Mortars firing 40 rounds each for 4 minutes. One gun on the ruins for 1 minute, then lifting on to KEEP for 3 minutes. One gun on hedge S. of KEEP for 1 minute, lifting on to KEEP for 3 minutes, the third gun firing on to the KEEP for 4 minutes., also 14 field guns which fired for 4 minutes on the KEEP, lifting 200 yards for 2 minutes, then a further 200 yards, remaing for 2 minutes and gradually dying away.	
			There were two 4.5 Howitzers firing on to buildings and roads 400 yards N.E. of the KEEP.	
			Dispositions were as follows:-	
			~~5~~ ~~Coy.strength 150~~	
			50 men of the 10th SCOTTISH on the RIGHT of the road leading to the KEEP. These men were detailed to attack and capture the ruins 100 yards S.E. of ROUTE A KEEP.	
			"D" Coy,strength 150 were given the task of capturing the main KEEP.	
			The attack commenced punctually at 12 midnight.	
			The 10th SCOTTISH quickly reached their objective, taking the garrison by surprise and capturing 9 men and light M.G. by which it was held.	
			"D" Coy on the left of the road had a more difficult task on account of many uncut belts of wire and deep wide ditches full of water.	
			Despite very heavy machine gun fire, all these obstacles were overcome and the KEEP taken. Heavy casualties were inflicted on the enemy and one Officer and several wounded men were taken prisoner. Three M.G. were captured.	

Army Form C. 2118.

WAR DIARY
or
INTELLIGENCE SUMMARY.   13TH BN THE KING'S (LIVERPOOL) REGT.

(Erase heading not required.)

Instructions regarding War Diaries and Intelligence Summaries are contained in F. S. Regs., Part II. and the Staff Manual respectively. Title pages will be prepared in manuscript.

Place	Date	Hour	Summary of Events and Information	Remarks and references to Appendices
FIELD	13		The enemy made several determined attempts to recapture the KEEP but was repulsed with heavy losses. TUNING FORK LINE was also heavily bombarded.	
	14		The Battalion was relieved by elements of 10TH SCOTTISH and 5th and 6th KING'S (relief completed by 5.30 a.m.) and marched to the CANAL BANK at E.6.c where they rested for the day. They now rejoined the 9th Brigade. At 8 p.m. the Battalion marched to RESERVE TRENCHES in X19-20 E.of CANAL DE LA LAWE, and relieved elements of 166th Bde. Congratulatory messages were received from G.O.C.165th Infy Bde and from BRIG:GENL H.C. POTTER commdg 9th Infy Bde upon the successful capture of ROUTE A KEEP, congratulating the Colonel and the Battalion upon the complete success of this important operation.	
	15		Remained in Brigade Reserve in MANCHESTER LINE AND SWITCH. "D" Coy dug in position facing GORRE WOOD from X.26.b.70 to E.2.b.4.4.	
	16		Remained as above.	
	17		Remained as above. A letter was received from the O.C. 1/5 The King's Regt.,expressing his appreciation of the work done by the Officers and men of "C" Coy.	
	18		The Battalion was relieved by 2nd BN THE ROYAL SCOTS and marched back to billets in ANNEZIN. (Divisional Reserve).	
	19		Remained in Divisional Reserve. The Officers reconnoitred the positions allotted to the reserve Brigade on LA BASSEE CANAL.	
	20		The Corps Commander was pleased to announce that the following N.C.O's and men had been awarded the MILITARY MEDAL for acts of gallantry in the FIELD:- 19783 Sgt J.F.Hill.;52423 Sgt J.Sutherland.;19127 Sgt J.Unsworth.;48542 Sgt W.G.Brodie., 235169 Cpl C.Randell,19583 Cpl J.W.Baker.,19287 L/Cpl I.Goddard.,19192 L/Sgt H.Cromer.; 48445 L/Cpl J.H.Myers.,19039 L/Cpl F.J.Duffy.,20542 L/Cpl A.E.R.Henstridge.,48707 Pte.W.D.Fowler., 18928 Pte S.Walker.,88167 Pte R.Smales.,268388 Pte G.Carroll.,90895 Pte R.Maddocks.,	

Army Form C. 2118.

WAR DIARY
or
INTELLIGENCE SUMMARY. 13TH BN THE KING'S (LIVERPOOL) REGT.

(Erase heading not required.)

Instructions regarding War Diaries and Intelligence Summaries are contained in F.S. Regs., Part II. and the Staff Manual respectively. Title pages will be prepared in manuscript.

Place	Date	Hour	Summary of Events and Information	Remarks and references to Appendices
ANNEZIN	21		27797 Pte L.Harrison.,22533 Pte A.Simpson.,53158 Pte J.Foddy.,10765 Pte A Roberts., 20300 Pte H.Henley.,26065 Pte W.Smith.,24923 Pte H.Marsden.,52671 Pte P.Murphy., 88012 Pte G.Sloan.,57810 Pte S.Maltman.,8660 Pte J.Kelly.,240286 Pte G.Marland., 48935 Pte L.G.Orme.,17507 Pte A.Drom.	
	22.		Remained at ANNEZIN.	
	23		Brig:Genl: H.C.Potter C.M.G. D.S.O. commdg 9th Infantry Brigade had pleasure in presenting M.M. ribbons to the N.C.O's and men who had been awarded same for gallantry during the operations 21/29th March 1918. At 8.15 p.m. The Battalion marched to the relief of the 2nd SUFFOLK REGT in the LEFT SECTION.	
	24		Remained as above. Our positions were heavily shelled at 3.30 a.m.,and again at dusk.	
	25/26		The enemy remained fairly quiet. Our trenches were strengthened and consolidation proceeded with. Our patrols located the enemy at several points. On the evening of the 26th our boundaries were slightly readjusted,with "A" and "D" Coys in the front line.	
	27		Remained as above. Identification was secured from several wounded Germans who came into our lines.	
	28. 29		Further identification was secured from enemy dead found near our lines. Remained in the left section. Enemy shelling increased during the day.	
	30		The Battalion was relieved by 2nd Bn The Royal Scots and marched back to billets at ANNEZIN.	
	30/4/18		Lieut:Col: commdg 13th Bn The King's (Liverpool) Regt.	

13th The Kings Regt.

Situation previous to the operations
commencing 10th April 1918

9/4/18   At about 8-15 p.m orders were
received that the Battalion would embus
at a point between GOUPIGNY and
BETHUNE at 9 p.m.
  Battalion was conveyed to BETHUNE
and from there marched to GORRE CHATEAU and
were placed under the orders of G.O.C.
165 Brigade who placed them in
Brigade Reserve

Account of the part taken by
13" Bn The Kings Regiment in
the operations, from 10th to 20th April

10/4/18 Early in the morning "D" Coy under
LIEUT J R ELLIS was sent to replace a Coy of
the 165 Brigade in a position lining a
stream N.W. of GORRE WOOD in X.27.a.

In the evening CAPT. BARRETT with "C"
Coy was ordered to report to O.C. 5TH KINGS at
FESTUBERT. This he did and was instructed
temporarily to put 2 platoons in FESTUBERT
KEEP and the remainder of his Coy under
2/LIEUT. F.D. BARTLEY was placed in shell hole
position in S.25.a to form a defensive flank
to the Battalion.

At about 10·30 p.m. CAPT. BARRETT received
orders to send one platoon of the two from
FESTUBERT KEEP to strengthen the garrison of
FESTUBERT CENTRAL at about S.25.a.7/9. (which
was the front line at that point)

At about 7 p.m. CAPT. N.A.R. VAN-GRUISEN
with "B" Coy was ordered to take up the following
positions :- two platoons in TUNING FORK SWITCH
and two platoons in TUNING FORK LOCALITY.

11/4/18 At about dawn CAPT. G.T. HICK with A
Coy was ordered to take his Coy and dig a

position running N.W - S.E in X.27.c. behind a belt of existing wire. By night he had completed 250 yards of continuous trench and the remainder of the line was held with small posts and rifle pits.

About noon on the 11th inst enemy artillery became very active in and about FESTUBERT and at about 4 p.m the garrison of FESTUBERT KEEP EAST (S.26.c. 7/3) and of CAILLOUX KEEP NORTH and SOUTH (near BREWERY CORNER) were driven back

CAPT. BARRETT was ordered by O.C. 5th KING'S to retake FESTUBERT EAST with his platoon in FESTUBERT KEEP.

This counter-attack was entirely successful and 'C' Coy continued to hold this position till relieved on night 13/14th April

2/LIEUT F.D.BARTLEY also received orders that when the barrage lifted he was to retake CAILLOUX KEEP. This was also done and the position held until the Coy was relieved on night 13/14th April.

In the afternoon two platoons of 'B' Coy in TUNING FORK LOCALITY were placed under the orders of O.C 5th KING'S and were ordered to take up positions in shell holes immediately on the left of BREWERY CORNER (S.25.b.6/5) where they remained till relieved

2

| | | CAPT G.T. HICK with 'A' Coy was ordered to relieve elements of 5th KING'S in FESTUBERT AREA and came under orders of O.C. 10th SCOTTISH. |
| | 12/4/18 | LIEUT. COL: T.B. LAWRENCE, M.C. D.C.M took over command of the TUNING FORK AREA from O.C. 6TH KING'S. |

One platoon of 'A' Coy under 2/LIEUT W.F. GALLEY was sent to strengthen the garrison at FESTUBERT EAST.

The platoon of C Coy in FESTUBERT CENTRAL was moved to hold a flank position near the barrages at about A.1.b. 7/4.

During the afternoon orders were received from O.O.C. 165 Brigade that ROUTE A KEEP was to be retaken by one Coy. 13TH KING'S and one Coy 10TH SCOTTISH.

LIEUT. J.R. ELLIS of D COY and CAPT. McSWINEY of X Coy 10TH SCOTTISH received full instructions and personal explanations from LT. COL. LAWRENCE and reconnoitred the position during the light. ZERO HOUR was fixed for 12 midnight.

The night was very dark and great difficulty was experienced in getting through the wire and over the many ditches between BATTN H.Q and the point of assembly.

The barrage came down punctually

3

and consisted of 3 Trench Mortars firing 40 rounds each for 4 minutes. One gun on the ruins for 1 minute then lifting on to KEEP for 3 minutes. One gun on hedge S of KEEP for 1 minute, lifting on to KEEP for 3 minutes, the third gun firing on to the KEEP for 4 minutes.

Also 14 field guns, which fired for 4 minutes on the KEEP, lifting 200 yards, for 2 minutes, then a further 200 yards, remaining for 4 minutes, gradually dying away.

There were two 4.5 HOWITZERS firing on to buildings and roads 400 yards N.E of the KEEP.

Dispositions were as follows:-
50 men of the 10TH SCOTTISH on the RIGHT of the Road leading to the KEEP. These men were detailed to attack and capture the ruins 100 yards S.E of ROUTE A KEEP.

"D" COY, strength 150, were given the task of capturing the main KEEP.

The attack commenced punctually at 12 midnight.

The 10TH SCOTTISH quickly reached their objective taking the garrison by surprise and capturing the gunmen and light M.G by which it was held.

"D" COY on the LEFT of the Road had a more difficult task on account of many

4

uncut belts of wire and deep wide ditches full of water.

Despite very heavy Machine Gun Fire all these obstacles were overcome and the KEEP taken. Heavy casualties were inflicted on the enemy and One Officer and several wounded prisoners were taken.

Three M.G's were captured.

13/4/18 — The enemy made several determined attempts to recapture the KEEP but was repulsed with heavy losses.
TUNING FORK LINE heavily bombarded.

14/4/18 — The Battalion was relieved by elements of 10TH SCOTTISH, 5TH and 6TH KING'S (relief completed by 5.30 a.m) and marched to CANAL BANK at E.6.c.d. where they rested for the day. coming under shell fire of 9" &15"

At 8 p.m the Battalion marched to RESERVE TRENCHES in X.19-20. E of CANAL DE LAWE and relieved elements of the 166 Brigade.

15 to 18th — Remained in Brigade Reserve in MANCHESTER LINE & SWITCH. D Coy to dig in position facing CORBE WOOD from

5

X.26.a.70 10 F.2.b.4/4.

Night 18/19.4 — Relieved by 2nd ROYAL SCOTS and moved back to billets in ANNEZIN.

20/4/18 — Remained in DIVISIONAL RESERVE.

25/4/18

[signature] Lieut. Col.
Commdg 13th Bn The King's (Liverpool) Regt

Copy

SECRET   MESSAGE N° 3
                       14/4/18.
To O.C. REF.   REF MAP.
                    GORRE 1/40000.

     Herewith report on minor operation undertaken by No 10 Platoon of 'C' Coy. on afternoon of 11th April 1918.

     At about 4.30 pm it was reported that the garrison of FESTUBERT KEEP EAST (S.26.c.7.3) had been driven out and I was ordered to get out my No 10 Platoon garrisoning FESTUBERT KEEP (S.25.d.55.38.) and have them ready to counter attack. I got them out by sections in shell holes near by, and almost immediately the CO of the 5th KING'S & Major KEAT came up. Major KEAT led the way (as I & the platoon were all new to the place) and sections followed at a distance in single file.

This formation had to be maintained, as it was the only way of getting through the wire, although, naturally the men scattered somewhat.

There was a very heavy barrage of HE and very heavy MG fire as the platoon crossed the open. Several belts of apron wire and a broad ditch had to be crossed.

The platoon entered the breastwork known as FESTUBERT EAST at about 5.30 p.m. where no signs of enemy were seen.

Strength was about 25 or 26 — the original strength being 42.

Very heavy shell fire was undergone until about 8.pm.

At night we put out shell hole posts to protect flanks.

At about 3.AM a Platoon of 5th King's came to increase garrison. This Platoon was however relieved again by a Platoon of our "A" Company, at 4.30 AM.

Major KENT who worked splendidly, left sometime after midnight.

At the request of OC 10th Liverpool Scottish, I remained to the post until the next night.

SIGNED. R.J. BARRETT. CAPT
OC. "C" COY
13th KING'S

15/4/18.

From "O.C" PEK

To Brigade Major P.o.B.

Apl. 24/1918.

Report of action taken by PEK in the operations from Apl 10th to Apl 20th

Apl. 10. On the night of April 9th/10th we embussed at BRACQUEMONT and debussing at BETHUNE we marched to ESSARS where we laid in Brigade Reserve all day, at W 30 b 9.1. About 5 pm we left there and marched to HINGES where we stayed the night

Apl. 11. Under the command of Capt. J.H. HOGSHAW we left HINGES about 11 am & proceeded to the Right of les CHOQUAUX where we started to dig in in front of the road running from W 13 c 0.7 to W 13 c 8.0 About 1 pm fresh orders being received we left there & took up a position to the Left of LOCON digging a line approx W 6 d 5.7 to X 1 a 0.1. We held this line until 2 am Apl 12 when we were relieved by elements of the 51st Division. On relief we proceeded back to HINGES where we spent the night

— over —

PEK Report — contd —

Apl. 12. We left HINGES at midday, proceeding to E6C5.2 (BETHUNE DOCK) where we laid in Brigade Reserve.

Apl. 13. Still in Brigade Reserve at E6C5.2

Apl. 14. We left E6C5.2 and relieved the 166th T.M.B. whose H.Q were at les GLATIGNIES (X14C 65.20) with 6 guns in position on the SOUTH side of the rivulet running approx X14C 3.0 to X14C 0.3. These were all SOS positions and owing to the wet state of the ground it was not possible to build positions forward sufficient to hide the flash of the guns.

Apl. 15 }
    16 } In position on SOS
    17 }

Apl. 18 We were relieved by the 8th TMB and came out to rest and reorganize at ANNEZIN

Apl. 19 }
    20 } At ANNEZIN

J A Fisher Capt
O.C. PEK.

Army Form C.2118.

13TH(S) BN THE KING'S (LIVERPOOL) REGT.

Instructions regarding War Diaries and Intelligence Summaries are contained in F. S. Regs., Part II. and the Staff Manual respectively. Title pages will be prepared in manuscript.

WAR DIARY
or
INTELLIGENCE SUMMARY.

(Erase heading not required.)

MAY 1916

Place	Date	Hour	Summary of Events and Information	Remarks and references to Appendices
ANNEZIN	1st		Arrived in Billets ANNEZIN by 4 a.m. The day being devoted to cleaning up. At 8 p.m. orders were received for the Battalion to move to CHOQUES E.ABBAYE owing to the enemy having heavily shelled ANNEZIN with YELLOW CROSS (gasshells). At 10 p.m. the Battalion moved.	
	2nd		Arrived at CHOQUES at 1 a.m. - 2 Coys being billeted in a large barn and the remaining 2 Coys by the river bank in bivouacs. In the evening the 2 Coys in the barn & H.Q. moved to BREASTWORK N. of CHATEAU.	
	3rd		Remained as above all day and Officers were lectured by the Brigadier-General at 12 noon. Fairly heavy shelling in the vicinity all day.	
	4th		Remained as above. At 9 p.m. the Battalion moved into the SHROPSHIRE LINE - all 4 Coys being in the one line. It was announced by the G.O.C. 3rd DIVISION that the Field Marshal Commanding in Chief, had, under authority granted by His Majesty The King, awarded the u/n decorations for gallantry in the Field:-	
			THE DISTINGUISHED SERVICE ORDER - LT.COL:T.B.LAWRENCE,M.C.,D.C.M. - MAJOR J.D.ATKINSON	
			BAR TO THE MILITARY CROSS - CAPTAIN F. AKED SELLERS,M.C.	
			THE MILITARY CROSS - CAPTAIN B.A.M.CLEVELAND - CAPTAIN G.T.HICK - 2/LIEUT.W.R.GALLEY	
			BAR TO THE DISTINGUISHED CONDUCT MEDAL - 52569 Sergeant F.DOLEMAN,D.C.M.	
			THE DISTINGUISHED CONDUCT MEDAL - 4805 R.S.M. T.ADAMS - 14842 C.S.M.R.FAIRHURST,M.M.	
			19304 L/Cpl J.DOUGLAS	
			The Commanding Officer also had great pleasure in announcing that the BAR TO THE MILITARY MEDAL had been awarded to:- 48547 L/S EVANS M.M. "A" Coy - 23212 Pte S.DENNISON,M.M. - 8660 Pte KELLY,M.M. "B" Coy.	
	5th		Remained in SHROPSHIRE LINE all day and at night the Battalion was out digging a new trench from Left of Brigade Boundary to join up GORDON LINE.	
	6th 7th		Remained in same position and at night continued work on the new trench.	
	8 & 9th		Remained as above and at night continued work on the new trench. Remained in SHROPSHIRE LINE until mid-night of 8th when the Battalion moved into the SUFFOLK LINE. Dispositions being as follows:- "A" "C" & "D" in line. "B" Coy in SWINCH.	
	10th		In the evening of 9th BN.H.Q. moved up to SHROPSHIRE LINE. Remained as above, consolidating and strengthening the position.	
	11th		Remained as above, consolidating and improving the position.	

Wt. W14422/M1160 350,000 12/16 D. D. & L. Forms/C./2118/14.

WAR DIARY or INTELLIGENCE SUMMARY.

13TH (S) BN THE KING'S (LIVERPOOL) REGT

MAY 1918

Army Form C. 2118.

Place	Date	Hour	Summary of Events and Information	Remarks and references to Appendices
	12th		The Battalion was relieved in Brigade Support by 2nd ROYAL SCOTS. On relief the Coys moved back to their former positions in SHROPSHIRE LINE to await the relief of the BRIGADE.	
	13th		BRIGADE relief was duly completed and as ordered the Battalion then moved back to trenches at CHOCQUES and the day was devoted to cleaning up.	
	14th		Remained in this position and the day was spent in cleaning up, re-organisation, inspections and lectures etc.	
	15th 16th		Remained in this position and a programme of training was carried out. Remained as above devoting the day in re-organisation, lectures and inspections. In the evening the Battalion moved up to relieve 2nd SUFFOLK REGIMENT in the RIGHT SUB-Section.	
	17th		On completion of relief the disposition of the Coys was as follows:- "A" & "D" Coys in SUPPORT. "C" & "B" Coys in FRONT LINE All work was taken over and carried on and the usual patrols and carrying parties provided.	
	18th		Remained in above position - the usual patrols being organised, carrying parties provided and the position being consolidated and strengthened. "A" Coy relieved a post held by "D" Coy at the locks and "D" Coy manned a post near the CANAL BRIDGE.	
	19th		Remained as above and work of consolidation of position proceeded with and usual carrying parties provided and patrols organised.	
	20th		Remained as above. At night-time "A" Coy took over from "C" Coy on RIGHT FRONT and "D" Coy took over the SUPPORT LINE from "A". "C" Coy moving back to RESERVE. All work in hand was duly handed over and carried on and the usual patrols organised.	
	21st & 22nd		Remained as above carrying on the work of consolidation and providing the usual carrying parties and organising the usual patrols. At mid-night of the 21st as ordered a RAID was carried out on the enemy outpost line in accordance with a Scheme submitted by LT.COL:T.B.LAWRENCE,D.S.O.,M.C.,D.C.M.(Commanding Officer) "C" Coy were chosen to carry out the Raid and the strength of the party was 3 OFFICERS. & 50 OTHER RANKS - ALL VOLUNTEERS. 2/LIEUT.W.L.DOCKING & 16 O.R. formed one party 2/LIEUT.J.P.FOULKES & 16 O.R. - do - 2/LIEUT.L.WHITEHOUSE & 18 O.R. with 2 Lewis Guns forming a covering party. A telephone was established in the front line at a point where the attacking party had to pass each way. An Officer being there to report everything that happened to BN.H.Q. The British Wire was cut waiist waiting for the Barrage to commence.	

WAR DIARY or INTELLIGENCE SUMMARY

13TH (S) BN THE KING'S (LIVERPOOL) REGT

MAY 1918

Army Form C. 2118.

(Erase heading not required.)

Place	Date	Hour	Summary of Events and Information	Remarks and references to Appendices
			The Barrage opened to time and was very good. At ZERO the attackers moved forward at a steady pace, cutting their way through 2 belts of enemy wire. As soon as the barrage lifted two enemy posts in front of main line, from which attackers were fired on, were immediately rushed. Sentries were shot and a prisoner taken from each. One surrendered quietly, the other made a fight, striking an N.C.O. in the face. He was overpowered and brought in but gave considerable trouble on the way back. 4 of the enemy are known to have been killed in these two posts by rifle fire, & the shelters were bombed. Posts in lines of SHELL HOLES were evidently caught in our barrage as enemy dead were seen in several of these, and others were bombed by the Raiding party. OUR CASUALTIES were 2 men slightly wounded. The first prisoner passed the advanced Telephone Station at ZERO plus 7 and the second at ZERO plus 11. All men were back in our line at ZERO plus 15. The Raid was not rehearsed nor was there any previous Artillery preparation.	
	23		Remained as above strengthening and consolidating the position. Usual patrols and carrying parties.	
	24		Remained as above until night-time when the relief of the Battalion was commenced by 4th Bn. ROYAL FUSILIERS. All work in hand was duly handed over and on completion of relief the Battalion moved into BRIGADE RESERVE. The Coys were disposed as follows:- INVERNESS LINE - "A" Coy RIGHT "B" Coy LEFT DUMBARTON LINE - "C" Coy RIGHT "D" Coy (less 1 platoon) LEFT. 1 platoon "D" Coy at AVELETTE BRIDGE.	
	25		Remained in Brigade Reserve the day being devoted to cleaning up.	
	26		Remained as above. Inspections were carried out and carrying party organised. Work on posts was commenced with a view to joining up all by a waving trench.	
	27		As above. Work on the trench was completed. The Commanding officer was very pleased to announce that the MILITARY MEDAL had been awarded to the u/m for gallantry in the Field. Date of Award 15th May. 94447 L/Cpl G.H.MOORE "D" Coy 94531 Pte C.DARBYSHIRE "D" Coy 95105 Corpl W.BURNS "D" Coy 19528 Sgt F.H.GREENHALGH "D" Coy 21764 L/Cpl G.N.MITCHELL "C" Coy 306612 L/Cpl A.ALLEN "D" Coy 260275 Pte L.DRESSER "C" Coy 29534 Pte T.STEWARD "B" Coy 94496 Pte R.DAGGER "C" Coy 235187 Pte W.C.BROWN "B" Coy 52468 Sgt A.HODKIN "C" Coy.	

13TH (S). BN. THE KING'S (LIVERPOOL) REGT   MAY 1918   Army Form C.2118.

WAR DIARY
or
INTELLIGENCE SUMMARY
(Erase heading not required.)

Place	Date	Hour	Summary of Events and Information	Remarks and references to Appendices
	28		Remained in same position until night-time when the Battalion moved up to relieve The 1st NORTHUMBERLAND FUSILIERS in the LEFT SUB-SECTION.	
	29		On completion of relief the Disposition of the Coys was as follows:— "D" "A" & "C" Coys in FRONT LINE. "B" Coy in SUPPORT	
	30		All workmen taken over and carried on, patrols organised and carrying parties provided. Remained in position until night-time when the relief of the Battalion was commenced by the 1st ROYAL SCOTS FUSILIERS.	
	31		Relief was duly completed and the Battalion moved into Divisional Reserve occupying trenches near CHOCQUES. The Commanding Officer had great pleasure in announcing the following further Rewards for gallantry in the field:— 2/LIEUT. F.D.BARTLEY, D.C.M. MILITARY CROSS — 12327 SERGEANT G.MAYLETT — 21399 CORPORAL G.M.CUNLIFFE THE DISTINGUISHED CONDUCT MEDAL.	
31/5/18			[signature] Lieut.Col: Commanding 13th Bn. The King's (Liverpool) Regiment.	

Army Form C.2118.

13TH (S) BN THE KING'S (LIVERPOOL) REGT

Instructions regarding War Diaries and Intelligence Summaries are contained in F. S. Regs., Part II. and the Staff Manual respectively. Title pages will be prepared in manuscript.

WAR DIARY
or
INTELLIGENCE SUMMARY

(Erase heading not required.)

JUNE 1918

Place	Date	Hour	Summary of Events and Information	Remarks and references to Appendices
CHOCQUES	1st		At CHOCQUES. The Divisional Commander inspected the Battalion at work during the morning and inspected the Officers and Men who took part in the successful Raid on 21/22 May.	
	2nd		Remained as above. Church Services being held for all denominations. At night a working party of 5 Officers, 25 N.C.O's and 250 men was provided to dig a cable burying trench in HINGES SECTION.	
	3rd		Remained at CHOCQUES. The Commanding Officer was pleased to announce the award of the following decorations:-	
			THE MILITARY CROSS	
			CAPT. R.J. BENNETT "C" COY (Authority A.R.O. 2728)	
			BAR TO MILITARY MEDAL	
			52463 SERGT. A. HODKIN "C" COY	
			THE MILITARY MEDAL	
			21764 CORPL. C. MITCHELL "C" COY	
			23895 SERGT V. FAIRS "C" COY } Authority C.R.O. 1711	
			105364 PTE. J. HARDON "C" COY	
			300284 PTE W. HARRISON "C" COY	
			For conspicuous gallantry during raid on the enemy's lines	
	4th		Remained as above. The usual inspections were held prior to going into the line and at night the Battalion moved up to the relief of the 2nd SUFFOLK REGT in the RIGHT SUBSECTION HINGES SECTION.	
	5th		On completion of relief the Battalion was disposed as follows:-	
			"A" COY RIGHT FRONT "D" COY LEFT FRONT "C" COY SUPPORT "B" COY RESERVE	
			All work was duly taken over and the usual patrols organised and carrying parties provided.	
	6th		Remained in this position. About 12.15 a.m. the enemy attempted to raid one of our posts but was easily repulsed with rifle and Lewis Gun Fire before he got within 20 yards of the post. One dead enemy remained in our hands. LIEUT. J.K. WHITTLE M.C. joined for duty.	
	7th		Remained as above, consolidating and strengthening the position and the usual patrols were organised. A strong enemy patrol was encountered opposite one of our posts and was fired at and soon dispersed by Rifle and M.G. Fire.	
	8th		As above. The work of consolidating the position was proceeded with, patrols organised and carrying parties provided.	
	9th		As above. Patrols were organised as usual and the work of consolidation proceeded with. 2/LIEUT. J. McA. AMERIGAN joined for duty.	
	10th		As above. Work and patrols as usual.	
	11th		Remained as above and the work of consolidating the position was carried on and patrols were organised and carrying parties provided.	
	12th		As above. Work and patrols and carrying parties as usual.	

Army Form C. 2118.

WAR DIARY
or
INTELLIGENCE SUMMARY.
(Erase heading not required.)

13TH (S) BN THE KING'S (LIVERPOOL) REGT

JUNE 1918

Place	Date	Hour	Summary of Events and Information	Remarks and references to Appendices
	13th		Remained in the RIGHT SUB-SECTION until night when the relief of the Battalion commenced by the 2nd SUPPORTS, 1st NORTHUMBERLAND FUS. & 6th ROYAL FUSILIERS.	
	14th		On completion of relief the Battalion occupied trenches near CROQUES. The day was devoted to cleaning up arm inspections etc.	
	15th 16th		Remained near CROQUES, and a programme of training was carried out. As above. Church Parades were held for all denominations. The Commanding Officer had great pleasure in announcing that THE MILITARY CROSS had been awarded to 2/LIEUT W.H.DOCKING for gallantry in the field (A.F.G.2769). 2/LIEUT J. MURDOCH joined this day for duty.	
	17th		Remained as above until 9.30 p.m. when the Battalion moved to the relief of elements of 1st ROYAL SCOTS FUS.(attached 7th K.S.L.I.) 2 platoons 1st NORTHUMBERLAND FUS.(attached 4th ROYAL FUSILIERS) 4th ROYAL FUSILIERS and 2nd SUFFOLK REGT in newly gained FRONT LINE POSTS. The Commanding Officer was pleased to announce the following awards of the MILITARY MEDAL:- 95057 L/CPL C. BRINDLEY "D" COY for conspicuous conduct and example during an attempted hostile raid. 18928 PTE S. WALKER "A" COY for conspicuous gallantry in bringing in a wounded (C.R.O. 26926 PTE D. KIRK "A" COY officer under severe machine gun fire.) 1753)	
	18th		On completion of relief the COYS were disposed as follows:- 2 COYS IN FRONT LINE POSTS "B" on the RIGHT "A" On the LEFT 2 COYS IN SUPPORT "D" on the RIGHT "C" on the LEFT Work was commenced in joining up the posts and generally strengthening and consolidating the position. Usual patrols also being organised.	
	19th		Remained as above continuing the work of consolidation of the new position, the usual patrols and carrying parties being organised.	
	20th		As above. The work of consolidating and strengthening the position was carried on and the usual patrols organised and carrying parties provided.	
	21st		Remained as above until night when the relief of the Battalion in the FORWARD ZONE was commenced by the 1st NORTHUMBERLAND FUS.	
	22nd		On completion of relief the Battalion moved to the disposition of the COYS was as follows:- BATTLE ZONE (SUPPORT POSITION) where "C" COY - PENTH LINE "B" COY - W.BANK OF LA BASSEE CANAL "A" COY SUFFOLK LINE "D" COY - GORDON LINE MAJOR H.N.GILES joined the Battalion for duty.	
	23rd		Remained in SUPPORT. Work and carrying parties being provided.	

13TH (S) BN THE KING'S (LIVERPOOL) REGT

Army Form C. 2118.

WAR DIARY
or
INTELLIGENCE SUMMARY.

(Erase heading not required.)

JUNE 1918

Place	Date	Hour	Summary of Events and Information	Remarks and references to Appendices
	24th		Remained in SUPPORT.	
	25th		Remained as above. The following Officers joined for duty; CAPT.G.A.E.CLARKE, CAPT.R..HEYWOOD,M.C., 2/LIEUT.L.A.POPE. At night the relief of the Battalion was commenced by the 1st NORTHUMBERLAND FUSILIERS.	
	26th		On completion of relief the Battalion moved into BRIGADE RESERVE and occupied trenches near CHOCQUES. The day was devoted to cleaning up and the usual inspections. 2/LIEUT.L.E.CURRY joined the Battalion for duty.	
	27th		Remained near CHOCQUES and a programme of training was carried out the platoons were re-organised in accordance with the new establishment of Infantry Battalions.	
	28th		Remained as above and a programme of training was carried out. The Commanding Officer had great pleasure in announcing that the MERITORIOUS SERVICE MEDAL had been awarded to 12089 R.Q.M.S. J.H.CROSS "B" COY. and 14235 C.S.M. A.McNAMEE "C" COY.	
	29th		As above, a programme of training being carried out and a Divine Service was held for R.C's in the Parish Church CHOCQUES at 7 p.m.	
	30th		Remained near CHOCQUES and Divine Services were held during the day for all denominations.	

30th June 1918.

[signature] Lieut.Col:
Commanding 13th Bn. The King's (Liverpool) Regt.

Army Form C. 2118.

13TH (S) BN THE KING'S (LIVERPOOL) REGT.

WAR DIARY
or
~~INTELLIGENCE SUMMARY~~

JULY 1918

(Erase heading not required.)

Instructions regarding War Diaries and Intelligence Summaries are contained in F.S. Regs., Part II. and the Staff Manual respectively. Title pages will be prepared in manuscript.

Place	Date	Hour	Summary of Events and Information	Remarks and references to Appendices
CHOCQUES	1st		At CHOCQUES. The usual preparations and inspections were made prior to going into the trenches and at night-time the Battalion moved up to the relief of the 4th ROYAL FUSILIERS in the forward zone AVELETTE SECTION.	
	2nd		On completion of relief the disposition of the Coys was as follows:- "C"Coy - Right FRONT "B"Coy - LEFT FRONT "D"Coy - RIGHT SUPPORT "A"Coy - LEFT SUPPORT All work on hand was taken over and carried on and patrols organised.	
	3rd		The Battalion remained in the Front Line and work of consolidating and strengthening the position was proceeded with, the usual patrols and carrying parties being organised.	
	4th		As above. Work, patrols and carrying parties as usual.	
	5th		Remained as above. Work, patrols and carrying parties as usual.	
	6th		Remained in the Front Line consolidating and strengthening the position. The usual carrying parties being found and patrols organised.	
	7th		As above until night when the relief of the Battalion was carried out by the 1st NORTHUMBERLAND FUSILIERS all work in hand being handed over.	
	8th		On completion of relief the Battalion moved to the relief of the 4th ROYAL FUSILIERS in the Battle zone. Dispositions being as follows:- "C"Coy occupying PERTH LINE "B"Coy occupying W.BANK OF LA BASSEE CANAL "D"Coy -do- GORDON LINE "A"Coy -do- SUFFOLK LINE All work on hand was taken over and carrying parties required in this position being furnished.	
	9th		Remained as above.	
	10th		As above.	
	11th		As above.	
	12th			
	13th		Remained in the Support position until night-time when the relief of the Battalion was commenced by the 1st NORTHUMBERLAND FUSILIERS. All work on hand being handed over.	
	14th		On completion of relief the Battalion moved into Brigade RESERVE CHOCQUES. 2/LIEUT. H.B. BRAMLEY was wounded and later the Commanding Officer heard with much regret that this officer had died. After resting the Battalion spent the day in cleaning up and Divine Services were held. 2 Companies visited the baths and were inspected by the Medical Officer.	
	15th		Remained at CHOCQUES and a programme of training was carried out. 2 Coys visited the Baths and were medically inspected. A Board to audit the Canteen Accounts assembled at H.Q.Mess, MAJOR W.J.H.HOWARD being PRESIDENT and MAJOR H.N.GILES & CAPT.S.T.J.PERRY,M.C. MEMBERS.	
	16th			

13TH (S) BN THE KING'S (LIVERPOOL) REGT.

Army Form C. 2118

WAR DIARY
or
INTELLIGENCE SUMMARY

(Erase heading not required.)

Instructions regarding War Diaries and Intelligence Summaries are contained in F. S. Regs., Part II. and the Staff Manual respectively. Title pages will be prepared in manuscript.

JULY 1918.

Place	Date	Hour	Summary of Events and Information	Remarks and references to Appendices
CHOCQUES	16th		At CHOCQUES. A working party was found composed of 400 men with a proportion of officers and N.C.Os in addition for burying cable. MAJOR H.N.GILES was in charge of the whole party. The Commanding Officer was pleased to announce that the Meritorious Service Medal had been awarded to No.19552, Sgt.J.HUDSON, B.Coy.	
	17th		Remained in Brigade Reserve and in the afternoon a Tactical Scheme for Officers, Sergeants, and Section Commanders was carried out. Zero hour was 3p.m.	
	18th		Remained as above and training was carried out in accordance with a programme issued to all concerned.	
	19th		Remained as above the day being devoted to usual preparations preparatory to proceeding to the Front Line and at night the Battalion moved up to the relief of the 4th ROYAL FUSILIERS in the forward zone AVELETTE SECTION.	
	20th		On completion of relief the Coys occupied the following positions:- "A"Coy - RIGHT FRONT "D"Coy - LEFT FRONT "C"Coy - RIGHT SUPPORT "B"Coy - LEFT SUPPORT All work was taken over and proceeded with and the usual patrols organised.	
	21st		Remained in the Front Line consolidating and strengthening the position and the usual working parties were provided and patrols organised.	
	22nd		As above.	
	23rd		As above.	
	24th		As above.	
	25th		Remained as above until night-time when the relief of the Battalion in the forward zone was commenced by the 1st NORTHUMBERLAND FUSILIERS.	
	26th		All work on hand in the forward zone was handed over to the 1st NORTHUMBERLAND FUSILIERS and on completion of the relief the Battalion moved to the relief of the 4th ROYAL FUSILIERS in the Battle zone. All work was taken over and proceeded with.	
	27th		Remained in Support the usual working and carrying parties being provided.	
	28th		As above.	
	29th		As above.	
	30th		As above.	
	31st		Remained in the Battle Zone until nighttime when the relief of the Battalion was commenced by the 1st NORTHUMBERLAND FUSILIERS.	

31st July, 1918.

[signature] LIEUT.COL:
Commanding 13th Bn. The King's (Liverpool) Regt.

13TH (S) BN THE KING'S (LIVERPOOL) REGT

Army Form C.

WAR DIARY
or
INTELLIGENCE SUMMARY

(Erase heading not required.)

AUGUST 1918

Instructions regarding War Diaries and Intelligence Summaries are contained in F.S. Regs., Part II. and the Staff Manual respectively. Title pages will be prepared in manuscript.

Place	Date	Hour	Summary of Events and Information	Remarks and references to Appendices
CHOCQUES	1st		On completion of relief the Battalion moved into Brigade Reserve CHOCQUES. After resting the Battalion spent the day in cleaning up.	
	2nd		At CHOCQUES. Training was carried out in accordance with a programme and Baths were arranged and all men were medically inspected at the Baths.	
	3rd		A programme of training was carried out special attention being paid to Wiring Instruction and practice and the use of the Entrenching Tool.	
	4th		Remained at CHOCQUES until 2p.m. when the Battalion moved via LABEUVRIERE - LAPUGNOY - LOZINGHEM - AUCHEL to RAIMBERT arriving there about 5 p.m. where billets were occupied.	
	5th		At RAIMBERT. The day was spent cleaning up generally, inspections and work under Company arrangements.	
	6th		The morning was occupied in Demonstrating and Rehearsing the formation for attack and the afternoon was devoted to Recreational Training.	
	7th		The Battalion paraded at 9 a.m. on the FLORINGHEM-RAIMBERT Road and marched to the Training Area where a programme was carried out. The afternoon was devoted to Recreation.	
	8th		During the morning the Commanding Officer inspected the Battalion in full marching order and Platoon Training was carried out.	
	9th		At RAIMBERT. The Battalion visiting the Training Area and carrying out a programme of Training and in the afternoon Recreational Training.	
	10th		As above.	
	11th		At RAIMBERT. Divine Services were held for all denominations. At noon Officers and men interested in new Educational Scheme met the Divisional Education Officer who explained the Scheme.	
	12th		Platoon Training was carried out on Company Parade Grounds until 11a.m. when all who wished to visit the Corps Horse Show at FERFAY paraded and marched there. 2/LIEUT.W.F.GALLEY,M.C. was a Competitor in the Sports and was successful - obtaining 2 prizes.	
	13th		The Battalion moved by train to the LE SOUICH area, entraining at PERNES.	
	14th		At LE SOUICH. After the usual cleaning up Coys paraded under Coy arrangements.	
	15th		The Battalion paraded and marched to Training Area and practiced a Company attack on a strong point, combining movement across Country in Artillery Formation, The Assault and Consolidation.	
	16th		As above.	
FOREST	17th		At LE SOUICH. The Battalion (less D.Coy) paraded and marched to W.side of LUCHEUX	

Army Form C. 2118.

13TH (S) BN THE KING'S (LIVERPOOL) REGT

Instructions regarding War Diaries and Intelligence Summaries are contained in F.S. Regs., Part II. and the Staff Manual respectively. Title pages will be prepared in manuscript.

WAR DIARY
or
INTELLIGENCE SUMMARY

(Erase heading not required.)

AUGUST 1918

Place	Date	Hour	Summary of Events and Information	Remarks and references to Appendices
	17th (Ctd)		FOREST for Company Training according to programme arranged by Company Commanders. "D" Coy used the Range	
	18th		At LE SOUICH. Divine Services were held for all denominations and in the evening a Football Match was played between the Battalion and the ROYAL FUSILIERS.	
	19th		The Battalion (less "A" Coy) paraded and marched to the Training Ground where Company Training was carried out. "A" Coy using the Range. In the evening the Battalion commenced marching to HANNESCAMP. On the early morning of 20th August the Battalion arrived at HANNESCAMP and went into close bivouacs. There was no movement during daylight and the presence of troops was concealed.	
	20th		During the morning of the 20th Orders were received that the Third Army were to advance on BAPAUME and that the 9th Brigade would take part in the operations. The Battalion were to take the Left Front of the attack with the 1st NORTHUMBERLAND FUSILIERS on the Right. The line of the advance was roughly from AYETTE to the Southern side of the COURCELLES LE-COMPTE with the ARRAS - ACHIET LE GRAND RAILWAY as the objective. The ground was reconnoitred as far as was possible during the afternoon. The Brigade and Battalion boundaries - the BLUE LINE - the RED LINE - the GREEN LINE were shewn on a map issued with the Operation Orders.	
		11 p.m.	The Battalion moved off from bivouacs at HANNESCAMPS to Assembly positions. During the early hours of the morning, assisted by a bright moon, the Battalion formed up in rear of our front line. "B" & "A" Coys were in Support on the right and left respectively.	
	21st		There was slight and intermittent shelling of the assembly area. The Battalion was in position well before Zero Hour. Zero Hour was fixed for 4.55 a.m. 21st August. At Zero Hour the Battalion moved forward in Artillery Formation behind the 2nd Division who were to capture the BLUE LINE before we passed through them to capture the RED LINE. Tanks co-operated with the 2nd Division. At dawn a thick mist hung on the ground. This was increased to great density by the smoke cloud put out to cover the tanks. Direction was extremely difficult. Troops could not be distinguished at 20 yards. All Officers were moving by the compass and this alone enabled a general direction to be kept.	

13TH (S) BN THE KING'S (LIVERPOOL) REGT.

Army Form C. 2118

WAR DIARY
or
INTELLIGENCE SUMMARY
(Erase heading not required.)

AUGUST 1918

Instructions regarding War Diaries and Intelligence Summaries are contained in F. S. Regs., Part II. and the Staff Manual respectively. Title pages will be prepared in manuscript.

Place	Date	Hour	Summary of Events and Information	Remarks and references to Appendices
	21st9(contd)		Throughout the whole advance the troops never hesitated in moving forward even though nothing could be seen of their objective or of troops on their flanks. The advance to the BLUE LINE was about 2000 yards. Before reaching the leading Companies came into action rushing Machine Guns and killing and capturing their crews. From the BLUE LINE to the RED LINE was approximately another 2500 yards. Fresh tanks were to have led this advance to the objective but these did not arrive and the men pushed on to the barrage. Several strong points were encountered. Lewis Gun and Rifle fire was brought to bear on them and the points eventually outflanked. On the way to the railway the fog became so thick and direction so uncertain that progress inevitably slackened. By the time our troops reached the railway the barrage had lifted from it. The arrival at the railway was known to all by the heavy Machine Gun fire which they suddenly came under. "D" Coy on the Left had skirted the Southern side of COURCELLES-LE-COMPTE where many prisoners were taken and aided by one tank from the Left Brigade established themselves on the railway. "C" Coy on the Right had no tank assisting but advancing by short rushes they eventually rushed the Machine Guns on the railway and established themselves on the Right of "D" Coy. Some of the two Supporting Companies had closed up previous to the railway being attacked and the total casualties were heavy. Three Company Commanders became Casualties and many men were caught by the heavy Machine Gun fire. Units were considerably mixed up on the railway but re-organisation immediately took place and the East Side of the Railway was consolidated. On our Right the troops were not actually on the railway but were dug in about 50 yards to 100 yards on the Western side. This left our Right flank very exposed and the enemy took the greatest advantage of harassing our position on the railway. Towards mid-day the mist lifted slightly but it was not found possible for Cavalry to go through and no Whippet Tanks advanced on our front. Enemy heavy artillery was active throughout the day. At night "A" & "B" Companys dug in on a Support line approximately 200 yards West of Railway and "C" & "D" Coy's held the Railway line.	
	22nd		At dawn there was mutual suspicion and heavy barrages were put down on both sides. Both then and during the day there was some fighting but we held our ground.	

WAR DIARY or INTELLIGENCE SUMMARY

13TH (S) BN THE KING'S (LIVERPOOL) REGT

AUGUST 1918

Army Form C.2118

Place	Date	Hour	Summary of Events and Information	Remarks and references to Appendices
	22nd (contd)		Our men suffered heavy casualties however from the exposure of our Right flank. Ammunition, Stores etc were carried forward and the position further consolidated. At night, the 76th Brigade assembled to go through us for the capture of GOMIECOURT on the 23rd August.	
	23rd		Orders were issued for "C" Coy tp push down to their Right and clear the Machine Gun Nest which was a serious obstacle to progress. At 4 a.m. simultaneously with the advance of the 76th Brigade, "C" Coy moved down the railway to the South and engaged the Machine Gun Nest. The point was attacked with Lewis Gun & Rifle fire and Rifle Grenades and Bombs. 150 prisoners and many Machine Guns were captured and the point thoroughly cleared. "A" & "B" Coys came up on the Right of "C" & "D" and all four Companies in line consolidated on the railway line. During the afternoon orders were received to move forward to the East of the railway. The Battalion dug in and rested for the night. There was intermittent shelling in the vicinity of our bivouacs. At 3 p.m. the Battalion moved back to bivouac near AYETTE. The Officer Casualties were:- KILLED CAPT.R.J.BARRETT,M.C.- 2/LIEUT.J.B.FRIEND- 2/LIEUT.H.WASHBROOK. WOUNDED CAPT.N.A.R.VAN-GRUISEN (Since DIED OF WOUNDS),-CAPT.J.A.C.JOHNSON - CAPT.R.P.HEYWOOD,M.C.(At duty).- 2/LIEUT.T.McA.KERRIGAN,- 2/LIEUT.T.W.CONE,-2/LIEUT.P.E.HEMMING 2/LIEUT.W.POTTS,- 2/LIEUT.L.K.POPE	Cornell Gr. 263.
	24th		Remained near AYETTE and re-organisation was proceeded with.	
	25		As above.	
	26		In the afternoon the Battalion moved to BOIRY ST.MARTIN where re-organisation and training was carried out.	
	27		As above.	
	28			
	29		In the afternoon the Battalion moved up to the relief of the 76th Brigade in HAMEL SWITCH.(Support)	
	30			

13TH (S) BN THE KING'S (LIVERPOOL) REGT

Army Form C. 2118.

WAR DIARY
or
INTELLIGENCE SUMMARY.
(Erase heading not required.)

AUGUST 1918

Instructions regarding War Diaries and Intelligence
Summaries are contained in F. S. Regs., Part II.
and the Staff Manual respectively. Title pages
will be prepared in manuscript.

Place	Date	Hour	Summary of Events and Information	Remarks and references to Appendices
	30 31		At night-time the Battalion moved up in preparation for an attack on ECOUST. The Battalion attacked and were successful in obtaining their objective as also did the 1st GORDON HIGHLANDERS on their Left. The Battalion on the Right flank however did not get their objective and this necessitated a withdrawal temporarily and subsequently the Battalion re-took the objective though suffering heavy casualties. Estimated Casualties 9 Officers 200 Other Ranks.	
	1/9/18			

CWWoward

Major for Lieut.Col:
Commanding 13th (S) Bn. The King's (Liverpool) Regiment.

"13th (S) BN THE KING'S (LIVERPOOL REGT)

WAR DIARY or INTELLIGENCE SUMMARY.

SEPTEMBER 1918

Army Form C. 2118.

Place	Date	Hour	Summary of Events and Information	Remarks and references to Appendices
ECOUST	1st		In the morning patrols pushed out down PONTEFRACT TRENCH and got into touch with the enemy who were round derilict huts. About mid-day verbal orders were received from G.O.C. 9th Brigade that the battalion had to move on and occupy the RED LINE some 400 yards S.E. of SYDNEY AVENUE overlooking the NOREUIL VALLEY. If this could not be done by "peaceful penetration" an attack would take place at 6 p.m. Further patrols were sent out and the ground to our front was found to be clear of the enemy as far as the SYDNEY AVENUE RIDGE where small parties of the enemy were observed. It was decided not to move until the barrage came down at 5.55 p.m. Then two Companies went forward "B" on the right & "D" on the left supported by "A" & "C". Opposition was met at SYDNEY AVENUE but by moving up by the Sunken Road at IGGAREE CORNER the objective was gained and consolidated. The ROYAL FUSILIERS were on our right but the troops on our left had failed to come up. "A" & "C" Companies were placed in the Sunken Road to watch that flank. On night 1/2nd the 8th Brigade assembled behind us	
	2nd		8th Brigade passed through us and attacked NOREUIL. The Battalion watched the left flank throughout the day. On the night 2/3rd the GUARDS took up assembly positions and at 1 a.m. the battalion withdrew to bivouacs N. of ERVILLERS.	
	3rd		At ERVILLERS. The day being devoted to rest and cleaning up.	
	4th		As above. Re-organisation was carried out and the usual inspections of kit etc. held.	
	5th		As above. The Commanding Officer inspected Coys in 'Battle Order'.	
	6th		As above. During the morning the Battalion practised the attack and in the afternoon moved to the HANNESCAMPS AREA	
	7th		The Battalion paraded at 9 a.m. and marched to area occupied by the 4th ROYAL FUSILIERS and witnessed a demonstration by the Model Platoon of the 4th ROYAL FUSILIERS.	
	8th		At HANNESCAMPS AREA. Divine Services were held for all denominations.	
	9th		Remained as above and a programme of Training was carried out.	
	10th		As above.	
	11th		The Battalion paraded in column of route at 9 a.m. and moved to area S. of ERVILLERS	
	12th		In new area and a programme of training was carried out.	
	13th		As above. During the morning a Tank exdemonstration was witnessed and "Co-operation with Tanks" was practised.	
	14th		As above. A training programme was carried out the afternoon being devoted to Recreational Training.	
	15th		As above. The day was spent in preparations for the Line and the usual inspections were held and in the evening the Battalion moved up to BRIGADE RESERVE.	

WAR DIARY
or
INTELLIGENCE SUMMARY.
(Erase heading not required.)

Army Form C.2118.

13TH (S) BN THE KING'S (LIVERPOOL REGT)

Instructions regarding War Diaries and Intelligence Summaries are contained in F.S. Regs., Part II. and the Staff Manual respectively. Title pages will be prepared in manuscript.

SEPTEMBER 1918

Place	Date	Hour	Summary of Events and Information	Remarks and references to Appendices
	16th		On taking up new positions the Coys were disposed as follows:- 2 Coys in Sunken Road near BOGGARTS HOLE and YORKSHIRE BANK. and 2 Coys in CHEETHAM SWITCH & CHEETHAM RESERVE.	
	17th		Remained in Brigade Reserve.	
	18th		The Battalion was in Brigade Reserve disposed as follows:- 1 Coy - KITTEN & KNIFE TRENCHES, 1 Coy - YORKSHIRE BANK, 1 Coy - CHEETHAM SWITCH & SHROPSHIRE TRENCH, 1 Coy - CHEETHAM RESERVE. About 3.30 p.m. an intense bombardment fell on this area and seemed to extend well away on both flanks but there did not appear to be any shelling of the front line of this Brigade. The Battalion stood to. As the bombardment continued and no news of the situation was forthcoming a message was sent by lamp to 1st NORTHUMBERLAND FUSILIERS and they replied that they were all right. Runners were also sent to their H.Q. and they returned with the same reply. Runners were also despatched to the 4th ROYAL FUSILIERS and it was some time before they returned. Their message was to be forwarded through our Battalion to Brigade H.Q. and stated that the enemy had penetrated their line in places but the situation was restored. Since no information came from the right where the main attack seemed to be taking place patrols were sent Southwards from KNIFE TRENCH, SHROPSHIRE TRENCH & CHEETHAM RESERVE. They could get into touch with no one of the Right Brigade. An Officer from the HERTS REGT returning from the line reported that the enemy had broken through their line. This news turned out to be false but in view of this information a defensive flank was formed on the Divisional Boundary. This was held throughout the night. The Three Companies holding KITTEN TRENCH, CHEETHAM SWITCH & CHEETHAM RESERVE respectively each kept 2 platoons in these positions the remaining 2 platoons per Company forming the defensive flank.	
	19th		During the night 18/19th the situation became normal. Two platoons from KITTEN TRENCH reinforced the NORTHUMBERLAND FUSILIERS and the Company from YORKSHIRE BANK were placed under the orders of O.C. 4th ROYAL FUSILIERS and were moved into LONDON SUPPORT with left battalion boundaries.	
	20th		At night the Battalion moved to the relief of the 1st NORTHUMBERLAND FUSILIERS in the right sub-section.	
	21st		On completion of relief dispositions were as follows:- "C" Coy on the right, "D" Coy in the centre, "B" Coy on the left & "A" Coy in Support.	
	22nd		During the early hours of the morning there was considerable gas shelling round Bn. H.Q. causing a number of casualties to officers and men. Officer casualties were as follows:-	

Army Form C. 2118.

WAR DIARY
or
INTELLIGENCE SUMMARY
(Erase heading not required.)

13TH (S) BN THE KING'S (LIVERPOOL REGT)   **SEPTEMBER 1918**

Instructions regarding War Diaries and Intelligence Summaries are contained in F.S. Regs., Part II. and the Staff Manual respectively. Title pages will be prepared in manuscript.

Place	Date	Hour	Summary of Events and Information	Remarks and references to Appendices
	22nd (CON'D)		LIEUT.COL:T.B.LAWRENCE,D.S.O.,M.C.,D.C.M.(Commanding Officer) CAPT.F.AKED SELLERS,M.C. (Adjutant) LIEUT.J.C.TINKLER. The following were also 'gassed' but remained at duty:- MAJOR W.J.H.HOWARD & LIEUT.G.M.REDDICK,M.O.R.C.,U.S.A.	
	23rd		Remained as above, consolidating and strengthening the position and the usual patrols being organised.	
	24th		Ditto.	
	25th		Ditto.	
	26th		Ditto.	
	27th		The Battalion was ordered to attack and capture the German Defensive System West of RIBECOURT within the Battalion boundary. This attack was carried out at 5.20 a.m. on the 27th September after a continuous tour in the trenches (Front Line & Supports) for 12 days prior to the attack. PRELIMINARY PREPARATIONS The attacking Companies actively patrolled 'NO MAN'S LAND' for 5 days - The enemy's G.T's were harassed nightly by the Battalion Lewis Guns - N.C.O's & officers were afforded opportunities of carefully studying the terrain over which they were about to operate - Patrols cut wire in 'NO MAN'S LAND' on Y night - A good hot meal was provided for the men at 3 a.m. on Z day. DISPOSITIONS The attack was carried out with "C" Coy on the right & "D" Coy on the left. Inter-Coy boundary RAILWAY from KEATING'S LANE to STATION AVENUE. "A" Coy was in support to "C" Coy and "B" Coy to "D" Coy. "B" Coy in addition were responsible for the capture of the RED LINE. This objective was allotted to "B" Coy owing to its being overrun by the 1st NORTHUMBERLAND FUSILIERS in their intermediate attack on RAVINE AVENUE leaving "D" Coy & "C" Coy prolonging their line to the right ready to move forward in conjunction with them in the attack on the final objective. OPERATIONS. From Zero hour to Zero plus 8 "C" Coy formed up for their attack on KEATING'S LANE during which period 4 Trench Mortars had been detailed to bombard KEATING'S LANE and also the saps leading to SUNKEN ROAD. When "C" Coy went forward they found themselves confronted with the full garrisons of KEATING'S LANE, the two saps South of it and Sunken Road. This 'hold-up' entailed heavy casualties to "C" Coy but with great resolution 2/LIEUT.N.MORLAND (Commanding "C" Coy) eventually cleared KEATING'S LANE but decided owing to the strength of the saps and Sunken Road not to again attack these until the final advance from the RED LINE. On Z-1 Adjutant "D" Coy found similar difficulty in getting into the N.E. portion of KEATING'S LANE but eventually stormed it.	

Army Form C. 2118.

WAR DIARY
or
INTELLIGENCE SUMMARY.
(Erase heading not required.)

13TH (S) BN THE KING'S (LIVERPOOL REGT)

SEPTEMBER 1918

Instructions regarding War Diaries and Intelligence Summaries are contained in F.S. Regs., Part II. and the Staff Manual respectively. Title pages will be prepared in manuscript.

Place	Date	Hour	Summary of Events and Information	Remarks and references to Appendices
	27th		"B" Coy met with little resistance on their portion of the RED LINE. *1st objective* During the long interval between this attack and the attack on STATION AVENUE "C" Coy re-organised and called 1 platoon of "A" Coy into line with them. On re-attacking the two saps and Sunken Road our barrage although directed against BILHELM TRENCH succeeded in intimidating the German Machine Gunners on the Western edge of the Sunken Road who ran down the dugouts and the saps were now easily stormed. Rifle Grenadiers co-operating. In the Sunken Road the nest of dugouts were found full of Germans in all some 200. They readily surrendered and the attack went forward smoothly receiving well timed reinforcements from the supporting Companies. The Division on our right did not hug their barrage but followed some distance behind their tanks. This resulted in several isolated hostile M.G. posts between their tanks and Infantry shooting men of "C" & "A" Coys in the back. *The final objective* The line was again held up about 50 yards short of STATION AVENUE where a few Machine Guns were still holding out. The remaining platoons of "A" Coy now merged into the firing line and swept it forward on to its final objective. "D" Coy's attack on the final objective was carried out with 2 platoons in front line and 2 platoons in file moving along GRAND RAVINE. These 2 platoons were completely concealed from view and on several occasions captured hostile Machine Guns in rear who were opposing the advance of the 2 platoons in front line. This means of progress proved most satisfactory and STATION AVENUE was captured without heavy casualties in this Coy. "B" Coy was not called on to re-inforce but supported the other 3 Companies right up to the final objective. This Company on one occasion seeing hostile snipers on the high ground sniping at our advancing Companies silenced them with long range Lewis Gun Fire. Consolidation and Re-organisation in depth was carried out. About 600 prisoners and 100 Machine Guns and Automatic Rifles were captured. Casualties:- 6 officers 125 Other Ranks. On being withdrawn the battalion spent the time in cleaning up and re-organisation. Re-organisation etc carried on.	
	28th		Ditto.	
	29th			
	30th		The Commanding Officer is pleased to announce that during the month that 5 BARS TO THE MILITARY MEDAL & 60 MILITARY MEDALS have been awarded to W.O's, N.C.O's & MEN of the Battalion.	

W. J. N. Howard. MAJOR
COMMANDING 13TH (S) BN THE KING'S (LIVERPOOL REGIMENT).

SECRET & CONFIDENTIAL

Army Form C. 2118.

13TH (S) BN THE KING'S (LIVERPOOL REGIMENT)

Instructions regarding War Diaries and Intelligence Summaries are contained in F.S. Regs., Part II. and the Staff Manual respectively. Title pages will be prepared in manuscript.

WAR DIARY
or
INTELLIGENCE SUMMARY.
(Erase heading not required.)

OCTOBER 1918

Place	Date	Hour	Summary of Events and Information	Remarks and references to Appendices
RIBECOURT	1st		Re-organisation etc. carried on.	
	2nd		Smartening up parades - Close Order Drill etc.	
	3rd		Ditto. Firing Practice on Range.	
	4th		Ditto. Sports.	
	5th		Ditto.	
	6th		Divine Services. In the afternoon a Football Match was played versus 4th ROYAL FUSILIERS 13TH KING'S winning 6 - 0.	
	7th		Officers reconnoitred approaches to RUMILLY. In the evening the Battalion moved up to intermediate area (about L.28) preparatory to moving up the line. About 11 p.m. the battalion proceeded to assembly positions E of RUMILLY. Ref. attached "REPORT ON OPERATIONS".	
	8th		Bn. withdrawn - marched to area W of FLESQUIERES.	
	9th		Bn. spent time in cleaning up and re-organisations. Bathing parades were also held.	
	10th		Ditto. Football was played and a Concert held in the evening.	
	11th		Close Order Drill - Smartening up parades - Firing on Range. Bn. Football Match V 1st KING'S. 13TH KING'S won 2 - 1. Inter-Battalion Concert followed the Match.	
	12th		Bn. moved to area W of NOVELLES. Rest of day being spent in cleaning up.	
	13th		Billets were transferred into Village of NOVELLES. Cleaning up & re-organisation parades and Bathing Parades being held.	
	14th		Drill & Musketry Parades. Firing on Range & L.G. Training.	
	15th		Bn. practised the Attack. Collecting Salvage from 2 - 3 p.m. Football Match versus 142 FIELD AMBULANCE. Victory for 13th KING'S 4 - 1.	
	16th		Drill & Musketry Parades, L.G. Training & Firing on Range. Collecting Salvage in the afternoon. Football Match v 4th ROYAL FUSILIERS. 13TH KING'S won 2 - 0.	
	17th		Practice Attack. Firing on Range. Fitting of new clothing & Collecting Salvage in the afternoon.	
	18th		Drill & Musketry Parades, L.G. Training, Battn Parade for Close Order Drill & practice in Deployment Movements.	
	19th		Battalion moved to BEVILLERS.	
	20th		Close Order Drill - Lewis Gun Training.	
	21st		Officers reconnoitred approaches to SOLESMES & ST PYTHON. Bn. moved to QUIEVY & billeted in QUIEVY during night 22/23rd.	
	22nd			

Army Form C. 2118.

WAR DIARY
or
INTELLIGENCE SUMMARY
(Erase heading not required.)

13TH (S) BN THE KING'S (LIVERPOOL REGIMENT)

OCTOBER 1918

Instructions regarding War Diaries and Intelligence Summaries are contained in F. S. Regs., Part II. and the Staff Manual respectively. Title pages will be prepared in manuscript.

Place	Date	Hour	Summary of Events and Information	Remarks and references to Appendices
	23rd) 24th) 25th) 26th)		Ref attached 'REPORT ON OPERATIONS'.	
	27th		Bn. remained in Brigade Support. Enemy shelled RUESNES & BEAUDIGNES areas with H.E. & Gas causing inconvenience but no casualties. On night 27/28th Bn. was relieved by 7th K.S.L.I. and withdrew to ESCARMAIN.	
	28th		On being withdrawn the Battn spent time in cleaning up, re-organisation, inspections Bathing Parades etc.	
	29th		Bn. moved to SOLESMES. Remainder of day spent in cleaning up.etc. Arms Drill - Specialist instruction - Bathing Parades.	
	30th		Bn. moved to CATTENIERES. Remainder of day being devoted to cleaning up.	
	31st		The Commanding Officer is pleased to announce that during the month the following awards have been granted to officers, W.O's, N.C.O's and Men of the Battalion:-	

2rd BAR TO THE MILITARY CROSS
CAPT.(A/MAJOR)R.P.HEYWOOD,M.C.
CAPT.F.A.KED SELLERS,M.C.

THE MILITARY CROSS
LIEUT.G.H.REDDICK,M.O.R.C.,U.S.A.
2/LIEUT.(A/CAPT)L.M.MILTON,D.C.M.
2/LIEUT.J.W.BARKER.
2/LIEUT.T.W.CONE.

BAR TO THE DISTINGUISHED CONDUCT MEDAL
4803 R.S.M.T.ADAMS,D.C.M.

1 SECOND BAR TO THE MILITARY MEDAL   2 BARS TO THE MILITARY MEDAL   17 MILITARY MEDALS
and 1 FRENCH CROIX DE GUERRE.

1/11/18

K.Heywood
Capt.(A/Major)
Commanding 13th (S) Bn. The King's (Liverpool Regiment).

13TH. BN. THE KING'S.

SECRET + CONFIDENTIAL

REPORT ON OPERATIONS.

Ref Map. 57B. N.W. 1/20,000.

1. OBJECT IN VIEW. "THE KING'S" were ordered to advance behind the 4th ROYAL FUSILIERS on to the RED LINE starting at 4.30 a.m. on the 8th October 1918, and on its capture to go forward through the 4th ROYAL FUSILIERS on to the GREEN LINE – ROADWAY between LA-TARGETTE and FORENVILLE, both places exclusive to the 13th KING'S.

2. OPERATIONS.
(a) 1st. Phase. The Battalion assembled and moved forward according to plan at ZERO HOUR. The German barrage fell in the vicinity of our two Companies as they moved forward shortly after ZERO. They therefore doubled forward to minimise casualties. The RED LINE was captured, the Battalion suffering casualties; prisoners were sent back to P.O.W. Cage. As the barrage left the RED LINE half an hour later our Companies who had in the meantime formed up behind it, followed it into the GREEN LINE, which they captured, sending back prisoners and lighting Success Signals. This road was held notwithstanding direct enfilade fire into it from FORENVILLE where there were Machine Guns in the houses and from the vicinity of LA-TARGETTE which contained "NESTS" of Machine Guns. Both these places looked down into our position in the GREEN LINE. The Battalion which had gone into action only 320 rifles strong was now so weakened in their extended position (about 1,000 yds. frontage) on the two GREEN LINE, that they were unable to detach men to capture either of these places but held on in the hopes that the Battalion on their right and the battalion of the 2nd Division on their left would soon clear these places which were within their bounderies. This, however, didi not take place, and the fact that, from the behind the Ridge E. of LA-TARGETTE, a German Tank came out to mop up our infantry in this road together with the untenable nature of the position decided the Senior Company Commander (CAPT. L.M. MILTON, M.C. D.C.M.) to withdraw his men before they were annihilated by Machine Gun fire back to a position conforming with the 2nd Division on our Left and the 2nd SUFFOLKS on our Right. This withdrawal took place in good order, but owing to the fog of war was carried back into the first trench position i,e, the RED LINE which the 4TH ROYAL FUSILIERS were holding. Capt. MILTON was also influenced in the above decision by the appearance of German Infantry working through the houses of TARGETTE down towards SERANVILLERS apparently with the object of cutting him off from the SUFFOLKS and getting in between him and the RED LINE. The strength of the troops under him, as previously pointed out, eliminated the possibility of dropping a strong right flank guard.

Companies re-organised and pushed out Lewis Gun posts to the crest in front to establish observation and to maintained touch with the BERKSHIRES on our left whose right Comapny was stretched out between approximately H.7. Central to H.7.d.5.0. The same German tank from the neighbourhood of TARGETTE came right across TARGETTE-FORENVILLE road about 500 yards S. of FORENVILLE, making in a westerly direction, firing Machine Guns broadsides into the BERKSHIRES who hurriedly withdrew right over the RED LINE and to the rear and west of it back towards the vicinity of G.18. Central, where two Battalion H.Q. officers of the 13TH KING'S who had been supervising consolidation of the RED LINE got up with them and ordered them to go back to the RED LINE, which they eventually did. These officers also obtained assistance from two Machine Guns to repel any possible counter-attack which the appearance of the German Tank led one to believe was coming. These M.G. went forward to crest line 500 yards W. of RED LINE. The services of an British Tank were also requisitioned and directed to engage the hostile tank which however was set on fire by L.G. or Rifle fire.

(b). 2nd. Phase.
Orders were received about 10.45 a.m. that a second attack would take plave on the GREEN LINE in conjunction with the 2nd. Division and in co-operation with 2ND. SUFFOLKS on the right who were holding RIBECOURT. this attack was to be carried out by the 4TH ROYAL FUSILIERS and the 13TH KING'S.
The C.Os. of these two Battalions mutually arranged to divide the 1,000 yards frontage of RED LINE as a jumping-off point in the following manner:-
4TH ROYAL FUSILIERS from SUNKEN ROAD H.13.c.9.4. SOUTHWARD.
13TH KING'S from above point to junction with ROYAL BERKS about H.13.a.8.3. -the objective of 13TH KING'S being the GREEN LINE from H.8.c.6.2. to H.14.b.3.3.
A barrage on the objective was ordered from 11.35 a.m. to 12 noon.
The barrage was afterwards postponed to 1 hour later.
The KING'S & ROYALS mutually arranged to leave their trenches at 12.40 p.m.
An officer of the M.G. Corps reported himself to O.C. 13TH KING'S in the RED LINE asking if his guns could assist. His offer was gladly accepted and a M.G. barrage from 12.35 to 12.40 p.m. was arranged at which houb the Infantry proposed leaving their trenches. O.C. 13TH KING'S then proposed approched the nearest officer of the ROYAL BERKS in RED LINE about H.7.c.4.5. to find out if he had received orders to attack in conjuction.
He said he had not, but on the request of O.C. KING'S he promised to take about 60 of his men, who were collected, to attack FORENVILLE which it was anticipated would render 13TH KING'S position untenable on the GREEN LINE. O.C. KING'S then re-joined his companies just in time to lead them to the assault.
The BERKS did not co-operate, thus leaving the 4TH ROYAL FUSILIERS & 13TH KING'S with their left flank 'in the air'.
The strength of 13TH KING'S was only 25 rifles per Coy. and these advanced in two lines of Platoons- "A" Coy. on the right & "B" Coy. on the left forming the first line. "C" & "D" Coys. supporting them. As we approched the ridge about H.13.b.9.5. we were raked with M.G. fire from Road about H.7.b.9.1. and on gaining the ridge M.G. fire was opened on us from houses in FORENVILLE, also along our whole front from positions some 200 to 300 yards N.W. of our objective, also on our Right front from the ground about and in TARGETTE. To gaurd against any possible counter-attack on our exposed left flank, the platoons of "D" Coy. eschelonged outwards in rear of "B" Coy. The attack was too weak to make headway so I determined to dig-in on the crest line where my 2 front Comapnies lay, and was about ot order the Support Coys. to re-inforce the front line which then extended along ridge from about H.13.b.9.5. Southward, when I saw the 4TH ROYAL FUSILIERS withdrawing on to the RED LINE. About this time a heavy hostile Trench Mortar barrage was put down on the ridge we occupied from positions which could not be located even through Field Glasses. Our own Artillery barrage was too weak to interfere with the hostile M.G. fire on our front.
The battalion lay out some 5 minutes thus exposed on the crest line to the various harrasing fire already described and seeing further sacrifice was useless I gave the Signal to withdraw, which "B" Coy. carried out by alternate sections as if on parade.
On re-gaining the RED LINE the battalion was again re-organised and L.G. posts were pushed out in conjuction with the 4TH ROYAL FUSILIERS some 200 to 3000 yards in front of our line.

(c) **3rd phase.**
Orders were received some hours later for consolidation along our outpost line working S.E. towards Eastern edge of SERANVILLERS, but later on, I understand, both battalions returned to RED LINE when 8th KING'S OWN advanced through us. 13TH KING'S now about 80 strong lay in the RED LINE until orders were received for relief.

LESSONS.

1. The enemy barrage fell some 500 yards in rear of our front line shortly after Zero, again emphasising the necessity of supporting battalions hugging the leading battalions in the initial stages of the fight.
2. Information was slow in coming through but this I attribute to the strenuous nature of the fighting.
Success Signals and Eye Witnesses Reports being the only indications of the progress of the battle.
3. Advanced Anti-tank Guns proved invaluable on our front where they were posted if the enemy had pushed Tanks through RED LINE. An enemy Tank was used with great skill and an issue of Anti-Tank Rifles would be of great value when the topography of the Battle Zone presents a likelyhood of hostile tanks being encountered, as infantry fire is almost futile in dealing with them.
4. Our advanced and Supporting M.G. Coys. worked well and were most willing to assist, which they did in the 12.35 p.m. barrage, giving confidence by the continuous sheets of lead which they sent on the enemy's position over our heads, and I only regret that the nature of the ground did not permit of their supporting us when we left our trenches.
5. A thin Artillery barrage cannot itself silence hostile M.G. fire, but should be supported by M.G. & Infantry fire. More practice will be required to perfect "FIRE & MOVEMENT" than it has been possible to obtain recently.
6. High Morale will carry troops anywhere, but their Officers, in my opinion, will only be trusted and continue to retain their confidence so long as they do not sacrifice their men needlessly. In this respect I consider CAPT. MILTON's decision to withdraw from XXXXXXXXX between FORENVILLE & LA TARGETTE was not only justifiable under the circumstances under which he did so, but a duty in accordance with FIELD SERVICE REGULATIONS, Part 1, Chap. 2. Para. 13, Sub.para. (11). It must be borne in mind that he was taking a grave responsibility.

I regret to report the following casualties:-

	KILLED	WOUNDED	MISSING
OFFICERS	1	8	Nil.
OTHER RANKS	9	103	18.

I am glad to say, however, that the Wounded were mostly from M.G. fire and not of a grave nature.

I shall have the honour to submit, under separate cover, recommendations for Honours & Awards in connection with the above operations.

(Signed) W.J.H. Howard.
Lieut. Col;
Commanding 13th Bn. The King's (Liverpool Regiment).

11/10/18.

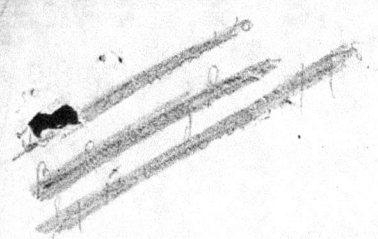

SECRET & CONFIDENTIAL

13th. BATTALION THE KING'S.

REPORT ON OPERATIONS.

REF. MAP SHEETS. 57.B.N.E.) 1/20,000.
            57.A.S.E.)

---

1. OBJECT IN VIEW.

The attack on the 1st. and 2nd. objective was to be carried out by the 76th. Brigade on the Right and the 8th. Brigade on the left, with the 9th. Brigade in Div. Reserve.

The attack on the 3rd. objective was to be carried out by the 76th. Brigade, with the 9th. Brigade in support.

The attack on the final objective, the BROWN LINE, running from R.31.,D.6.9. N.W. to R.31. Central. Thence along Sunken Road to R.36.B.15.25., thence to R.36.C.15.60., was to be carried out by the 9th. Brigade.

The 8th. Brigade was to attack with the 1st. Northumberland Fusiliers on the RIGHT and the 4th. Royal Fusiliers on the LEFT. The 13th. King's were ordered to support the attack and be prepared to support either of the front Battalions within their boundries.

1. OPERATIONS
(a) 1st. PHASE.

At 07.40. hours on October 23rd. 1918, 13th.King's passed the Starting Point at B.14.C.9.2., as ordered and marches to SOLESMES, accompanied by the band in column of route with a hundred yards distance between Companies. A short halt was made West of the SOLESMES - ST. PYTHON Railway, where Lewis Gun Limbers Limbers were unpacked and tea served out to all Companies. At 09.00. hours the Battalion proceeded to cross the SELLE RIVER between ST. PYTHON and SOLESMES on two huriedly constructed foot bridges skirting the Northern outskirts of SOLESMES. Companies proceeded to ROMERIES in column of platoons in file at fifty yards distance. No Hostile Artillery was encountered till ROMERIES was reached; the village was being shelled by 5.9 hows. so the battalion skirted the left of the Village in Artillery Formation.

The assembly positions in rear of the 1st NORTHUMBERLAND FUSILIERS and 4th ROYAL FUSILIERS in W 22 a. and b. N.E. of ROMERIES were reached by 11.00 hours with the loss of only one casualty.

At 12.12 hours the battalion moved forward according to plan, conforming to the movements of the 1st NORTHUMBERLAND FUSILIERS and 4th ROYAL FUSILIERS, keeping about 500 yards in rear of them. The battalion advanced in lines of platoons in file, "C" & "D" Coys in front and "A" & "B" Coys in support. No hostile fire of any description was encountered till the R de ST GEORGES was reached about 15.30 hours; the enemy shelled this valley with Field Guns and 5.9 hows. but a very high bank afforded admirable cover, with the result that no casualties were sustained.

2nd phase

About 13.30 hours orders were received from 9th Brigade H.Q. that the 8th & 76th Brigades would now take the BROWN LINE in place of the 9th Brigade. As soon as this line was taken all available cavalry were to be pushed forward to RUESNES and the Railway beyond it. The 9th Infantry Brigade was ordered to support the advance of the cavalry with the 1st NORTHUMBERLAND FUSILIERS on the Right and the 4th ROYAL FUSILIERS on the Left. The 13th KING'S were ordered to support these two battalions. The advance was to be made in bounds, making good the following positions within our boundaries:-

(a) River ECAILLON.
(b) High ground North of it.
(c) RUESNES.
(d) The Railway between Halt at R.9.C.15. and R.15. Central.

During the halt at the R de ST GEORGES the 13th KING'S re-organised wherever necessary; the 1st NORTHUMBERLAND FUSILIERS and 4th ROYAL FUSILIERS re-organised behind the bank running from W 12.b.8.8 N.W. & W 6.c.6.4.

About 16.10. hours the Brigade resumed its advance, 13th. King's moving forward in lines of Platoons in file on a two Company frontage as before, keeping about 500 yards in rear of 1st. N.F's., and 4th. R.F's., As soon as the area of the Ridge in W.6.B. and X.1.A. was reached the Battalion came under a most accurate, oblique Machine Gun fire from the direction of CAPELLE and the Ridge North of river ESCAILLON in Q.29.B. and 30.A. At this juncture 16.50. hours the Commanding Officer Lieut. Colonel W.J.H. Howard was wounded in the knee by a Machine Gun bullet. Captain G. Carson.M.C. took over Command of 13th. King's and informed Brigade immediately. Battalion Scouts brought back information that 1st. N.F's. had been called upon by 2nd. Suffolks to assist them in the capture of the BROWN LINE, that the objective had been taken and was being consolidated by the 2nd. Suffolks 1st. N.F's., 4th. R.F's., owing to the forward slope of the hill being in full view of the hostile Machine Guns and the inevitability of casualties if the Battalion dug in on this forward slope with O.C. King's decided to consolidate about 70 yards below the crest of the Ridge on the rear slope, with observation posts pushed out in advance to the crest of the hill. Two Companies therefore dug a line of half Platoon Posts from X.1. C.3.5. to W.6.B.1.2., the remaining two Companies dug a support line 200 yards in rear. Battalion Head Quarters was established in the ravine at W.6.c.9.1. This operation was successfully accomplished without a casualty. 1st. N.F's. and 4th. R.F's., were informed. Touch was gained with N.Z. on right and 8th. Brigade on the left, as well as with Suffolks. N.F's., R.F's and Shropshires who consolidated the BROWN LINE.

About 17.45.p.m. the 1st. Gordon Hdrs. came up in the rear of 13th. King's and commenced consolidation.

The Valley of R. de ST. GEORGES was subjected to desultory shell fire throughout the night, ESCARMAIN also was shelled by a hostile H.V. Gun at irregular intervals. At 24.00. hours Capt. (A/Major) R.P. Heywood.M.C., arrived at Battalion Head Quarters and took over Command of 13th. King's.

Consolidation was continued throughout the night, which passed very quietly.

3rd. phase.

During the night 23/24 October 1918 orders were received to the effect that 9th. Brigade at 04.00. hours on 24th. October would advance to capture high ground N.E. of RUESMES in R.14.B.15.4, and 21.b. The 1st. N.F's. were to attach on right and 4th. R.F's. on the left. 13th. King's were ordered to support N.F's., but be prepared to help the 4th. R.F's., if asked. On capture of objective patrols were to be sent out to the Railway beyond.

The Battalion was assembled at 03.20.hours, 300 yards South of BROWN LINE, within Brigade boundries, in a dip in the ground, C. and D. Companies in front with A. and B. Companies following up in support. Battalion Head Quarters was to remain in R. de ST. GEORGE'S valley, W.6. C. 9.1., till a report was received that the Battalion had crossed the ESCAILLON river.

At 04.00. hours, our Artillery Barrage came down on the line of the ESCAILLON river, where it remained for 24 minutes, thus allowing the two front Battalions to close up to it from the BROWN LINE. As soon as The BROWN LINE was evacuated by the 1st. N.F's and 4th R.F's., the two leading Companies of 13th. King's occupied it while the two support Companies remained 300 yards South of it under natural cover, as previously arranged. At 04.24. hours the barrage lifted off the ESCAILLON river and moved forward at the rate of 100 yards in 6 minutes, a point 400 yards North of the river. Here the barrage rested for one hour. During this period the 1st. N.F's. and 4th. R.F's., crossed the ESCAILLON river, taking up a position close to the barrage. 13th. King's moved forward to 100 yards South of river Escaillon and reconnoitred various passages across the river, whilst the barrage was stationary. During this reconnaissance two of King's Scouts captured 10 enemy Machine Gunners on the South bank of the ESCAILLON and sent them back to Brigade. At 05.48. hours the barrage lifted, moving forward at the rate of 100 yards in 4 minutes. The two fron Battalions followed close to the barrage and 13th. King's crossed the ESCAILLON suffering a few casualties from hostile Machine Gun fire. Little opposition was offered to our advance up the Ridge North of the River ESCAILLON, but when the leading Battalions reached the crest in R.19.d. and 20 C. our barrage appeared to cease. Accordingly the 1st. N.F's. and 4th. R.F's., pushed on and the 13th. King's moved forward to conform with the general advance, but suddenly our barrage came down on the crest of the Ridge between 13th. King's and the two leading Battalions in R.22.B., King's were then held up for a time until our barrage overtook the leading Battalions, inflicting several casualties on them. During this advance O.C. B. Company, 13th. King's caught up 4th. R.F's., and lent them two Platoons, which they had asked for prior to the attack, but which the 4th. R.F's., Guide failed to guide to proper destination. An enemy 77.c.m. Field Gun was captured about R.25. A. 9.1., with a great quantity of abandoned amunition. Numerous Machine Guns were also captured.

The 1st. R.F's., following the creeping barrage entered RVESNES and observed enemy transport, guns and Red Cross Wagons retreating in great haste through the Northern and Eastern outskirts of the village. Fires were still burning. The 1st. R.F's., continued the advance, till held up on slope about R.20. D. 9.8. and 21.C. by a heavy concentration of Machine Gun fire from the wooded valley in R.21.C. and D. and Machine Gun Posts about R.21. D.9.7. and R.22 C.3.4. Here consolidation was commenced.

On the left the 4th. R.F's., entered the S.W. outskirts of RVESNES, and a little later were reported to have gained the objectives 13th. King's followed 1st. R.F's., to line of Sunken Road, running S.S.E. from the village in R.20. B. and D. A report was received at Batt. Head Quarters, which had moved up to ravine at R.25. C. 7.8., that all four Companies were consolidating in Sunken Road from R.20. D. 5.5. to R.20. B.2.8. Orders were immediately issued to consolidate in depth, whereupon two Companies withdrew to following positions.

A. Coy. R.20. C. 75.80. to R.20. A.40.15.
B. Coy. R.20.A. 40.15. to R.20. A. 5.5.

During the afternoon the 1st. R.F's., asked for assistance, and were reinforced by C. Company, 13th. King's. They continued the advance and secured crest in R.21. D. and 22.C., being about 500 yards S.E. of Divisional Boundary. On this line they consolidated. During the night they re-organized and pushed forward to road running S.E., from RVESNES in R.21. A. and B., and R.22. C. Consolidation was begun on this road and posts pushed forward on to Ridge N.E., of it. Simultaneously, remaining three Companies of 13th. King's advanced from Sunken Road in R.20. B. and D., and consolidated the following positions:-

A. Coy. R.21. C. 60.15. to R.21. C. 15.65.
B. Coy. R.21. C. 15.65. to R.20. B. 45.26.
B. Coy. R.21. C. 15.40. to R.20. D. 8.9.

During the night 24/25. all Battalions pushed forward patrols to Railway beyond objective. One patrol of 13th. King's captured two prisoners. Save for intermittent shelling of RVESNES and vinicity by 5.9.Hows., the night was quiet.

On the 25th. Company patrols reached the Railway about 12.00. hours and the 8th. Brigade advanced through our positions.

At 14.30., hours 13th. King's moved their Battalion Head Quarters to BENVDIGNIES, R.26. D. 7.1.

After darkness C. Company, 13th. King's, was relieved by N.Z. Div. and rejoined its Battalion, taking up the following position:-

R.20. D. 4.8. to 20. B. 15.55.

During the night 25th. October, the enemy shelled RVESNES and BENVDIGNIES with H.E. and Gas. Several Field Batteries of N.Z. Artillery moved up in close proximity to our positions. Consequently, O.C. King's considered it adviseable to withdraw the Battalion to the following positions:-

B. Coy. R.26. B. 5.5. to R.26. B. 2.2.
A. Coy. R.20. D. 15.05. to R. 20. D. 04.
C. Coy. R. 20. C. 7.1. to R. 20. C. 50.55.
D. Coy. R.26. A. 8.4. to R. 26. A. 7.9.

About 17.00 hours on 26th. October the Battalion withdrew and consolidated these positions.

CONCLUSION.

1. During the 24th and 25th of October our lack of Low Flying Aeroplanes was most apparent. The enemy Reconnoitring planes flew over our lines whenever they chose, gaining valuable observations with practically no interference.
2. The Artillery Barrage appeared to rest both W. of and on Ruesnes, thus hampering to a large extent the movements of our Infantry.
3. During consolidation, our Machine Guns remained too far behind and could not possibly have rendered any assistance with overhead fire in the event of a hostile Counter-attack.

I regret to report the following casualties:-

	Killed.	Wounded.	Missing.
Officers.	-	1	-
Other Ranks.	5	34	-

I am pleased to say, however, that the majority of these casualties are slightly wounded as a result of Machine Gun fire.

I shall have the honour to submit, under separate cover, recommendations for Immediate Honours and Awards in connection with the above operations.

(Signed). R.P. Heywood. Capt. (A/Major).

27.10.18.   Commanding, 13th Bn. "The King's" Liverpool Regt.

SECRET

Army Form C. 2118.

WAR DIARY
or
INTELLIGENCE SUMMARY. 13TH (S) BN. THE KING'S (LIVERPOOL) REGT.
NOVEMBER 1918.

(Erase heading not required.)

WO 39

Place	Date	Hour	Summary of Events and Information	Remarks and references to Appendices
CATTENIERS	1st.		On being withdrawn, Bn. spent time in washing & cleaning equipment, re-organization & thorough inspections. Football match v. 1st. N.F's. - King's lost - 5-1.	
	2nd.		Close Order Drill. Firing on range with L.Gs. & Rifles. Specialist training of Scouts, Signallers, S.Bs. Bathing parades in afternoon.	
	3rd.		Divine Services. Bn. moved to QUIEVY.	
	4th.		" " Bn. spent time in cleaning up.	
	5th.		" " Bn. under orders to move at 1 hours notice.	
	6th.		Specialist instruction.- Drill. Arrival of Col. T.B. Lawrence, D.S.O., M.C., D.C.M.	
	7th.		Drill - Specialist training - Firing on range with L.Guns in afternoon.	
	8th.		Bn. moved to ROMERIES. Spent rest of day cleaning up.	
	9th.		Drill parades - Specialist instruction. Cleaning up of billets & collection of salvage.	
	10th.		Bn. moved to LE GRAND SART. Rest of day spent in cleaning up.	
	11th.		Bn. on march to LA LONGUEVILLE; suddenly recalled to LE GRAND SART. Cessation of hostilities at 11.00 hrs. General cleaning up of limbers, transport & billets. - Lecture by Divisional Educational Officer.	
	12th.		Bn. clearing roads. Bn. concert in the evening.	
	13th.		-ditto-	
	14th.		Cleaning up parades. Inter-Coy., football match in afternoon. Concert in the evening.	
	15th.		Clearing roads - Cleaning up parades - Football - Concert. Lt.Col. T.B. Lawrence, D.S.O. M.C., D.C.M., to hospital.	
	16th.		Bn. moved to LA LONGUEVILLE.	
	17th.		Divine Services.	
	18th.		Cleaning up parades. Bn. moved to SOUS LE BOIS.	
	19th.		Smartening up parades. - Drill - Practice marching. Lecture on Educational Scheme by Educational Officer.	
	20th.		Bn. moved through MEABEUGE to COLLERET. Rest of day spent in cleaning up.	
	21st.		Two Coys. clearing roads. Remainder cleaning billets & equipment. Bn. team played 142nd. Field Amb. - King's won. 4-2.	
	22nd.		Cleaning up parades. - Smartening up drill. - Physical training - Practice in Guard Mounting. Inter-Coy. football in the afternoon. Small party visited Mons.	
	23rd.		Clearing roads. - Smartening up drill for remainder of Bn. Bn. match v. Bds. in afternoon. - King's won. - 7-2.	
	24th.		Bn. moved to BOIS DE VILLERS.	

SECRET.

Army Form C. 2118.

13TH (S) BN. THE KING'S (LIVERPOOL REGIMENT).

WAR DIARY
or
INTELLIGENCE SUMMARY.   NOVEMBER 1918.

(Erase heading not required.)

Instructions regarding War Diaries and Intelligence Summaries are contained in F.S. Regs., Part II. and the Staff Manual respectively. Title pages will be prepared in manuscript.

Place	Date	Hour	Summary of Events and Information	Remarks and references to Appendices
	25th.		Bn. moved to BERZEE, through THUIN.	
	26th.		Bn. moved to GOUGNIES.	
	27th.		Cleaning up parades. Foot inspections - Bn. concert in the evening.	
	28th.		Bn. moved to BIOUL.	
	29th.		Bn. moved to SPONTIN. - crossed R. Meuse at YVOIR.	
	30th.		Bn. moved to SOVET. Rest of day spent in cleaning up.	
			The Commanding Officer is pleased to announce the following awards during the month:-	
			THE MILITARY CROSS.	
			2/Lieut. E. Baldwin, D.C.M.	
			2/Lieut. E.G. Sturgeon.	
			2/Lieut. H. Morland.	
			2/Lieut. (A/Capt) J. Hockenhull.	

Capt. (A/Major):
Commanding 13th (S) Bn. The King's (Liverpool Regiment).

/SECRET.

Army Form C. 2118.

WAR DIARY
or
INTELLIGENCE SUMMARY.

13TH (S) BN. THE KING'S (LIVERPOOL) REGT.

DECEMBER. 1918.

Instructions regarding War Diaries and Intelligence Summaries are contained in F.S. Regs., Part II. and the Staff Manual respectively. Title pages will be prepared in manuscript.

Place	Date	Hour	Summary of Events and Information	Remarks and references to Appendices
SOVET.	1st.		Bn. spent day in cleaning equipment, limbers and cookers.	
	2nd.		Commanding Officer inspected the Bn. - Inter-coy Football Final, "B" beat "D" 5 - 2.	
	3rd.		"All Present" parade to check strength. Close Order drill and cleaning up parades. Football, H.Q., v Rest of Bn. - Victory for H.Q., 2 - 0.	
	4th.		Bn. moved to PESSOUX.	
	5th.		Bn. moved to NOISEUX and Gd. EMEILLE.	
	6th.		Bn. moved to EREZEE.	
	7th.		Bn. moved to FANZEL.	
	8th.		Bn. moved to ODEIGNE.	
	9th.		Bn. moved to COMTE & PROVEDROUX.	
	10th.		Cleaning and inspection parades. - Interior Economy.	
	11th.		Bn. crossed the German frontier - billeted in ESPELER. Order of march:- 1st N.F's., 4th R.F's and 13th King's. 9th Bde followed 76th Bde.	
	12th.		Bn. moved to THOMMEN.	
	13th.		Bn. moved to HEUEM.	
	14th.		" " " DAHLEM.	
	15th.		" " " SCHONAU.	
	16th.		" " " ROTZHEIM.	
	17th.		" " " EUSKIRCHEN. - Cleaning up parades.	
	18th.		" " " ZULPICH.	
	19th.		" " " LUXHEIM, KELZ, JAKOBWULLESHEIM, area.	
	20th.		Cleaning up and inspection parades. - Football.	
	21st.		Divine Services. - Football - Recreation.	
	22nd.		Commanding Officer's inspection. - Football.	
	23rd.		-do- -do- -do- - Football.	
	24th.		Divine Services. - Recreation.	
	25th.		Coy. arrangements - Football.	
	26th.		Bn. moved to KERPEN.	
	27th.		Cleaning equipment and Billets.	
	28th.		Divine Services.	
	29th.		Instructional Parades under Education Scheme. Drill parades, - Ceremonial parades. Recreation and Football.	
	30th.			

SECRET.

Army Form C. 2118.

WAR DIARY

or

INTELLIGENCE SUMMARY.

13TH (S) BN. THE KING'S (LIVERPOOL REGT).

DECEMBER. 1918.

(Erase heading not required.)

Instructions regarding War Diaries and Intelligence Summaries are contained in F.S. Regs., Part II. and the Staff Manual respectively. Title pages will be prepared in manuscript.

Place	Date	Hour	Summary of Events and Information	Remarks and references to Appendices
	31st		Instructional, drill and ceremonial parades - recreation and football. The Commanding Officer is pleased to announce the following award during the month:- THE MILITARY CROSS. 2/Lieut. J.W. McCutcheon.	

[signature] Lieut. Col:
Commanding, 13th Bn. The King's (Liverpool Regt).

SECRET

Army Form C. 2118.

WAR DIARY
or
INTELLIGENCE SUMMARY. 13TH (S) BN. THE KING'S (LIVERPOOL) REGIMENT.

JANUARY 1919.

(Erase heading not required.)

Instructions regarding War Diaries and Intelligence Summaries are contained in F.S. Regs., Part II. and the Staff Manual respectively. Title pages will be prepared in manuscript.

Place	Date	Hour	Summary of Events and Information	Remarks and references to Appendices
KERPEN.	1st.		Drill, Ceremonial Parades and Instructional Classes. Inter-Platoon Football and Recreational Training.	
	2nd.		- ditto -	
	3rd.		- ditto -	
	4th.		Bn. Route March - Route - SINDORF - HORREM - MODRATH - KERPEN. Inter-Platoon football Competitions.	
	5th.		Divine Services.	
	6th.		Inspecting of Billets, Educational Training, Ranges and Regimental Institutes by G.O.C. Bde. Inter-Platoon Competitions, Football, Rugby, Battalion Concert in evening.	
	7th.		Educational Training - Lecture on "Agricultural Science" by Lieut. T.L.Davies. Drill and Ceremonial parades. Inter-Platoon football Competitions. - Officers Rugby.	
	8th.		Educational Training - Drill, Musketry and Ceremonial Parades. Battn.Drill parade - Football match v 4th. R.Fs. - King's lost 3 - 1. Inter-Platoon football.	
	9th.		Educational Training - Drill, Musketry and Ceremonial parades, Semi - finals Inter-Platoon Competition. - Recreational Training. - Divisional Cinema in evening.	
	10th.		Educational Training - Drill, Musketry, Ceremonial Parades - Recreational Training - Replayed Semi-final Inter-platoon Competition.	
	11th.		Route March - MODRATH - BALKHAUSEN - GYMNICH - KERPEN. Inter-Company Competition football - Recreational Training - Cinema. victory	
	12th.		Divine Services - Footballmatch - Reglt. XI v Officers XI/for former 4 - 0.	
	13th.		Educational Training - Drill, Ceremonial and Musketry parades - Recreational Training.	
	14th.		Inspection of Coys. by G.O.C. Bde. Officers' Association XI v 42nd. Bde. R.F.A. at KREUSAU - Draw 1 - 1.	
	15th.		Educational Training - Drill, Ceremonial and Musketry parades - Recreational Training - Concert given by the "Elegant Extracts" of 4th. R.Fs.	
	16th.		Educational Classes - Drill, Ceremonial and Musketry parades. Inter-Platoon Competition - Final.	
	17th...		Educational Classes - Drill, Ceremonial and Musketry parades. Recreational Training - Rugby Match- Officers v Rest of Bn. Victory for the latter.	
	18th.		Route March - SINDORF - KOPPENDORF - AHE - SINDORF - KERPEN. Recreational Training. Battalion Concert in evening.	
	19th.		Divine Services - Competition "A" - Divisional Silver Bugle - 13th.King's v 40th. Bde.R.F.A. Victory for the King's 4 - 0.	
	20th.		Educational Classes - Drill, Ceremonial and Musketry parades. Recreational Training - Inter-Company Competition - "B" v "C" - "C" Coy. won 4 - 0.	

SECRET.

Army Form C. 2118.

Instructions regarding War Diaries and Intelligence Summaries are contained in F.S. Regs, Part II. and the Staff Manual respectively. Title pages will be prepared in manuscript.

WAR DIARY
or
INTELLIGENCE SUMMARY. 13TH.(S) BN. THE KING'S (LIVERPOOL) REGIMENT.

(Erase heading not required.)

JANUARY 1919.

Place	Date	Hour	Summary of Events and Information	Remarks and references to Appendices
KERPEN.	21st.		Educational Classes - Bn. "Hare Drive" - Recreational Training - Football Match - Officers v N.C.Os. - Drew 2 - 2.	
	22nd.		Educational Classes - Drill, Ceremonial and Musketry Parades - Recreational Training - Rugby Bn. Paper Chase.	
	23rd.		Educational Classes - Drill, Ceremonial and Musketry parades . Recreational Training - Lecture in evening by Capt. Beagley, 4th. R.Fs. on "Prospects of Demobilization".	
	24th.		Bn. Route March - BERGENHAUSEN - ELATZ HEIM - KERPEN. Football - Inter-Company Competition Final - "C" Coy. 3 - "A" Coy. 1.	
	25th.		Visit of Official Photographer - Battalion, Companies, Officers and Sergeants photographed on parade. Recreational Training.	
	26th.		Divine Services. - Range Practice.	
	27th.		Drill and Musketry parades, Range Practices - Educational Classes - Recreational Training.	
	28th.		" " "	
	29th.		" " "	
	30th.		Concert given by "H.Q." R.A.F. Concert Party. Drill, Ceremonial Parades - Lewis Gun Instruction - Range Practices - Educational Classes - Recreational Training.	
	31st.		Drill, Ceremonial parades - Range Practices - Lewis Gun Instruction - Educational Classes - Recreational Training.	

The Commanding Officer is pleased to announce the following awards during the month:-

THE MILITARY CROSS.

Capt. (A/Major) J. H. Jackman.

THE MERITORIOUS SERVICE MEDAL.

C.Q.M.S. H. Leigh - Hunt. 14399.
Corporal J. Sinclair. 21620.
Corporal J. McDonough. 19707.

[signature] Lieut. Col.
Commanding 13th. Bn. The King's (Liverpool) Regiment.

SECRET.

Instructions regarding War Diaries and Intelligence Summaries are contained in F.S. Regs., Part II. and the Staff Manual respectively. Title pages will be prepared in manuscript.

Army Form C. 2118.

WAR DIARY or INTELLIGENCE SUMMARY

(13TH. (S) BN. THE KING'S (LIVERPOOL REGIMENT).

FEBRUARY, 1919.

(Erase heading not required.)

Place	Date	Hour	Summary of Events and Information	Remarks and references to Appendices
KERPEN	1st.		Route March MODRATH - BOTTENBROICH - KERPEN. Recreational Training - Lecture at 17.00 hrs. by Col. The Earl of Denbigh, H.A.C. A.D.C. on "The Worlds escape from German Domination".	
"	2nd		Divine Services.	
"	3rd		Drill, Musketry Parades, Range Practice - Educational Classes - Recreational Training - Singing Competition in evening.	
"	4th		Drill - Range Practice - Educational Classes - Recreational Training.	
"	5th		Drill - Range Practice - Educational Classes - Recreational Training - Concert.	
"	6th		Battn. Parade - Ceremonial Drill - Competition "C" 2nd. Round - Result 13th. King's 5 40th. Bde. R.F.A. 1.	
"	7th		Inspection of Battn. at work by G.O.C. Bde. - Drill - Musketry - Lectures by Os.C. Coys. - Recreational Training.	
"	8th		Coy. arrangements - Recreational Training.	
"	9th		Divine Services	
"	10th		Inspection of Billets and Battn. at work by Divl. Commander - Recreational Training.	
"	11th		Battn. Parade - Ceremonial Drill - Recreational Training.	
"	12th		Battn. Parade - Ceremonial Drill - Competition "A" 13th. King's v 23rd. Bde. R.F.A. - Recreational Training. (C.S.M. Fairhurst - Italian Decoration)	
"	13th		Battn. Parade - Ceremonial Drill - Recreational Training.	
"	14th.		Battn. Parade - Ceremonial Drill - Battn. Football Match.	
"	15th.		Battn. Route March.	
"	16th.		Divine Services	
"	17th.		Educational Classes - Inspection of Billets - Recreational Training.	
"	18th.		Inspection of Billets, Educational Training - Recreational Training.	
"	19th.		Inspection of Billets - Educational Training - Visit by Brig. Gen.	
"	20th.		Moved to Cologne, 58, Siemens Strasse, EHRENFELD.	
EHRENFELD	21st.		Cleaning of Billets - Inspection of Billets.	
"	22nd		Practice for Colour Presentation by Army Commander.	
"	23rd		" " " " " " " " Divisional Commanders Inspection.	
"	24th		Presentation of Colours by Army Commander.	
"	25th.		Cleaning of Billets and preparing for move to BEUEL.	
"	26th		Moved to BEUEL. The Battalion proceed by Train from NIPPES to BEUEL to join a new Division. The 3rd. Divisional Commander said Good-Bye to the Battalion on NIPPES Station along with the Brig. Comnd	
BEUEL	27th.		Recreational Training and cleaning up. Rugby Match 13th. King's v 1st. N.Fs.	
"	28th		Recreational Training. Football Match (Rugby) 13th. King's 3 pts. R.Fs. Nil	

2nd. March, 1919. Commanding 13th. Bn. The King's (Liverpool Regiment). Lawrence Lieut. Col.

SECRET.

Instructions regarding War Diaries and Intelligence Summaries are contained in F. S. Regs., Part II. and the Staff Manual respectively. Title pages will be prepared in manuscript.

Army Form C. 2118.

WAR DIARY (13th.(S) BN.THE KING'S (LIVERPOOL REGIMENT)
or INTELLIGENCE SUMMARY

(Erase heading not required.)

MARCH 1919.

Place	Date	Hour	Summary of Events and Information	Remarks and references to Appendices
BEUEL	1st.		Recreational training. Football match 13th.K.L.R. v 1st. N.Fs.	
	2nd.		Cleaning and inspection of billets. Football match A.Coy. v B.Coy.	
	3rd.		Cleaning and inspection of billets. Educational training. Recreational training.	
	4th.		Cleaning and inspection of billets. Educational Classes. Rugby match played at Duren.	
	5th.		Cleaning and inspection of billets.Educational Classes - lecture by M.O. on "Venereal Disease" and Recreational training.	
	6th.		Cleaning and Inspection of billets -Educational Classes - lecture Drill,Musketry,-Recreational training.	
	7th.		Cleaning and Inspection of billets.Educational Classes-Drill,Musketry,Recreational Training.	
	8th.		Battalion Route March - Recreational training.	
	9th.		Divine Services - Inter-platoon Semi-final at Cologne - 11 platoon 2 v 1st.N.Fs. Nil.	
	10th.		Battalion inspected on parade by the Divisional Commander - Inspection of A.Coy's Kits and billets. Inter-Coy.relief of the 5/6th.Royal Scots in the outpost line by "D" Coy. Rec.training	
	11th.		Educational Classes - Drill parades - Ceremonial - Officers Rugby Final v 2nd.Royal Scots. 3rd. Division Cup - 2nd. Royal Scots 26 points 13th.King's Nil. Regtl.Soccer match 13th.King's 1 90th. Field Ambulance 1.	
	12th.		Inspection of Draft by Commanding Officer - Reorganisation - 3rd.Div.Inter-Platoon Soccer Final 13th. King's 1. v 1st. R.Fs. 1.	
	13th.		Cleaning of billets - Educational Training -Reorganization - Recreational training.	
	14th.		Cleaning of billets - Educational Training - Drill - Ceremonial - Musketry - Recreational Training	
	15th.		Route March - RAMERSDORF - OBERKASSEL - RAMERSDORF - BEUEL. Football Officers v 151 Bde.R.F.A.	
	16th.		Divine Services. (Officers.)	
	17th.		Educational Training - Drill, Musketry - Baths - Recreational Training.	
	18th.		Drill - Ceremonial - Educational Training - Recreational Training.	
	19th.		Drill - Ceremonial - Educational Training - Officers v N.C.O's-Football N.C.Os' won 1 - 0	
	20th.		Drill - Ceremonial - Lecture on "Search for British Prisoners in Germany" by Capt.A.P.Hart	
			Recreational Training. A.W.C.	
	21st		C.O's inspection by Coys. - Transport, inspected. Football Regtl.XI. 6 v Rest of Bttn 1.	
	22nd.		Route March - JULICH - GEISLAR - VINICH - MULDORF - BEUEL. Recreational Training. Officers	
	23rd.		Rugger v 52nd. King's lost 12 points to 3.	
	24th.		Divine Services.	
			Football Officers Cleaning up - Educational Classes - Drill - Ceremonial and Musketry - B.Coy.1	
			Recreational training - Football Officers 13th.King's 13 v 51st.King's 1. Football - D.Coy. 1.	

SECRET

Continued –

Army Form C.2118.

WAR DIARY 13th.(S)BN.THE KING'S (LIVERPOOL REGIMENT)
or
INTELLIGENCE SUMMARY   MARCH 1919.

(Erase heading not required.)

Place	Date	Hour	Summary of Events and Information	Remarks and references to Appendices
BEUEL	25th.		Educational Classes – Drill – Guard Mounting – Musketry. Football – Officers 13th.King's 5 v 161 Bde. R.F.A. 1.	
	26th.		Cleaning up etc., – Drill – Technical Instruction – Recreational Training Football "A" Coy. 13th. King's 7 v D.Batty. 161 Bde.R.F.A. 4.	
	27th.		Educational Classes – Drill – Ceremonial Parades. Recreational training.	
	28th.		Educational Classes – C.Os. Inspection of Coys. H.Q. and Transport – Drill – Ceremonial. Regtl.Football match – 13th.King's 5 v 52nd. King's Mil.	
	29th.		Interior Economy – Lectures – Recreational Training.	
	30th.		Divine Services.	
	31st.		Educational Classes – Ceremonial Drill – Musketry – Physical Training – Football Regtl.XI. 2 v 90th. Field Ambulance 2.	

The Commanding Officer is pleased to announce the following awards
during the Month:-

51840 Pte. S. Leigh – Medaille Baratie si Credinta 3rd. Class (Roumanian Decoration).

19495 C.Q.M.S. J.R. Galloway – The Military Medal.

Keith Hall   Capt.

1st.April 1919.   Commanding 13th.Bn.The King's (Liverpool Regiment).

3rd Division
9th Infantry Brigade
1st Lincolnshire

From 1st January, To 30th June
1915

9th Bde.
3rd Div.

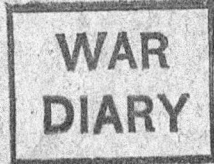

1st LINCOLNSHIRES

JANUARY 1915.

On His Majesty's Service.

121/4261

9th Brigade

1st Bn. Lincoln.

Vol VI. 1—31.1.15

Army Form C. 2118.

1st Bn. Lincolnshire Regt.

WAR DIARY
or
INTELLIGENCE SUMMARY
(Erase heading not required.)

Instructions regarding War Diaries and Intelligence Summaries are contained in F. S. Regs., Part II. and the Staff Manual respectively. Title pages will be prepared in manuscript.

Hour, Date, Place	Summary of Events and Information	Remarks and References to Appendices
1 – 1 – 1915	Our artillery duel continued throughout the day. Our Artillery made very good practice, some of the shell bursting directly over the enemies' trenches. Capt Carruthers hit. Lieut SMELY joined the Battalion. Information had been received that troops opposite Chapelles had been reinforced the preceding day.	
2 – 1 – 1915	The artillery duel re-commenced at daybreak and continued except for several short intervals until dusk. Casualties 3 killed 4 wounded. C & D Companies were relieved in the fire trenches by A & B Companies during the evening.	
3 – 1 – 1915	Occasional artillery from the enemy, artillery throughout the day. 2 Officers and 2 NCOs (2nd Lt Hopkins Light Infty) spent the previous night and the day in the trenches. Casualties 2nd Lieut A MOODY severely wounded, other Ranks 1 wounded.	
4 – 1 – 1915	The day passed very quietly. Our artillery again shelled the enemies trenches, without reply; a very meagre reply from the Germans	OR stout

Army Form C. 2118.

WAR DIARY
or
INTELLIGENCE SUMMARY
(Erase heading not required.)

Hour, Date, Place	Summary of Events and Information	Remarks and References to Appendices
5-1-15	During the evening the Bn. was relieved by the 2nd Royal Irish Rifle and marched to Billets at WESTOUTRE.	
6-1-15	2nd Lieut SHAW and RICKETTS proceeded on leave to England. Lieut Col. Clerke, Seymour Bt. CB. DSO Commanding Battery Corps visited the Headquarters of the Battalion.	
	The Battalion was paraded at 11 a.m and Maj General Mullane inspected the whole of the B.E. Held.	
	2nd Lieut Mustard, "A" Company from ENGLAND Capt ?? of "C" Boys and 2nd Lieut WALKER, with a draft of 15 NCOs and men joined the Battalion.	
7-1-15	Bn. in billets at WESTOUTRE. Routine work.	
8-1-15	Bn. left WESTOUTRE at 2 p.m. marched via Kemmel to the trenches to relieve the 9th Br. Royal Irish Rifles Capt Copeland the Adjutant tried to go in support to Cy. Reserve then and the Trench Commander H. Quar then in a Ravine near Douve	a Return

Army Form C. 2118.

WAR DIARY
or
INTELLIGENCE SUMMARY.
(Erase heading not required.)

Instructions regarding War Diaries and Intelligence Summaries are contained in F.S. Regs., Part II. and the Staff Manual respectively. Title pages will be prepared in manuscript.

Hour, Date, Place	Summary of Events and Information	Remarks and references to Appendices
9-1-15	The day passed quietly except by occasional exchange of artillery fire & sniping. No casualties.	
10-1-15	A few of the enemy's shells fell close to "C" Coy of trench, but no damage was done. During the evening disputes between C & D Coys in the trenches. Casualties 1 man wounded.	
11-1-15	The day passed quietly. Lt. C.G. SHAW and A. RICKETTS returned from leave. Casualties 1 wounded.	
12-1-15	The day passed quietly. In the evening 2nd in Command Lt-Col. Ron Royal Irish Rifles, after which they marched to 10thRE to Billets. Casualties 1 wounded.	
13-1-15	In Billets. Refitting, cleaning up. Capt E.M. GRANT-HAMILTY and 2nd Lt Thomson Regt joined from England. Lt Roberts Report — J.	
14-1-15	—	
15-1-15	—	
16-1-15	Bn. left 10thRE trenches to the ? and relieved the 2nd Bn. Royal Irish Rifles	A/Relief

WAR DIARY or INTELLIGENCE SUMMARY

Army Form C. 2118.

(Erase heading not required.)

Instructions regarding War Diaries and Intelligence Summaries are contained in F.S. Regs., Part II and the Staff Manual respectively. Title pages will be prepared in manuscript.

Hour, Date, Place	Summary of Events and Information	Remarks and references to Appendices
17 - 1 - 15.	Div. 18 Coys reinforced by a party of 1 Officer & 50 NCO's and men employed supplying respirators to firing line & in supporting trench. C.Coy in reserve Chavasse Chantilles hill.	
18 - 1 - 15.	Received exchange of artillery fire during Capt. Julian's relief.	
19 - 1 - 15.	An on 17th. Enemy was fairly active. Greater part of the day 2nd. Coy Companies were relieved by Coy of 1st Regiment. Chavasse hill.	
20 - 1 - 16.	Very quiet day. 1st Chambers 1 wounded. A quiet day in the evening the Bn. turned out the interim Rafael Sangh. Ripol after which the Bn. returned to OCRE. After Chantilly kill hun to HR BOXER and G.E.L. TICH proceeded to England on leave.	
21 - 1 - 15.	In billets. Repairing clemency.	
22 - 1 - 15.	Do	
23 - 1 - 10.	Do	
24 - 1 - 15.	Bn. left OCRE at 5pm and marched to Brigade Reserve in billets there are formed.	or Ration

WAR DIARY or INTELLIGENCE SUMMARY.

(Erase heading not required.)

Army Form C. 2118.

Hour, Date, Place	Summary of Events and Information	Remarks and references to Appendices
25-1-15.	Still in Reserve Bn: being employed in various Brigade duties.	
26-1-15.	Still in Reserve Bn: employed as in the previous day. 2 Lieut. DESBROWE proceeded to ST. OMER for machine gun course & 2/Lt. PARRISH rejoined from Machine Gun Course at ST. OMER.	
27-1-15.	Still in Brigade Reserve. Brigade duties continued.	
28-1-15.	Still in Brigade Reserve. In the evening the Bn. was relieved by Composite of the Honourable Artillery Company after which the Bn. marched to WESTOUTRE and billeted. Majors EDWARDS & 2/Lieut. S.H. JEUDWINE rejoined & a draft of 100 N.C.O.'s & men joined the Bn: at WESTOUTRE. 2/Lieut. T.G. NEWBURY proceeded on leave to England.	a return
29-1-15.	In billett. Refitting & cleaning of Bn.	
30-1-15.	Billett during two days & staff	
31-1-15.	Sgt. 169 R.W. Cremen joined the Battalion. Bn. received	

9th Bde.
3rd Div.

WAR DIARY

1st LINCOLNSHIRES

FEBRUARY 1915.

On His Majesty's Service.

9th Brigade.

1st Lincolns.

Vol VII. 1 – 28.2.15.

Nil

WAR DIARY
or
INTELLIGENCE SUMMARY.
(Erase heading not required.)

Army Form C. 2118.

1 Leicestershire Regt.

Hour, Date, Place	Summary of Events and Information	Remarks and references to Appendices
1 – 2 – 15.	The Bn. left WESTOUTRE at 4-15 pm and marched via LOCRE to the trenches, relieving the 2nd Bn. K.O. Rifles between 8 and 9 pm. C & D Coy. in the firing line. A & B in support. The Commanding Officer Lieut. Col. WER. SMITH was unable to accompany the Bn. owing to illness. He proceeded to BETHUNE Convalescent Hospl. for treatment. Major L EDWARDS taking over command of the Bn. 2nd Lieut A. SHEARMAN joined the Bn. and was posted to A. Coy.	
2 – 2 – 15.	Except for occasional artillery fire the day passed quietly. Between 9 and 10 an aeroplane (ours) returning from the trenches was fired on by the enemy's artillery. Casualties 1 killed 2 wounded.	
3 – 2 – 15.	The day passed quietly. In the evening A & B Coys. relieved C & D Coy. in the trenches. Casualties 2 wounded.	

WAR DIARY
or
INTELLIGENCE SUMMARY.
(Erase heading not required.)

Army Form C. 2118.

Instructions regarding War Diaries and Intelligence Summaries are contained in F. S. Regs., Part II and the Staff Manual respectively. Title pages will be prepared in manuscript.

Hour, Date, Place	Summary of Events and Information	Remarks and references to Appendices
4 - 2 - 15.	a horse which was in front of our trench was thought to be killed by snipers, our trenches by our artillery causing considerable damage to the lines. The enemy's artillery shelled KEMMEL doing a certain amount of damage to the village and casualties were inflicted on a working party of the 9th Brigade in which 2 of the R.F. were wounded. Casualties for the day 7 wounded.	
5 - 2 - 15.	Unusual activity between artillery of both sides during the day. Nothing further happened. In the evening the Bn. was relieved by the 2nd H.L.I. after which we marched back to LOCRE and billeted. Casualties 1 killed 3 wounded.	
6 - 2 - 15	In billets cleaning up. [2nd Lieut T.G. NEWBURY rejoined off leave] still in billets. Bn being on duty.	
7 - 2 - 15		
8 - 2 - 15	2nd Lieut on killed. 2nd Lieut L.T.S. BOWER and 2nd Lieut Regt joined the Battn with a draft of 33 N.C.O's & men. Lieut Col W.E.D. SMITH proceeded	

WAR DIARY
or
INTELLIGENCE SUMMARY. 1st Lincolnshire Regt.

(Erase heading not required.)

Army Form C. 2118.

Hour, Date, Place	Summary of Events and Information	Remarks and references to Appendices
9 – 2 – 15	To England on sick leave from WERTHEIM. Still in field. Capt C.E.F. RICH proceeded by MONT NOIR to take over the duties of APM to the 2nd Div. 2nd Lieut R.W. Gen. CAVE ORME joined the Batt. from England. In the evening the Battn proceeded to the trenches relieving the 2nd Bn R.I. Rifles. A & B Coy being in the firing & C & D Coy in support. Casualties Nil	
10 – 2 – 15	The day passed very quietly. A part of the trench held by the Bn being in such a very bad state is now being reconstructed. Casualties 1 wounded.	
11 – 2 – 15	Very quiet day. C & D Coys relieves A & B Coys in the trenches. Casualties 1 wounded.	
12 – 2 – 15	Very quiet day. The heavy rain made the trench very wet which made bailing necessary. Casualties 1 killed 1 wounded	

Army Form C. 2118.

WAR DIARY
or
INTELLIGENCE SUMMARY.
(Erase heading not required.)

1st Inverness-shire R.G.

Hour, Date, Place	Summary of Events and Information	Remarks and references to Appendices
13 – 2 – 15	The morning passed very quietly. In the afternoon there was a heavy artillery duel. In the evening the Bn. was relieved by the 2nd R.S. Rifles & 2nd Essex Regt. after which we proceeded to LOCRE to billets. [2nd Lieut. A.B.S. PARISH proceeded on leave to England] Reached billets	7/10
14 – 2 – 15	Resting in billets	
15 – 2 – 15	Still in billets. Bn. being on duty from 5pm in the evening	0P 9/10
16 – 2 – 15	Still in billets. Bn. still ready up to 5pm.	
17 – 2 – 15	About 12-0 noon a sudden order was received for the Brigade to move to YPRES to support the 5th Corps who had been some trouble [An Infantry Barracks]. The march from LOCRE to YPRES was very difficult owing to heavy rain & the march throughout. 2nd Lieut. L. TROOP and A.J. Eilby joined the Battn. In the evening we arrived at YPRES the Bn. billeted in the Refugee	11/10

Army Form C. 2118.

WAR DIARY
or
INTELLIGENCE SUMMARY.
(Erase heading not required.)

1st Lincolnshire Regt

Instructions regarding War Diaries and Intelligence Summaries are contained in F.S. Regs., Part II. and the Staff Manual respectively. Title pages will be prepared in manuscript.

Hour, Date, Place	Summary of Events and Information	Remarks and references to Appendices
	were informed the Brigade was transferred to the 5th Corps relieving the 84th Brigade. The Brigade is now forming part of the 28th Division.	XXVIII
18 - 2 - 15	The Brigade paraded at 8-30 am and proceeded to take up a position on the YPRES Canal in support of the 84th Brigade as the reserve. The day proving very windy the Bde were relieved at 4pm by the 1st of November afterwards returned to billets (Belgium Infantry Barracks) Canal side. 1 man wounded.	
19 - 2 - 15	Still in billets near gate turned at crossroads notice.	
20 - 2 - 15	Still in billets. The very high wind is unlikely to move off in anything approximately. In the enemy the Commanding Officer was today ordered to proceed to visit the trenches for the purpose of gaining information about the line which the Bn is going to take over.	

Army Form C. 2118.

WAR DIARY
~~INTELLIGENCE SUMMARY.~~
(Erase heading not required.)

1st Lincolnshire Regt

Instructions regarding War Diaries and Intelligence Summaries are contained in F. S. Regs., Part II. and the Staff Manual respectively. Title pages will be prepared in manuscript.

Hour, Date, Place	Summary of Events and Information	Remarks and references to Appendices
21-2-1915.	The Battalion remained in the Infantry Bks during the day, at 7.40 P.M. Bn paraded to proceed to the trenches to relieve the Welsh Regt. "B" & "D" Coys forming the firing line, "A" Coy in support. Owing to it being a first line taken up by the Battalion the relief took some considerable time to carry out. The trench taken over by "B" Coy was considered dangerous, as it was a continuation of a trench held by the Germans. A hurricane rundown on from the latter, eventually the relief was successfully carried out - being completed just after midnight. Casualties:- 3 other Ranks Wounded. 2nd Lieut WALKER [having been overcome with seizure or on his way up to the trenches was sent back & admitted to hospital.	1/10 ST 4/22
22-2-1915.	The day passed rather quietly. The enemy shelled the trenches occupied by "C" Coy which was close to the YPRES CANAL and on top of a hill, thereby making the trench conspicuous. In the evening a report was received that the was a party of the enemy had worked round behind the trench held by "B" Coy. A message was sent to "D" Coy to	

Forms/C. 2118/10 (9 20 6) W 4141-463 100,000 9/14 HWV

Army Form C. 2118.

WAR DIARY
or
INTELLIGENCE SUMMARY.
(Erase heading not required.)

1st Bedfordshire Regt

Hour, Date, Place	Summary of Events and Information	Remarks and references to Appendices
22.2.15 (Cont'd)	Sent a party forward and drove them out. 2nd Lieut. M.H. WILSON who was in command of "D" Coy took this party forward and succeeded in driving them out and he was severely wounded in following them up. Casualties:- 1 Killed, 1 Died of wounds 5 wounded. Artillery very active on both sides. The enemy's Artillery which was at very close range shelling "C" Coy trenches, but without doing any damage. Snipers were also very active, causing several casualties in "D" Coy. In the evening the Battalion was relieved by the R.S. Fus. after which it proceeded to Billets. A Coy going to ROSENTHAL CHATEAU. B Coy being billeted in VANIKHOF CHATEAU. B.H.Qrs. Chateau being on the LILLE ROAD outside YPRES. "A" Coy found a post on the bank of the YPRES CANAL as a supporting point for the troops holding the line on the South side of the CANAL. Casualties 2 Killed 1 Died of wounds 12 Wounded & 1 missing	
23.2.15		

WAR DIARY
or
INTELLIGENCE SUMMARY.
(Erase heading not required.)

Army Form C. 2118.

1st Monmouthshire Regt

Hour, Date, Place	Summary of Events and Information	Remarks and references to Appendices
24.2.1915	In reserve at ROSENTHAL and LANKHOF CHATEAUX. Artillery very active all day, the enemy's artillery shelled the post on the CANAL Bank held by "A" Coy. Casualties:- 2 killed 3 wounded. Captain J.N. PHILLIPS, LIEUT F.N. WAKES and a draft of 165 N.C.Os & the Battalion arrived [at YPRES.]	1/10th
25-2-1915	The draft previously mentioned joined the Battn. at 5-30 a.m. Capt. J.N. PHILLIPS being posted to "D" Coy, LIEUT WALES to "B" Coy.] In the evening Batt paraded & marched to the trenches, between the R.S.B. and "A" C" & "D" Coys forming the firing line with "B" Coy in support at Batt H.Qrs. Owing to the experience gained from a few previous visits to these trenches, we were able to do a great deal of work to improve the trenches & to strengthen our line and reduce the list of casualties. Casualties:- 4 wounded.	

Army Form C. 2118.

WAR DIARY
or
INTELLIGENCE SUMMARY.
(Erase heading not required.)

1st Shropshire Regt.

Hour, Date, Place	Summary of Events and Information	Remarks and references to Appendices
26-2-1915.	The Enemy continued to shell the trenches close to the Canal held by "C" Coy and except for sniping the day passed quietly. In the evening a reconnoitering party consisting of 2nd LIEUT JEUDWINE & 2 men accompanied by 2 men of the R.E. got forward to reconnoitre a house which was believed to hold snipers & to possible to blow the house up. They arrived at the house and found it unoccupied, charges of gun cotton were laid down and the house was successfully blown up. All the party returned back safely. Casualties:- 1 killed 1 died of wounds 11 wounded	
27-2-1915.	Enemy still continued to shell the trenches held by "C" Coy and late in the afternoon one of their shells destroyed a dug-out Captain F.N. GRANTHAM who was in the dug-out being killed. 2nd LIEUT DISBROW being slightly wounded. In the evening the Bath. was relieved by the P.S.L.I. & they marched to CRUIS STAAT to billet. Casualties:- Other Ranks 1 killed 1 died of wounds 10 wounded.	

Army Form C. 2118.

WAR DIARY
or
INTELLIGENCE SUMMARY.

(Erase heading not required.)

1st Herefordshire Regt.

Hour, Date, Place	Summary of Events and Information	Remarks and references to Appendices
28-2-1915.	The Battalion remained in billets at CRUIS STAAT, resting. A few of the enemy's shells came near the billets but without doing any damage.	

9th Bde.
3rd Div.

WAR DIARY

1st LINCOLNSHIRES

MARCH 1915.

On His Majesty's Service.

121/4816

J.8.
11 sheets

2ⁿ O'Brigan
1/3
1ˢᵗ Lincolns

Vol VIII. 1 — 31.3.15

Army Form C. 2118.

WAR DIARY
or
INTELLIGENCE SUMMARY
(Erase heading not required.)

1 Lincolnshire Regt.

Hour, Date, Place	Summary of Events and Information	Remarks and References to Appendices
1. 3. 15.	Battalion still in billets. At 8-15 the Bn paraded and proceeded to ROSENTHAAL CHATEAU and relieved 4th Royal Fusiliers. Casualties O.R. 2 wounded.	
2. 3. 15.	Bn at ROSENTHAAL CHATEAU in support to Brigade. Heavy artillery fire on both sides. The Bn moved at 7-15 pm & proceeded to the Trenches relieving R.S.F. A, B & D Coys in firing line, C Coy in support with Bn Headquarters at LA CHAPELLE FARM. Lieut Col WEBB SMITH C.M.G. rejoined from England off sick leave. Casualties O.R. 1 wounded. 2nd Lieut H.C. DISBROWE & 2nd Lieut J.W.HOULTON sent to Hospital.	
3. 3. 15.	Enemy's artillery very active. Town in vicinity of Bn Headquarters shelled. Casualties O.R. 1 killed. 3 wounded.	

Army Form C. 2118.

WAR DIARY
or
INTELLIGENCE SUMMARY
(Erase heading not required.)

1 Lincolnshire Regt.

Instructions regarding War Diaries and Intelligence Summaries are contained in F. S. Regs., Part II. and the Staff Manual respectively. Title pages will be prepared in manuscript.

Hour, Date, Place	Summary of Events and Information	Remarks and References to Appendices
4. 3. 15.	Enemy's artillery very active. 18 coys Munst. shelled during xxxx horse. Machine Guns in support shelled during xxxxxx to xxxx of the town. Bn Headquarters shelled. 27 shell xxx striking on falling and exploding about Headquarters causing many casualties in "C" Coy. The shelling lasted about 1 hour + 30 minute. Medical Officer decided to remove wounded, which kept xxx coming out without further loss. Bn relieved by 1st Dorset Regt + proceeded to YPRES and billeted in Infantry Barracks. Casualties. 1 killed, 1 M.O. wounded. 74 wounded.	
5. 3. 15.	Bn Paraded at 6-45 a.m. and proceeded to VLAMERTINGHE to rest in huts + act as Divisional reserve. Bn on duty from 5 p.m. 5-3-15 to 5 p.m 6-3-15. Casualties Nil.	
6. 3. 15.	Bn on duty to 5 p.m. Day passed quietly. Weather cold + wet.	

WAR DIARY
or
INTELLIGENCE SUMMARY

(Erase heading not required.)

Army Form C. 2118.

1 Inniskilling Regt

Hour, Date, Place		Summary of Events and Information	Remarks and References to Appendices
7.	3. 15.	Bn still resting at VLAMERTINGHE	
8.	3. 15.	- do - on duty from 5pm.	
9.	3. 15.	- do - " " No 5 pm	
10.	3. 15.	Bn paraded at 4-45pm and proceeded to YPRES. A, B Coys proceeded to Dug-outs and TUILERIES to act in support of R.S.F. in trenches. C & D Coys and Headquarters in reserve at Infantry Barracks. 2.9 Lieuts [A. RICKETTS & C.G. SHAW] to Hospital sick. Casualties Nil	
11.	3. 15.	2nd Lieut. A. STAPLETON posted to Bn. Enemy's artillery shelled support dug-outs occasionally during the day. Casualties Nil. C & D Coys with Headquarters left Barracks at 7-20pm to support A & B Coys who had relieved R.S.F in trenches. The enemy had succeeded in blowing up a trench held by the R.S.F. and an attack was expected, which however did not take place. A Coy under command of Major HER BNER	
12.	3. 15.		

Army Form C. 2118.

WAR DIARY
or
INTELLIGENCE SUMMARY

(Erase heading not required.)

1st Amershire Rgt

Instructions regarding War Diaries and Intelligence Summaries are contained in F. S. Regs., Part II. and the Staff Manual respectively. Title pages will be prepared in manuscript.

Hour, Date, Place	Summary of Events and Information	Remarks and References to Appendices
12. 3. 15.	H.E.R. BOXER reconnoitred the trench destroyed by explosion. Casualties, 1 wounded. 2nd LIEUT J.H. TOOLIS arrived at Infantry Barrack YPRES with draft of 61 NCO & men.	
13. 3. 15.	Enemy artillery very active. A number of shell burst near Bn Headquarters. 'A' Company heavily shelled causing many casualties. Occasional bursts of rifle fire from our side. The draft under 2nd Lieut J.H. TOOLIS proceeded to join the companies in the trenches about 8-30 p.m. Casualties: killed 16 wounded	
14. 3. 15.	Enemy's artillery active all day. Bn Headquarters again shelled without effect. In the afternoon our trench shelled causing casualties. Toward evening our batteries heavily shelled the enemy. Bn relieved about 9 p.m. by R.S.F. A & B Coys with HQrs proceeded to Infantry Barrack YPRES in reserve. C & D Coys remained in support in Dug-outs 1 & 2 TUILLE RIES. Casualties: 2 Lieut T.G. NEWBURY slightly wounded. O.R. returned.	

WAR DIARY
or
INTELLIGENCE SUMMARY

(Erase heading not required.)

Army Form C. 2118.

1 Incomplete Rgs

Hour, Date, Place	Summary of Events and Information	Remarks and References to Appendices
15. 3. 15.	Headquarters & A & B Coys in reserve at Monarch. C & D Coys in support of R.S.F. in Dug-outs at TUILERIES. 2nd Lieut [SHIEUDWINE] to hospital sick.	
16. 3. 15.	C & D Coys in support. Day passed quietly. A & B Coys with Headquarters proceeded at 4.15 p.m. and proceeded to join C & D Coys and relieve R.S.F. in the trenches. Trenches improved generally and wire entanglements put out by the 2nd Ruth. Casualties 3 wounded.	
17. 3. 15.	Major HERBOXER left the Bn and proceeded to join 2nd Ruth. During daylight nothing noteworthy occurred. Heavy rifle fire from the enemy commenced at dusk and continued in about 1 hour. Casualties 3 wounded. 2nd Lieut. J.W. HARRIS with 12 O.R. rejoined from Base	
18. 3. 15.	Situation normal. Improvements in trenches continued. Rand near Bn Headquarters shelled during the afternoon. Bn relieved by R.S.F. at about 8.30 p.m.	

Army Form C. 2118

WAR DIARY
or
INTELLIGENCE SUMMARY
(Erase heading not required.)

1 Lincolnshire Rgt

Instructions regarding War Diaries and Intelligence Summaries are contained in F.S. Regs., Part II. and the Staff Manual respectively. Title pages will be prepared in manuscript.

Hour, Date, Place			Summary of Events and Information	Remarks and References to Appendices
19.	3.	15.	A & B Coys remain in support of R.S.F. in Dug outs & TUILERIES. C & D Coys with Headquarters returned to Barracks. YPRES in ruins. 2 suspected spies dressed in Red Cross uniform of American Ambulance caught. Handed over to A.P.M. 9th Infantry Brigade	
			Headquarters Companies remained in barracks. A & B Companies in support at TUILERIES and Dug out. Capt. Hon W.H. LITTLETON 3rd Bn North Staffordshire Regt (S.R.) joined from 2nd Bn Lincoln Regt.	
20.	3.	15.	Headquarters Coys left Barracks at 7-15 pm relieved R.S.F. in the trenches. Casualties Nil	
21.	3.	15.	The day passed quietly. The Battn was relieved about 9 pm by Cheshire Regt (15th Brigade) and marched back to rest huts near VLAMERTINGHE, arriving 7-0 am 22.3.15. Casualties Nil.	LIEUT COL W.E.R SMITH C.M.G. leaves to take command of 80th Brigade. LIEUT C.B. FAREBROTHER joins from England.

Army Form C. 2118.

WAR DIARY
OR
INTELLIGENCE SUMMARY.
(Erase heading not required.)

1 Lincolnshire Regt.

Hour, Date, Place	Summary of Events and Information	Remarks and References to Appendices
22. 3. 15	Major L. EDWARDS assumes command of the Battalion. The Batln remained in rest huts, acting with other units of Brigade in Divnl reserve.	
23. 3. 15	— do —	
24. 3. 15	Capt. F.M. GREATWOOD rejoined from England and took over duties of senior Major. Still in rest huts. Baths on duty from 5-8 pm.	
25. 3. 15	" " " " 2nd Lieut A. AGELASTO, Dorset Regt. " " " " J.A.R. WESTON STEVENS, 2nd Dorset R. (SR) " " " " H.H.ST. TUFTON 2nd R. Sussex R (SR) joined the Batln from England.	
26. 3. 15	The Bn paraded at 4 - 15 pm and proceeded to the trenches S.E. of YPRES relieving R.W.KENT Regt (1st Batln) 1/2 Coy 10th Rl Liverpool Scottish attached to Bn for duty A.B.C & D Coys in fire trenches, Liverpool Scottish in support in dugouts with the Headquarters. Casualties O.R. wounded 1 (Niel fores) 2nd Lt. G.R. KEEP, 3rd R. Sussex R. (SR) joins the Bn.	

Army Form C. 2118.

1 Lincolnshire Regt.

WAR DIARY
or
INTELLIGENCE SUMMARY

(Erase heading not required.)

Instructions regarding War Diaries and Intelligence Summaries are contained in F. S. Regs., Part II and the Staff Manual respectively. Title pages will be prepared in manuscript.

Hour, Date, Place	Summary of Events and Information	Remarks and References to Appendices
27. 3. 15.	2nd Lieut S.H. JEUDWINE rejoined from hospital. B Coy heavily bombarded by trench mortars & lifted from. Considerable damage caused to trench & caused 13 casualties. Casualties O.R. 2 killed 1 died of wds. 10 wounded.	
28. 3. 15.	Artillery on both sides fairly active. [Several shell fell near support & Headquarters dugouts] Bns relieved about 10·25 p.m. by R.S.F. and proceeded to ROSENDAEL CHATEAU in support. Casualties O.R. 2 died of wds. 6 wounded.	
29. 3. 15.	Bns remained in support. [Chateau in vicinity of Chateau shelled by enemy during afternoon.] Casualties O.R. 1 wounded.	
30. 3. 15.	Day passed quietly. Bns paraded at 5 p.m. and proceeded to the trenches relieving R.S.F. A & C Coys. 1s Coy Liverpool Scottish in fire trenches. B & D Coys with Headquarters in support in dug out. Casualties nil.	

Army Form C. 2118.

WAR DIARY
or
INTELLIGENCE SUMMARY
(Erase heading not required.)

1 Warwickshire Rgt

Instructions regarding War Diaries and Intelligence Summaries are contained in F. S. Regs., Part II. and the Staff Manual respectively. Title pages will be prepared in manuscript.

Hour, Date, Place	Summary of Events and Information	Remarks and References to Appendices
31. 3. 15.	Day passed quietly. Trenches improved. Evening O.R. wounded 1 [signature]	

9th Bde.
3rd Div.

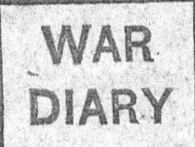

1st LINCOLNSHIRES.

April

1915

On His Majesty's Service.

Army Form C. 2118.

WAR DIARY
or
INTELLIGENCE SUMMARY

(Erase heading not required.)

1 Lincolnshire Regt

Hour, Date, Place	Summary of Events and Information	Remarks and References to Appendices
1. 4. 15.	Quiet up to nothing. At about 2 p.m. the enemy heavily bombarded trenches opposite being held by Bedfords Redoubt, with heavy howitzers and light guns. About 50 large shells burst over this trench each salvo interval of about 10 second causing many casualties. T trench held by one Company of Bedfords. Several shells burst where support dugouts which were in a wood about 150 yards in rear of firing line. The wounded had to be removed to a safer place. Eventually to Ypres hospital. OR 30 killed & wounded. A machine gun section was buried by shell explosion. Casualties, Lincolns Nil. At about 11-30 p.m. the Bn was relieved by R.S.F. and proceeded to & billets at KRUISTRAAT arriving about 1-0 a.m. 2nd Lieut G.R. HOPEHALL 2nd Devon R (SR) joined the Bn.	
2. 4. 15.	Remained in billets. Orders received to rejoin 3rd Division. The Bn paraded at 5-15 p.m. and proceeded to DICKEBUSCH [The Commanding Officer & Company Commanders proceeded to the trenches at 2nd Lieut H.H SHEARMAN sick & to BROOK regions. The Bn from hospital	

Army Form C. 2118.

WAR DIARY
or
INTELLIGENCE SUMMARY
(Erase heading not required.)

1 Lincolnshire Regt

Instructions regarding War Diaries and Intelligence Summaries are contained in F. S. Regs, Part II. and the Staff Manual respectively. Title pages will be prepared in manuscript.

Hour, Date, Place	Summary of Events and Information	Remarks and References to Appendices
3. 11. 15.	LIEUT C.D. FAREBROTHER to Hospital. The Bn rested in billets during the day. Paraded at 8.15 pm & proceeded to trenches near ST ELOI relieving E. SURREY Regt. B, D Coy occupied the firing line, A, C Coy with Headquarters in support in the Canadian Trench. Heavy rain had fallen all day. The route to trenches were in very bad condition & in consequence the relief took a considerable time to carry out.	
4. 11. 15.	Enemy artillery active. D Coy in trenches T1 shelled with howitzer causing casualties and damage to trench. Capt. J.W. PHILLIPS severely wounded. Several shells burst near H.Q. dugout & by which D Coy in fire trench at 8-0 p.m. During the evening a party of R.S.F. officers visited the trenches in view of that Bn's occupation of same. Casualties. 1 Officer wounded. O.R. 3 killed. 10 wounded. Major D.H.F. GRANT joined from England.	

(9 26 6) W 257—976 100,000 4/12 H W V 79
32087 Regt

Army Form C. 2118.

1 Lanarkshire Rgt.

WAR DIARY
or
INTELLIGENCE SUMMARY
(Erase heading not required.)

Hour, Date, Place	Summary of Events and Information	Remarks and References to Appendices
5. 4. 15.	Day passed quietly. when except out a loss of the fire trench, the Commanding Officer - Major EDWARDS was severely wounded by rifle shot. The same bullet also wounded Lieut. E W WALES. The Bn was relieved by R.S.F. about 10 p.m. and proceeded to rest huts at DICKEBUSCH. Casualties. 2 Officers wounded. Other Rank 4 wounded.	
6. 4. 15.	Resting in huts. 1/Lt A St JOHN PERKINS 3rd Devon Regt & 2/Lt T J NELLY 1 Lincoln R & 1/Lieut of 6 SCOTR. joined the Batln.	
7. 4. 15.	Resting in huts during day. 2nd Lieut A AGELASTO J A R WESTON STEVENS & J.S. HODGSON having been gazetted to commissions in 1st Dorset Regt. left to join their own unit. 2nd Lieut N H SHERMAN and L T BROOK sick to hospital. The Battalion at 6-40 p.m. and proceeded to the trench near S.S.E. 101 relieving R.S.F. about 10-0 pm. B/D Trench. M Gun suffered Casualties. 2/Lt T G NEWBOLY wounded. OR's wounds.	

Army Form C. 2118

WAR DIARY
or
INTELLIGENCE SUMMARY. 1 Inniskilling Rgt
(Erase heading not required.)

Instructions regarding War Diaries and Intelligence Summaries are contained in F. S. Regs, Part II and the Staff Manual respectively. Title pages will be prepared in manuscript.

Hour, Date, Place	Summary of Events and Information	Remarks and references to Appendices
8. 4. 15.	Quiet until noon. Our artillery opened fire lasting about 1 hr. The enemy replied with light gun. Several shells exploded between support trenches occupied by B & D Coys. Evening quiet. Enniskillen OR. 2 wounded. Very heavy artillery fire was heard from the direction of N E of YPRES during night.	
9. 4. 15.	Morning quiet. Artillery duel in afternoon. Several large shells burst in vicinity of support trenches without causing any damage. B & D Coys situation normal during evening. B & D Coys relieved A & C Coys in the firing line at about 10 pm. Enniskillen 2 O R wounded. Artillery on both sides active all day.	
10. 4. 15.	Enemy's artillery & T.M. heavier and Machine Gun damaged parapets of T.M. trench and Machine Gun emplacement. Enemy's snipers being carrying several enniskillen. A working party of about 30 of the enemy caught repairing their trench. Machine Gun fire opened, dispersing them.	

Army Form C. 2118.

WAR DIARY
or
INTELLIGENCE SUMMARY. (Inniskilling Rgt.)
(Erase heading not required.)

Instructions regarding War Diaries and Intelligence Summaries are contained in F.S. Regs., Part II. and the Staff Manual respectively. Title pages will be prepared in manuscript.

Hour, Date, Place			Summary of Events and Information	Remarks and references to Appendices
			About 9 p.m. 1st Movement walked into our lines, unopposed & unarmed. He stated he was an Alsatian and had effected his escape from the enemy's line when he comrade, were temporarily withdrawn from the trench he being left as sentry. He was handed over to R.E. H.Q. Casualties Killed 2 officers 4 wounded	
11.	4.	15.	Artillery active on both sides during day. No damage to our lines. The Rn was relieved about 10 a.p.m. by R.S.F. after 4 days strenuous hard duty by the trenches. 1 marched to billets at DICKEBUSCH Casualties 1 Killed, 2 died of wounds.	
12.	4.	15.	Bn remained in billets. Weather fine.	
13.	4.	15.	— do — — do — 2nd Lieut J H TOOLIS to Hospital sick.	
14.	4.	15.	Wet in morning, remainder of day fine. At 7.45 p.m. a working party of 150 of O.Ranks under Lieut ECHHAIT proceeded to trenches for the purpose of constructing a communication trench	

WAR DIARY
or
INTELLIGENCE SUMMARY.
(Erase heading not required.)

Army Form C. 2118.

1 Hertfordshire Regt.

Hour, Date, Place	Summary of Events and Information	Remarks and references to Appendices

under supervision of the R.E.

The enemy opened a heavy rifle fire & their artillery followed with a bombardment of our lines. A large shell exploded and destroyed a house in the line of the R.S.F. but causing few casualties.

At about 11-0 pm

Our artillery opened fire in reply and after a very heavy bombardment lasting about 1 hour the enemy's guns were completely silenced. Their infantry had intended to attack but were dispersed immediately they showed themselves above the trenches. Considering the severity of the hour's fighting very few casualties occurred on our side & the enemy must have suffered heavily.

During the bombardment the Bn. stood to arms. B & D Coys proceeded to support trenches, A & C Coy with HQrs remained in reserve at alarm post.

Casualties: O.R. killed 6 wounded
Lieut H MARSHALL & 14 O.R. joined from Base.

15.4.15.

The Bn. returned to billets at about 3-0 am

The day passed quietly. Weather fine.

The Bn. paraded at 7-15 pm. A & C Coys proceeded

WAR DIARY
or
INTELLIGENCE SUMMARY.
(Erase heading not required.)

Army Form C. 211

1 Herefordshire Regt

Hour, Date, Place	Summary of Events and Information	Remarks and references to Appendices
S. 16. 4. 15. 2nd July 17th ½ 21st just this relief on 15th 17th was ? 1st — attached H.M. 60	to 2nd line trenches followed by "B" "D" Coys with HQrs at half an hour's interval. This was a precautionary measure owing to an attack by the enemy being anticipated. The attack however did not take place. Gramillies Wed. The Regt remained in 2nd line trenches until 1·0 a.m. when orders were received from Bde HQrs that the relief was to be carried out. The Regt proceeded to relieve the R.S.F. in the trenches. B & D Coys in the firing line, A & C Coys with HQrs in support thereto. The day passed quietly until 7 pm when the enemy's artillery opened fire on ground between HQrs & T1 trench ("B" Coy) lasting about 30 minutes, causing no damage. Later (about 9 pm) our fire trenches were shelled by light field guns. The shelling lasted under 4·20 pm when our own artillery replied with shrapnel which burst over the enemies lines and silenced their guns. During the afternoon an order was received from Bde HQrs that this Coy in fire trenches were to open a rifle burst of rapid fire at 7·30 p.m.	

WAR DIARY
or
INTELLIGENCE SUMMARY.
(Erase heading not required.)

Army Form C. 2118

1 Lincolnshire Regt

Hour, Date, Place	Summary of Events and Information	Remarks and references to Appendices
17.4.15.	At 7-0 pm a violent explosion was heard from the left of our position and simultaneously an artillery opened a heavy fire. A message was received that one of the enemy at Hill 60 had been successfully mined and seized. The success was mainly due to the timely cooperation of the artillery at the moment the infantry were ready to rush and by the continuance of a most violent bombardment of the enemy trenches throughout the night; our infantry were enabled to establish themselves in the captured trench. Casualties OR. 1 killed & 1 wounded. The bombardment continued until daylight. After a period of quietness lasting until 9 am our artillery opened heavy fire lasting about 2 hours. During the night A.& C. Coys. relieved B. & D. in the fire trench. Casualties OR. 1 died of wounds. [signature]	

Army Form C. 211

WAR DIARY
or
INTELLIGENCE SUMMARY.
(Erase heading not required.)

1 Shropshire Regt

Hour, Date, Place	Summary of Events and Information	Remarks and references to Appendices
18. 4. 15.	Weather fine. Occasional bursts of artillery fire from either side continued throughout the day. During the evening very heavy rifle fire was heard from the left. Casualties. 2nd Lt. A J BUSBY wounded O.R. 1 wounded	
19. 4. 15.	Weather fine. Artillery on both sides active all day. The village of DICKEBUSCH was bombarded during the day doing damage to 2 houses & causing slight casualties amongst the troops in reserve. The Bn was relieved by the RSF about 10.0 pm and proceeded to billets at DICKEBUSCH. Casualties. 1 O.R. wounded	
20. 4. 15.	In billets at DICKEBUSCH. Weather fine. B & D Coys on duty ready to turn out at an instant notice.	
21. 4. 15.	In billets. A & C Coys on duty 2nd G M MOORE 1st N Reed Regt with draft of 94 O.R. joined weather fine.	

Army Form C. 211

1 Kruisstraat Kr-

WAR DIARY
or
INTELLIGENCE SUMMARY.
(Erase heading not required.)

Hour, Date, Place	Summary of Events and Information	Remarks and references to Appendices
22.4.-15.	In billets during the day. Artillery on duty weather fine. The Bn paraded at 7.30pm & proceeded to a new position on Bdge F 32 B (YPRES 1/40,000) in a distance of about 5,000 yds direct and 9,000 yds by road from DICKEBUSCH reformally 1st Bn D.C.L.I. (14th Bde) at about 11pm. A & C Coys in the fire trenches B Coy with Bn H.Q. in support dug-outs on W. Canal Bank near KANHOF CHATEAU- distance from fire trenches about 1000 yds. The enemy's lines were from 150 to 1300 yds from our front. The approach to our fire trenches was over open ground for about 600 yds. which during the day being exposed to the enemy's rifle fire. A heavy artillery and rifle fire continued throughout the night. YPRES was heavily bombarded considerable improvements to trenches, parapets, wire entanglements were effected by Battalion during the night. also the new communication trench was commenced (F in Summary) to the Battalion to left our trenches in a poor condition and much labour falls to the men in making them safe for both offensive defensive purposes and is resumed when none available generally. Casualties. O.R. 1 wounded. Lieut. E.C. HOPE-HALL proceed to join 1st DEVON REGT. transport remained at DICKEBUSCH. W.J.W.	

Army Form C. 2118.

1 Lincolnshire Regt

WAR DIARY
or
INTELLIGENCE SUMMARY.
(Erase heading not required.)

Instructions regarding War Diaries and Intelligence Summaries are contained in F.S. Regs., Part II. and the Staff Manual respectively. Title pages will be prepared in manuscript.

Hour, Date, Place	Summary of Events and Information	Remarks and references to Appendices
23-4-1915.	Situation on our front quiet. A heavy artillery duel over our position lasted throughout the day. Heavy rifle fire heard on our left throughout the afternoon. The Artillery duel continued during the night. Casualties O.P. 2 Killed 1 Died of wounds 3 Wounded. Some further casualties occurred (when men were crossing the open ground between the trenches) AM 1915. 2nd Lieut G.B. MOORE 3rd Ryl. Berks Regt sent to hospital. Weather cold windy. Bombardment of YPRES continues. Casualties 2 Killed. D/wounds 3 wounded when killed.	
24-4-1915.	At daybreak a violent cannonade, and a heavy rifle firing was heard from direction N.E. YPRES. The rifle fire subsided about 7 a.m. The artillery fire continued throughout the day. Enemy's cavalry was seen on our front. Everything quiet on artillery duel over our position continued all day. Two shells burst near 14Pt Hqrs, into on Canal Bank in afternoon. B Coy relieved A Coy in the trenches about 10pm. On that patrol reconnoitred the ground between our lines and the enemy's, reaching his wire entanglements. Four hand grenades were thrown in to the German trenches. Bombardment of YPRES continues. Weather dull. Rain at night. Casualties O.P. 3 Wounded.	

Forms/C. 2118/10

Army Form C. 211

1 Shropshire L.I.

WAR DIARY
or
INTELLIGENCE SUMMARY.
(Erase heading not required.)

Instructions regarding War Diaries and Intelligence Summaries are contained in F. S. Regs., Part II. and the Staff Manual respectively. Title pages will be prepared in manuscript.

Hour, Date, Place	Summary of Events and Information	Remarks and references to Appendices
25. 4. 1915.	Conditions quiet on our front during day. An occasional exchange of artillery fire in the daytime developed its a dual rifle & musket firing throughout the night. Bombs & rifle grenades from the front were opened on vigorously during the evening. Weather fine. Casualties O.R. 2 wounded. (A.W.)	

Army Form C. 2118

Shropshire L.I.

WAR DIARY
or
INTELLIGENCE SUMMARY.
(Erase heading not required.)

Hour, Date, Place	Summary of Events and Information	Remarks and references to Appendices
28-4-1915.	Conditions Quiet on our front during day at about 3 am the Battalion on our left opened heavy rifle fire lasting about 1 hour, the enemy replied with Shiller fire. Several shells burst in the vicinity of BANK OF CHATEAU. Our Artillery returned the fire which ceased about 4am. Quiet until about 11.0 am when enemy light field guns shelled was near chateau, two shells falling about thirty near Bath N°3 and support dug-outs. Artillery on both sides more or less active remained quiet day and night. A boy reliever boy in the trenches at about 10pm. Grenades were thrown into enemy lines during the night. Casualties Other Ranks 1 Died of wounds. 3 Wounded. DICKEBUSCH bombarded in afternoon. Engagement N.E. YPRES heard in progress during day & night. Weather fine.	
29-4-1915.	Quiet on our front all day. Artillery active on both sides until noon. DICKEBUSCH again bombarded. 2nd LIEUT L.T. BROOK who had returned from Divisional Rest Camp was wounded. LIEUT & Q.M. F.W. MASTERS slightly wounded. Sergt Drummer killed. A draft of 104 other ranks opened at DICKEBUSCH in the evening. Owing to DICKEBUSCH being shelled the transport was ordered to move to a place about 1 mile N.W. of the village. Casualties 2 Officers wounded. 1 O.R. Killed.	

Army Form C. 2118

1 Hooghe Ry

WAR DIARY
or
INTELLIGENCE SUMMARY.
(Erase heading not required.)

Hour, Date, Place	Summary of Events and Information	Remarks and references to Appendices
28-4-1915	The day passed quietly until about 3pm when a heavy cannonade was heard on our left which continued until about 6pm. Enemy's artillery shell LANK OF CHATEAU and again in the vicinity during evening and night. 7 Coy relieved B Coy in fire trenches about 11pm. All quiet on our front with the exception of occasional bursts of rapid rifle fire from our side. Reinforcements 9/79 other ranks arrived and billeted at ROSENTHAL CHATEAU. Casualties Other Ranks 5 Wounded. Weather fine.	
29-4-1915.	Enemy Artillery shelled LANK OF CHATEAU and road in the vicinity during the day. Several shells burst near support dug-outs without causing any damage. Towards evening artillery on both sides seemed very active. Reinforcement posted to Company 2nd LIEUTS F.N. FRAZIER, J.H. BARRETT, G.N.H. APPLIN and F.C. GREEN joined the Battalion. Casualties	

Army Form C. 2118.

WAR DIARY
or
INTELLIGENCE SUMMARY. Kruishilik Ry.
(Erase heading not required.)

Instructions regarding War Diaries and Intelligence Summaries are contained in F. S. Regs., Part II. and the Staff Manual respectively. Title pages will be prepared in manuscript.

Hour, Date, Place	Summary of Events and Information	Remarks and references to Appendices
30.4.1915	Artillery on both sides active at intervals during day, several shell from light guns knocked support dug-outs, causing no damage or casualties. B Coy relieved E Coy in the two blacks during the night. All quiet on our front during night. Artillery became active on both sides. Weather fine. Brouillis the Parks Wounded. 2ⁿᵈ J.R. HAMMOND joined from ENGLAND.	

9th Bde.
3rd Div.

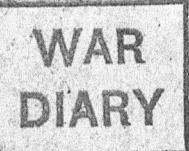

1st LINCOLNSHIRES.

May

1 9 1 5

On His Majesty's Service.

Army Form C. 2118

1st Bn. Kings Own Scottish Borderers Regt

WAR DIARY or INTELLIGENCE SUMMARY.
(Erase heading not required.)

Hour, Date, Place	Summary of Events and Information	Remarks and references to Appendices
1- 5- 1915.	Artillery active until about 6 am. All quiet until about midday when a most violent cannonade was kept up on our left and continued throughout the afternoon. Artillery on either side came again active at irregular intervals during the night. Weather fine. Casualties 2nd Lieut L.T.S. BOWER 3rd DORSET REGT (S.R.) severely wounded. Other ranks 2 killed, 4 wounded.	
2- 5- 1915.	All quiet on our front. During afternoon artillery on both sides became very active and on our left a most violent bombardment was heard. Bursts of heavy rifle fire now and again broke out at about ½ per minute for about half an hour. Several shells burst near Battn H.Qrs during afternoon and the roads in the vicinity of CHATEAU of BLANKAERT were shelled at irregular intervals during the night. A cry relieved C Coy in fire trench at about 11pm. Trench-gags soaked in a solution of robut water, kept issued to the Battalion as a precaution against asphyxiating gas which	N21

Forms/C. 2118/10

WAR DIARY or **INTELLIGENCE SUMMARY**

Army Form C. 2118.

1st Bn Cheshire Regt

Hour, Date, Place	Summary of Events and Information	Remarks and references to Appendices
3-5-1915.	The Germans were wiring. Casualties other ranks 1 Wounded. Very quiet throughout the whole day. A few shells from light field guns burst near Support. Dug outs, but caused no damage. Occasional bursts of rifle & machine gun fire from our side was heard at irregular intervals during the night. Casualties O.R. 4 Wounded. Captain H.M.C. ORR arrived at DICKEBUSCH with 50 O.R. Reinforcements.	
4-5-19.5.	All quiet on our front. During afternoon some heavy shells burst near Bn. H.Q., and LANKOF CHATEAU was again shelled at intervals throughout the day and the road from ROSENTHAL & LANKOF CHATEAUX was searched by the enemy's artillery. Our batteries opened fire at about 11 pm and continued throughout the night causing considerable damage to still enemy parapets. 'C' Coy relieved 'B' Coy in the fire trenches during the night. Captain J.M.C. ORR + 50 O.R. moved to ROSENTHAL CHATEAU in support. Captain R.H. JOHNSTON D.S.O. arrived at DICKEBUSCH. Casualties Nil. Weather fine.	

Army Form C. 2118.

1st Bn Lincolnshire Regt

WAR DIARY
or
INTELLIGENCE SUMMARY.
(Erase heading not required.)

Instructions regarding War Diaries and Intelligence Summaries are contained in F. S. Regs., Part II. and the Staff Manual respectively. Title pages will be prepared in manuscript.

Hour, Date, Place	Summary of Events and Information	Remarks and references to Appendices
5. 5. 15.	All quiet on our front. In the early hours of the morning heavy firing, both Artillery & rifle, was heard from the direction of Hill 60, and continued until about 9.30 A.m. Enemy's artillery shelled roads and fields near Battalion dressing station. During the afternoon and evening asphyxiating gases were actively floating from the German trenches towards our lines. Our artillery kept up a steady fire throughout the day in the direction of Hill 60. At about 9 P.m. Heavy artillery fire and rifle fire was heard and this continued for about an hour and a half when the Artillery fire died down. Later our Artillery became active and opened a very heavy fire on the German trenches, continuing until dawn. Sprays containing Carbonate of Soda solution were issued to the Battalion for use in the trenches to combat the effects of the gases used by the Germans. Weather fine. Casualties O.R. 2 Wounded	

Army Form C. 2118

1st Bn Lincolnshire Regt

WAR DIARY or INTELLIGENCE SUMMARY.
(Erase heading not required.)

Instructions regarding War Diaries and Intelligence Summaries are contained in F.S. Regs., Part II. and the Staff Manual respectively. Title pages will be prepared in manuscript.

Hour, Date, Place	Summary of Events and Information	Remarks and references to Appendices
6-5-1915.	A quiet day. Artillery on either side fired occasional rounds during afternoon. At dusk our artillery continued with bursts of fire which developed into a duel lasting into the night. Occasional bursts of rifle fire from our side drew fire to which the enemy replied. B Coy relieved A Coy in the fire trench and two platoons of D Coy were relieved and went into support at ROSENTHAL CHATEAU. Weather - Wet. Casualties NIL 1 killed 1 wounded.	
7-5-1915.	At 1 am our Artillery opened a steady fire in the direction of Hill 60 which developed into a most violent bombardment. By 2 am a very heavy rifle and machine gun fire was also opened at about the same time and this continued until 6 am when the firing gradually subsided down to 7 am. During the afternoon artillery exchanged shells & towards evening this firing increased and became a most violent duel by 7 pm and very heavy rifle and machine gun fire was also heard and continued throughout the night. 100 improvised respirators were issued for use in the fire trenches. Weather fine. Lieut A.B.L. PARISH sent to Hospital. Killed 3 wounded. NW Casualties OR 1 killed 1 wounded.	

(9 29 6) W 4141—463 100,000 9/14 H W V Forms/C. 2118/10

Army Form C. 2118.

1st Bn Blackie Regt

WAR DIARY
or
INTELLIGENCE SUMMARY.
(Erase heading not required.)

Hour, Date, Place	Summary of Events and Information	Remarks and references to Appendices
8-5-19/15.	Firing continued from previous night and at 2 am our artillery shelled trenches in front of our position, causing great damage to the enemy's parapets. Heavy artillery rifle fire was heard from the direction of HOOGE. Firing died down after 9 am & during the remainder of the day all was quiet. Casualties OR 3 Wounded. (Weather fine) LIEUT G.R.KEEP 3rd R.SUSSEX R'GT(S.R) to hospital-sick.	
9-5-1915.	All quiet on our front. Heavy artillery rifle fire was heard on our left throughout the day. After dusk our artillery opened with a steady fire throughout the night. The enemy fired numerous rifle grenades in our fire trenches causing a few casualties. Among B.Coy. Reinforcements 8/118 OR joined at DICKEBUSCH. LIEUT A. ST JOHN PERKINS 3rd Devon Regt (S.R.) to hospital - sick. Casualties OR 1 Killed 9 Wounded. (Weather fine)	
10-5-1915.	In the early hours of the morning a very heavy rifle fire was heard. All was quiet on our front until about midday when the enemy's artillery became very active. Our artillery replied to this fire and later this firing developed in a very fierce duel which lasted for nearly two hours. After dusk a very heavy artillery rifle fire was heard from the left of our position. This firing continued throughout the night. The road between	

Army Form C. 2118

WAR DIARY
—or—
INTELLIGENCE SUMMARY.
(Erase heading not required.)

1st Bn Lincolnshire Regt

Hour, Date, Place	Summary of Events and Information	Remarks and references to Appendices
10- 5- 15 (Contd)	LANKOT CHATEAU & BEDFORD HOUSE were shelled intermittently throughout the night. The Barricade on the bank of the YSER CANAL, which was being held by a party of the Bn, was heavily shelled during the day - but little or no damage and no casualties were caused. Reinforcements of 118 O.R. moved up & billetted at BEDFORD HOUSE. "A" Coy relieved B Coy in the fire trenches at about 11 P.M. Casualties O.R. 12 Wounded. Weather fine.	
11- 5- 15.	At about 2 am we opened a burst of rapid fire to which the enemy replied. The firing lasted for about an hour. Enemy's Artillery shelled wood near BEDFORD HOUSE ex how. Without doing any damage. Our fire trenches were subjected to fire from rifle grenades during the afternoon and later a rather severe fire. The trenches were shelled, but no damage was caused. Our Artillery replied to this fiercely shelling the German Trench in front of our position. This fire was very accurate and caused great damage to the enemy's fire trenches. All became very quiet and remained so with the exception of a few rifle shots heard at intervals during the night. Casualties 2nd Lieut S.H. JEUDWINE B. Lincoln Regt. slightly wounded. O.R. 3 Wounded (Weather fine)	

WAR DIARY
INTELLIGENCE SUMMARY.
(Erase heading not required.)

Army Form C. 2118

1st Bn Lincolnshire Regt

Instructions regarding War Diaries and Intelligence Summaries are contained in F.S. Regs., Part II. and the Staff Manual respectively. Title pages will be prepared in manuscript.

Hour, Date, Place	Summary of Events and Information	Remarks and references to Appendices
12-5-1915.	All quiet on our front throughout the day and night. 'C' Coy relieved 'D' Coy in the fire trenches about 10 pm. 'B' Coy moved back to BEDFORD HOUSE & 'D' Coy occupied dug-outs on Canal Bank. Casualties O.R. 2 (Wounded) (Reached line)	
13-5-1915.	All quiet on our front until about 9 am when enemy fired several rifle grenades into our fire trenches causing two casualties. Our artillery fired two rounds into the enemy's trench which had the effect of quieting the enemy's fire. The German artillery shelled road near the Barricade on the Canal Bank, but did no damage. later enemy's artillery shells a roads between ROSENTHAL & BANK OF CHATEAUX. Owing to darkness and raining falling heavily throughout the day, the paths approach to trenches were in a very bad condition and fatigue working parties found it most difficult to make even slow progress. During the night, whilst supervising the work being carried out by his Company Captain H.M.C. ORR slipped & falling heavily caused a fracture to his ankle. Rain fell continuously throughout the day & night. Captain H.M.C. ORR 1st Lincoln Regt. to hospital. Sick. Casualties O.R. 1 Died of Wounds 2 Wounded.	

WAR DIARY
INTELLIGENCE SUMMARY.
(Erase heading not required.)

Army Form C. 2118

1st Bn Lincolnshire Regt

Hour, Date, Place	Summary of Events and Information	Remarks and references to Appendices
14.5.15.	Heavy firing was heard on our left front which continued during afternoon and early evening. Enemy artillery again shelled our fire trenches causing no damage or casualties to this line. Our artillery replied shelling the German fire & support trenches and causing considerable damage to the enemy parapets etc. Our men on occupying the fire trenches fired rifle grenades into the German trenches, and it is believed caused numerous casualties among the enemy owing to the fire being very accurate. B Coy relieved A Coy in the fire trenches during night and occupied dug outs on the Canal Bank. A Coy moved back to BEDFORDE HOUSE in support. Lieut. A. STAPLETON 1st LINCOLN REGT. Sick to Hospital. Casualties O.R. 1 Killed 2 Wounded Reinforcements of 50 O.R. joined the Battalion at Dick[t?] Busch.	

WAR DIARY
or
INTELLIGENCE SUMMARY.
(Erase heading not required.)

Army Form C. 2118

1/8 Bn Hampshire Regt

Hour, Date, Place	Summary of Events and Information	Remarks and references to Appendices
15. 5. 1915.	Heavy firing was heard from our left and continued until about 9 a.m. when all became very quiet especially on our front. At about 11 a.m. our heavy batteries shelled the German trenches in front of our position, this firing continued for about half an hour. Enemy's artillery shelled the approaches to the firing line at irregular intervals during the night. After dusk a party (11 N.C.O's & men) of the Battalion sent out in front of our line trenches to remove some growing crops which were obstructing our field of fire. This party successfully carried their task & returned without casualty. A party of miners of the Battalion completed the construction of a tunnel under the bank of the YSER CANAL. Work was continued on the trenches and progress was also made in thickening the trench held by the Battalion. Casualties O.R. 1 died of wounds, 1 wounded.	

WAR DIARY
or
INTELLIGENCE SUMMARY.
(Erase heading not required.)

Army Form C. 2118.

Hour, Date, Place	Summary of Events and Information	Remarks and references to Appendices
16-5-1915	All quiet on our front. During the day heavy firing was heard from the direction YPRES SALIENT. At about 2pm our batteries shelled the German trenches in front of our position, causing considerable damage to the enemy's parapets. Later in the afternoon the enemy's snipers became active & Lieut. CAVE-ORME was severely wounded. During the evening rifle grenades were used by the enemy and some casualties were caused. "D" Coy relieved "C" Coy in the fire trenches during the night. "B" Coy occupied dug-outs on Canal Bank. "A" Coy moved back to BEDFORD HOUSE in support. Casualties. LIEUT. R.W. CAVE-ORME 1st Lincoln Regt Severely Wounded. O.R. 5 Wounded.	
17-5-1915	A quiet day. During the night a rapid fire was opened on our trenches at 11.15pm, but soon died down. Casualties 1 Died of Wounds 8 Wounded	
18-5-1915	All quiet on our front. Enemy's snipers were active during night, and occasional bursts of rapid rifle fire was heard. "A" Coy relieved "B" Coy in fire trenches. "B" Coy occupied dug outs on Canal Bank & "C" Coy moved back to Bedford House in support. Casualties O.R. 6 Wounded.	

WAR DIARY
or
INTELLIGENCE SUMMARY.
(Erase heading not required.)

Army Form C. 2118.

1st Bn. Lincolnshire Regt

Hour, Date, Place	Summary of Events and Information	Remarks and references to Appendices
19-5-15.	A very quiet day on our front. Several shells burst near our support trenches during the early evening. Casualties O.R. 3 Wounded	
20.5.1915.	All quiet on our front. The Barricade on the Canal Bank was shelled during the afternoon but no damage was caused. C Coy relieved B Coy in the fire trenches during the night. A Coy moved to BEDFORD HOUSE in support. Casualties O.R. 1 Died of Wounds 1 Wounded.	
21.5.1915.	Another quiet day. Patrols were sent out during the night in the direction of the enemy's line but no trace of hostile patrols could be seen. Casualties 1 Killed 1 Wounded.	
22.5.1915.	During early morning enemy snipers were very active, and later in the day the Germans used rifle grenades frequently, our men answered this fire & did a considerable damage to the enemy's parapets etc. A Coy relieved B Coy in the fire trenches during the night. B Coy moving to Bedford House in support. Casualties O.R. 1 Killed 1 Died of Wounds 7 Wounded.	

Army Form C. 2118.

1st Bn. Lincolnshire Regt

WAR DIARY
INTELLIGENCE SUMMARY.
(Erase heading not required.)

Instructions regarding War Diaries and Intelligence Summaries are contained in F.S. Regs., Part II. and the Staff Manual respectively. Title pages will be prepared in manuscript.

Hour, Date, Place	Summary of Events and Information	Remarks and references to Appendices
23-5-1915.	Our fire trenches and support trenches were shelled by the enemy's light field guns during the morning and early afternoon and several casualties were caused. Later the Germans opened fire with rifle grenades but very little damage was done. Towards evening all became very quiet. Casualties. O.R. 4 killed 7 wounded.	
24-5-1915.	With the exception of a few rifle grenades fired by the enemy the day passed very quietly. Bttn moved from Canal Bank & relieved 2 Coy in the fire trenches. Bttn moved to Brayon House in Support. Casualties Lieut H. MARSHALL 1st Kendal Regt Slightly Wounded. O.R. 4 Wounded.	
25-5-1915.	Day passed quietly, but during early evening the Germans again used rifle grenades inflicting several casualties in our fire trenches. Casualties. LIEUT G.W.H. APPLIN 1/Lincoln Regt Slightly Wounded O.R. 6 Wounded. A party of Officers & the 2nd K.O.S.B visited the trenches held by the Battalion, during the night, with view to latter Battalion occupying the same line of trenches.	

WAR DIARY
INTELLIGENCE SUMMARY.
(Erase heading not required.)

Army Form C. 2118.

2nd Bn. Oxf & Bucks L.I Regt

Instructions regarding War Diaries and Intelligence Summaries are contained in F.S. Regs., Part II. and the Staff Manual respectively. Title pages will be prepared in manuscript.

Hour, Date, Place	Summary of Events and Information	Remarks and references to Appendices
26-5-15	With the exception of a few rifle grenades fired into our fire trenches, the day passed very quietly. The Battalion was relieved by the 2nd K.O.S.B. during the night and proceed to billets at OUTERDOM, arriving in the early hours of the following morning. Casualties 2nd Lieut H.H. ST TUFTON 3rd Bn. Sussex Regt (S.R) Wounded. OR. 1 Killed 2 Wounded.	
27-5-15	Battalion remained at rest at OUTERDOM. MAJOR F.W. GREATWOOD proceeded to 2nd Battalion. MAJOR H.E.R. BOXER from 2nd Battalion joined the Battalion & assumed command of the Battalion. Casualties Lieut F.W.G. HOPPER (with draft 94) OR joined the Battalion.	
28-5-15	The Battalion paraded at 8 am and proceeded to VLAMERTINGHE where it billited in huts. A party of 600 men of the Battalion formed part of a large party digging trenches in rear of the ROYAL FUSILIERS. This was kept up the whole of the night. The Regimental Transport was moved to a position N of the YPRES-POPERINGHE Road, three kilometres W of VLAMERTINGHE. 2nd Lieut A. STAPLETON reported from Divisional Rest Camp at WESTOUTRE Casualties nil.	

Army Form C. 2118.

WAR DIARY
INTELLIGENCE SUMMARY.
(Erase heading not required.)

Instructions regarding War Diaries and Intelligence Summaries are contained in F. S. Regs., Part II. and the Staff Manual respectively. Title pages will be prepared in manuscript.

1st Bn. Argyll & Sutherland High[landers]

Hour, Date, Place	Summary of Events and Information	Remarks and references to Appendices
29-5-15	Battalion resting at VLAMERTINGHE. A fatigue party of 400 men was found by 1st Battalion to continue the work on support trenches in rear of Royal Fusiliers position. Casualties nil	
30-5-15	The Battalion at rest at VLAMERTINGHE. Casualties nil	
31-5-15	At rest at VLAMERTINGHE. The Battalion paraded to march to huts at OUTERDOM at 9.30 pm, arriving at about 11.10 pm. Lieut W.R. Pryn R.A.M.C. proceeded to 9th Field Ambulance. Lieut R.P. Nash R.A.M.C. took over the duties of Medical officer to the Bn. 2nd Lieuts W.H. Jacques and R.O. Pearson joined the Battalion. Casualties nil.	

9th Bde.
3rd Div.

WAR
DIARY

1st LINCOLNSHIRES.

JUNE

1915

On His Majesty's Service.

Army Form C. 2118.

WAR DIARY
or
INTELLIGENCE SUMMARY.
(Erase heading not required.)

1st Lincolnshire Regt.

Hour, Date, Place	Summary of Events and Information	Remarks and references to Appendices
1. 6. 15	The Bn remained on rest in huts near OUDERDOM during day. Paraded at 8.40 p.m. and proceeded to support the 6th Cavalry Bde. C & D Coys relieved the 5th Yorks Regt in ZOUAVE WOOD (I.18.c.3.5. Map 28) at about midnight, in dug-outs. A & B Coys & H.Q. were to relieve 4th E YORKS REGT in the HOOGE WOOD (I.18.c. Map 28) but owing to non arrival of guides to conduct the parties to new positions the relief was not carried out during this night. The companies remained on the fringe of the wood. The Transport moved to a position North of the VLAMERTINGHE - RENINGHELST ROAD (G.18.a.5.4. 28 map) near BUSSEBOOM. Casualties. O.R. 1 wounded.	
2. 6. 15	About 1-30 am 2 platoons of A Coy relieved a company of 4th E Yorks Regt in the support trench. B company & remainder of A Coy occupied dug-outs in ZOUAVE WOOD. H Coy moved into dug-outs in SHAMP WOOD. HQ	

Army Form C. 2118.

1 Lincolnshire Regt.

WAR DIARY
or
INTELLIGENCE SUMMARY.
(Erase heading not required.)

Hour, Date, Place	Summary of Events and Information	Remarks and references to Appendices
2. 15" (continued)	An enemy's machine Gun which was well concealed commanded a path passing through the wood. The moment any movement took place on this path, the Machine Gun became active. Continual sniping went about 7.15 pm. At about 8.0 pm the whole of C Coy moved back to dug-outs in HOOGE WOOD. B Coy moved forward & relieved the remainder of the 2nd Dragoon Guards in the fire trenches. D. D Coy occupied the trenches in rear of the trenches during the night. At 9.0 pm Headquarters & A & C Coy moved back to dugouts at the fringe of HOOGE WOOD. Casualties. O.R. 3 killed, 60 Wounded, 2 missing	
3. 6. 15	The fire trench occupied by D Company was shelled during the day. At dusk A Coy moved up from support to carry out an attack on some earthworks to the WEST of HOOGE CHATEAU, which was strongly held by the enemy. At midnight B Company successfully attacked and occupied the stables of the Chateau. The attack was evidently a complete surprise	

N.R.S.

WAR DIARY
or
INTELLIGENCE SUMMARY.

(Erase heading not required.)

Army Form C. 2118.

1 Lincolnshire Regt-

Hour, Date, Place	Summary of Events and Information	Remarks and references to Appendices

2. 6. 15. (Continued)

C & D Companies were supporting the 3rd Dragoon Guards who were in the fire trench. At about 5-0 a.m. the enemy's artillery commenced most violent bombardment with high explosive shells lasting until 7-0 p.m. The fire trench held by the 3rd Dragoon Guards were reduced to a series of shell holes. The ZOUAVE WOOD was subjected to a continuous ranging shell fire causing numerous casualties in C & D Coys. Nearly all the men in the wood were destroyed & their "dug outs" were unfavorable to reveal men being buried with the debris. The survivors were relieved. 2 platoons of C Company had occupied a support trench under command of Lieut. T. M. HARRIS. LIEUT HARRIS was killed by a shell bursting in the trench. dug out.

The 2 platoons of A Company in support trench were also subjected to a heavy shell fire all day.

At 6-15 p.m. D Company were ordered to reinforce the 3rd Dragoon Guards. This movement was successfully carried out at a period when the bombardment was at the height of severity and in consequence numerous casualties occurred.

Towards 7-0 p.m. the bombardment gradually subsided.

Army Form C. 2118.

WAR DIARY
or
INTELLIGENCE SUMMARY.
(Erase heading not required.)

1st Lincolnshire Regt.

Hour, Date, Place	Summary of Events and Information	Remarks and references to Appendices
3. 6.15 (Continued)	to the enemy, & was carried out with a loss to us of only 1 man wounded. Shrapnel fire. LIEUT C HUTCHINSON James Casualties 2 officers T R HAMMOND severely wounded and 2 killed, 17 wounded, 1 missing. Lieut J SKELLY died of his wounds. At 1.15 am A Company were ordered to advance and take the earthworks. A party of bombers under 2nd Lieut Ingram led the attack supported by the remainder of A Coy. The bombers reached to within 20 yards of the German lines when they were seen by the enemy who opened a rapid rifle & machine gun fire, three machine guns being in the chateau & one in the earthworks. Owing to the severity of this fire the attack was abandoned at 2.0 am. C Company were acting in support. A & C Companies moved back to dug-outs in HOOGE WOOD to act in support of B & D Coys in the firing trench.	
4. 6.15	During the remainder of day a party of men under Lieut HOPPER held two advanced sap heads of the MENIN ROAD which were only 15 yards from the German trenches. The small party received hand	Alt

Army Form C. 2118.

WAR DIARY
or
INTELLIGENCE SUMMARY.
(Erase heading not required.)

Hour, Date, Place	Summary of Events and Information	Remarks and references to Appendices
4. 6. 15 (Continued)	throughout the day bombing and rapid firing to prevent the enemy from entering our new slope. The enemy supplied further were several times dispersed. Enemy snipers were active throughout the day. During the night the Batln. were relieved by the 1st Wilts Regt. Casualties O.R. 5 killed, 1 officer, 13 wounded, 13 missing	
5. 6. 15	Owing to numerous delays the Batln. did not leave the Trenches until the early hours of the morning and Headquarters were unable to leave until later, but owing to a thick mist not having lifted the whole Batln. was able to get away unobserved, marched via YPRES & VLAMERTINGHE to the transport lines (G.18.a.5 & 28 m.p.) & bivouacked in a field adjoining, arriving about 6-0 am. Weather fine. Hot. 2nd Lieut J H P BARRETT rejoined from duty. Casualties. Nil.	

N.S.

Army Form C. 2118.

WAR DIARY
or
INTELLIGENCE-SUMMARY. 1st Bn Lincolnshire Regt.

(Erase heading not required.)

Instructions regarding War Diaries and Intelligence Summaries are contained in F. S. Regs., Part II. and the Staff Manual respectively. Title pages will be prepared in manuscript.

Hour, Date, Place	Summary of Events and Information	Remarks and references to Appendices
6-6-1915	The Battalion remained in rest. Church parades for C/E, R.Cs and Nonconformists were held in the morning. Bright sunshine all day.	
7-6-1915	Trench for bombing practice was made. Commanding Officers' parade was held at 10·0 am. Draft of 40 O.R. joined. Bright sunshine all day.	
8-6-1915	Parades were held at 7·30 am (Physical training) and during the day under Company Officers arrangements. Sallies of NCOs & men were practice in bombing. Lieut A.D. WALKER 1st Bn Lincoln Regt joined the Battalion. Lieut J.E. IMPEY 1st Bn Lincoln Regt. Weather warm but cloudy.	

Army Form C. 2118.

WAR DIARY
INTELLIGENCE SUMMARY.
1st Bn Lincolnshire Regt

(Erase heading not required.)

Instructions regarding War Diaries and Intelligence Summaries are contained in F.S. Regs., Part II. and the Staff Manual respectively. Title pages will be prepared in manuscript.

Hour, Date, Place	Summary of Events and Information	Remarks and references to Appendices
9-6-1915	Parades were carried out as on previous day. A demonstration in use of Respirators & Smoke Helmets was held under Divisional arrangements. Major Bowen, Capt & one Officer/man per Coy attended. Captain J.D.D. Wickham joined the Battalion. No 7690 Sgt W. Kitt B Coy " 9183 a/Sgt W. Dodson D Coy " 13904 L/Cpl A. Brownley B Coy " 9310 " G. Williams B Coy " 9658 Pte E.J. Smith A Coy " 8303 " N. Newby A Coy Weather dull but warm.	Awarded Distinguished Conduct Medal (early M.S.H./1645 V. Corps V.A./1444)
10-6-1915	A thunderstorm broke during the early hours and heavy rain fell, causing the men much inconvenience owing to shortage of binoculars. In spite of these trying circumstances the men remained very cheerful.	

WAR DIARY
INTELLIGENCE SUMMARY.
(Erase heading not required.)

Army Form C. 2118.

1/8 Bn. Argyle & Sutherland Regt

Hour, Date, Place	Summary of Events and Information	Remarks and references to Appendices
10-6-15 (Borre)	All ranks were lectured on the use of smoke helmets respirators at 9.45 am. Route marches, rifle exercises, bombing practice, physical and wire carried out under Company Officers' arrangements during remainder of day. The Battalion was on duty from 12 noon. Weather dull. Casualties 1 Other Rank Wounded.	
11-6-1915.	Heavy rain fell in the early morning. The Battalion remained on duty till 12 noon. Parades were carried out as on the previous day. An assault on hostile trenches was also practised. Reinforcements 7/60 Other Ranks joined. Weather dull & cool.	

Army Form C. 2118.

1st Bn Lincolnshire Regt

WAR DIARY
INTELLIGENCE SUMMARY.
(Erase heading not required.)

Hour, Date, Place	Summary of Events and Information	Remarks and references to Appendices
12.6.1915	The Divisional Commander, Major Genl J. A. L. HALDANE C.B. D.S.O. presented D.C. medal ribbons to No 7690 Sgt Kidd, 9183 Sgt Corban, 4940 L/Cpl Williams, 1858 Pte Smith & 8303 Pte Murphy. Parades were carried out as on previous day. Captain J.R.G. MAGRATH joined the Battalion. Weather cool & dull	
13.6.1915	Usual parades were carried out as on previous day. Weather fine	
14.6.1915	Similar parade were continued. Weather fine. Captain R H SPOONER [signature]	

Army Form C. 2118.

WAR DIARY or INTELLIGENCE SUMMARY.

(Erase heading not required.)

1st Bn Lincolnshire Regt

Hour, Date, Place	Summary of Events and Information	Remarks and references to Appendices
15. 6. 15.	The Bahn remained in bivouac resting during the day. The Bahn paraded at 4.15 pm ready to march to the assembly position, CAMBRIDGE Rd South East R 11 d. The order of march was D. C. H gun. A & B Coys. The Machine Gun Detachment accompanied the left column of the Brigade. – (5th & 9th). It took over 2 spare Coaths.). The Bn (less 1 & 2 Coys) formed the right column. The right column marched off from rest position H.17 Central at 5.0 pm and proceeded by the road through H.13. H.14. H.15. H.16. H.17. 9. H.23. to KRUISSTRAAT crossed the Canal at Bridge 13 A thence through YPRES to the LILLE GATE, at 8.30 pm continuing via railway track to S.10 N 0.2 thence by MENIN Rd. Casualties 4 OR. Wounded. Fine summer weather.	

Army Form C. 2118.

WAR DIARY
or
INTELLIGENCE SUMMARY.

(Erase heading not required.)

1st Lincolnshire Regt

Hour, Date, Place	Summary of Events and Information	Remarks and references to Appendices
16. 6. 1915. (1)	The Battn. occupied the assembly trenches J.11.b at 1.15 am. The 9th Rifle Bde supported by the 4th Rifle Bde were to attack the BELLEWAARDE FOUR at early morning, the objective was to seize thghts to the line J.12 & J.3.2. — Y.18 — Y.17. The 1st Lincolns supported the attack & were to pass through & consolidate with high explosives when front trenches were made in the Bombardment at 2-50 am, 2.40 am & 4-0 am. Our front line was occupied by Royal Fusiliers Roy. Lincs., & Wiltshires, Y.S. to Fusiliers, the Honorton and Liverpool Scottish in support. The Liverpool Scottish were on our left & the Wiltshires (4th Bde.) on our right, when the second Battn. Royal Fusiliers reached the Railway embankment line received a few casualties from the enemy & a few casualties were received, at 4-15 am Battn. our front line reached trenches and immediately seized the first line of hostile trenches from the East edge of wood Y.18 — Y.15 — NE corner of Railway wood and took prisoner all of the enemy in the trenches who had not been killed. The Roy Scot Fusiliers in conjunction with 5th Fusiliers on the Honorton, between Y.12 & Y.15. at the same time. The Battn. rushed forward in support of the Royal Fusiliers.	

Hour, Date, Place	Summary of Events and Information	Remarks and references to Appendices
16. 6. 15. (2)	reinforcing the new line. The line continued to advance, holding fire, forcing their way along the communication trench Y16-Y17 and along the trench Y16-Y10 driving the enemy at a run into his second line trenches. The attack was being covered on the right by rifle & machine gun fire from the MENIN RD. east from the South of it, and covered on the left by rifle & machine gun fire of the 6th Division from the railway. The Bedfs. & R Fus besieged the trench Y20-Y21. The artillery bombardment on the first line of trenches had been most effective, wrecking them considerably and now destroying the barbed wire entanglements. Many dead Germans were found in the trenches. The prisoners taken were put in to the rear. The attack now reached its objective which was the crossing of the trench running from BELLEWAARDE FARM to a force on road 100 yds South of Y17. Our artillery had already dealt with this trench which we reached at 4-20 am with very few casualties, to our side. No enemy being finally driven out and the bayonet. The first phase of the attack followed immediately. A party of 7 30 NCOs men led by Major HERAKER succeeded in occupying the line Y17-Y18. It was however found impracticable to remain, owing to	1 Lincolnshire Reg.

WAR DIARY
or
INTELLIGENCE SUMMARY.
(Erase heading not required.)

1st Warwickshire Regt.

Hour, Date, Place	Summary of Events and Information	Remarks and references to Appendices
16. 6. 15.	our own artillery not having ceased to shell this trench. The artillery observers were prevented from seeing the flags carried by the infantry denoting the margin of their advance, by mist and smoke from shell. Also commencing fire was difficult owing to the ground wires being cut by the enemy fire. The advance of the infantry had been extremely rapid and was carried out with great dash and fervour, and they had anticipated their objective too quickly for the our artillery, which caused many casualties to our side. The Commanding Officer - Major HER BOXER, was himself wounded when he ordered the men to fall back on the line 717-720. Their our their eagerness had rushed forward, mixed together, and were much disorganised in the captured trenches. The attack had been brilliantly carried out and many acts of gallantry were performed by all ranks of the Batn, both during the attack itself and during the subsequent enemy bombardment.	

(3)

- Army Form C. 2118.

WAR DIARY
or
INTELLIGENCE SUMMARY.
(Erase heading not required.)

1st Hertfordshire Regt.

Hour, Date, Place	Summary of Events and Information	Remarks and references to Appendices
16. 6.15	At 6.0 am the Batln. now under command of Major D.H.F. GRANT, received orders to fall back on to the first line of Captured trench Y16 – T17 and Y16 – Y15, to reorganise and hold the line at all costs which was done accordingly. The enemy heavily bombarded the captured trench throughout the day, the bombardment becoming most violent at 4 p.m. when it became evident that a counter attack was being developed. The counter attack was met by our artillery and by heavy rifle and machine gun fire, the enemy being repulsed with great loss to him. At 6 p.m. the enemy bombarded the trenches and ground behind with gas-shells and we were forced to resort to the use of respirators. At about 9.30 p.m. the Batln was relieved by the H. London (8th R. Bde) and marched back to bivouac 18 b 4 5 arriving about 5 am next day. AL.H.	

Army Form C. 2118.

WAR DIARY
or
INTELLIGENCE SUMMARY.
(Erase heading not required.)

1st Worcestershire Regt.

Hour, Date, Place	Summary of Events and Information	Remarks and references to Appendices
11. 6. 15	The Battn. having returned to bivouac rested during the day. A Roll Call was taken at 12 noon. The following casualties had been sustained during the previous days fighting. Officers. Major H.F.P. BOXER wounded & missing. K. Captain J.R.G. MAGRATH wounded. " R.H. SPOONER " Lieut. A.D. WALKER Missing 2Lieut. F.C. GREEN Killed " J.H.P. BARRETT Wounded " R.O. PEARSON Missing Other Ranks Killed 22 Died of Wds 3 Missing 96 Wounded 265	

Army Form C. 2118.

WAR DIARY
or
INTELLIGENCE SUMMARY.
(Erase heading not required.)

1st Lincolnshire Regt

Hour, Date, Place	Summary of Events and Information	Remarks and references to Appendices
18. 6. 15"	The Batt. remained in bivouac resting. Weather Cloudy. Reinforcement 61 otherwise joined	
19. 6. 15"	The Batt. rested in the morning, and further ready to proceed to the trenches at 3.15 p.m. that orders having been received two platoons of D Coy; the whole of B Coy were left at bivouac whilst the remainder of Batt. marched off at 4 p.m. proceeding via VLAMERTINGHE to KRUISSTRAAT, halting near the latter place at 6 p.m. when tea was provided. The march was resumed at 8 p.m. via Bridge 14 and ZILLEBEKE to SANCTUARY WOOD relieving 6th Northumberland Fusiliers in fire trenches B7 and B4 Bivouacks 11-ish	
20. 6. 15"	The Relief was completed at 1-15 a.m. The regiment remained in dug outs in SANCTUARY WOOD. The artillery exchanged fire occasionally during the day. Enemy aeroplanes hovered over our position	

Army Form C. 2118.

WAR DIARY
or
INTELLIGENCE SUMMARY.
(Erase heading not required.)

1st Hampshire Regt.

Hour, Date, Place	Summary of Events and Information	Remarks and references to Appendices
20. 6. 15	Towards evening firing very low. B Company & 2 Platoons of D Coy left behind to advance funnelled at 5.30 pm & proceeded to join the Bath. which they did at 11.0 pm. B Company remained in support trench which they had to dig. Lieut D'ENISON and 2 Lieut L.H.ROWEN joined the Bath & both posted to C Coy. Casualties. O.R. 2 wounded. Weather fine & very hot.	
21. 6. 15	The day passed very quietly. Weather hot. Capt J D WICKHAM was wounded about 11 pm by an enemy rifle grenade and died of his wounds about midnight. Casualties. O.R. 1 wounded.	
22. 6. 15	The day passed quietly. Weather fine & very hot. About 8 pm a heavy bombardment was commenced by our artillery on to the enemy lines near MOOSE CHATEAU also a heavy rifle fire was kept up during till midnight. Casualties. O.R. 1 wounded. [signature]	

Army Form C. 2118.

WAR DIARY
or
INTELLIGENCE SUMMARY.

(Erase heading not required.)

1st Lincolnshire Regt.

Instructions regarding War Diaries and Intelligence Summaries are contained in F. S. Regs., Part II. and the Staff Manual respectively. Title pages will be prepared in manuscript.

Hour, Date, Place	Summary of Events and Information	Remarks and references to Appendices
23. 6. 15.	The day passed very quietly. Weather very close. Slight thunder showers towards evening. Casualties O.R. 4 wounded	
24. 6. 15.	The day passed quietly. About 6 p.m. enemy large howitzer shell burst in ZOUAVE WOOD close to aid dept. Weather dull and slight showers. Casualties Nil.	
25. 6. 15.	The day passed quietly. Occasion shell bursting over our left. Carrier pigeons were introduced for signalling purposes. Officers joined. LIEUT H MARSHALL, LIEUT HC OSBORNE, 2 LIEUT MJ EDMUNDSON & 2 LIEUT GAHAN. Weather dull. Occasional heavy storms. Strength of 164 OR joined and draughts with draught. Casualties Nil. at RUSTE FARM.	

WAR DIARY
or
INTELLIGENCE SUMMARY.
(Erase heading not required.)

Army Form C. 2118.

1st Hertfordshire Rgt

Hour, Date, Place	Summary of Events and Information	Remarks and references to Appendices
26. 6. 15	On our front the day passed quietly. Artillery more active. Enemy shell burst over regimental left. Splinter falling on headquarters. Weather fine. B Company relieved A Company on the fire trench at 10 pm & A Company went into support. Casualties O.R. 3 wounded	
27. 6. 15	The day passed quietly on our front. Shelling of supports on our right & left took place at intervals. Weather dull. Several showers. Casualties O.R. 2 wounded. Lieut A.S.J. PERKINS rejoined from sick leave.	
28. 6. 15	All quiet on our front. The shelling of supports on right & left continued. Weather dull. Casualties O.R. 2 wounded. 120 O.R. from BUCERNON came up and relieved an equal	

Army Form C. 2118.

WAR DIARY
or
INTELLIGENCE SUMMARY.
(Erase heading not required.)

1st Lincolnshire Regt

Instructions regarding War Diaries and Intelligence Summaries are contained in F.S. Regs., Part II. and the Staff Manual respectively. Title pages will be prepared in manuscript.

Hour, Date, Place	Summary of Events and Information	Remarks and references to Appendices
29. 6. 15	number from the trenches. The relieved Frank's proceeded to ROBERROM at 11 p.m under Lt Jacques. Owing to all not a great heat to hill with slight shower. Casualties, O.R. wounded 2.	
30. 6. 15	The day passed quietly. C & D Companies were relieved at 2 pm and Blog. A Coy & Headquarters at 10.30 pm by 4th & 5th LINCOLNS (T.F.), all ranks feeling pleasure at meeting such an old Territorial Battalion. A contingent of 11 officers Capt R.J. TUCKER and 76 O.R. of the Kamaroka & Lundees Rifle Corps (France) and remained with Bn. and left at BUSSEBOOM. The Bath. proceeded via ZILLEBEKE, YPRES STRAAT and VLAMERTINGHE to BUSSEBOOM arriving about 3.30 am on 1.7.15.	

Army Form C. 2118.

WAR DIARY
or
INTELLIGENCE SUMMARY.
(Erase heading not required.) 1 Lincolnshire Regt.

Instructions regarding War Diaries and Intelligence Summaries are contained in F.S. Regs., Part II. and the Staff Manual respectively. Title pages will be prepared in manuscript.

Hour, Date, Place	Summary of Events and Information	Remarks and references to Appendices
19th to 20th June 1915	Summary The Bn. returned to Busseboom after 11 days in the trenches. During the period the casualties were Capt. J.D.D. WICKHAM died of wounds, and other ranks wounded 21. The Bn. occupied B3 & B4 trenches, with a frontage of about 300 yards. The front line was a strong one and varied in distance, from 40 to 450 yards from enemy trenches. The enemy line did not appear to be strongly held and their infantry were very inactive. The German artillery was considerable strength and continually shelled ZOUAVE WOOD and the Southern End of SANCTUARY WOOD but did not cause much damage. The 71st Brigade was on our left and a Brigade of the 50th Divn on our right. We were relieved by two Battns of the 138th Bde - 46 Divn (T.F.)	

1st Bn. Lincolnshire Regt.

Operation Orders by Major H.E.R. Boxer, Commanding. 3/6/15.

1. The stable in front of our trenches will be taken by 'B' Company after dark.
  'A' Company will attack the earthwork to the West of the Chateau occupied by the Germans. 1 officer and 30 men will attack the earthwork and another party of 1 officer and 30 men will be ready to reinforce or make a second attack. Hand grenades will be taken by 10 bombers who will accompany the first party of 30 men. One party of 20 men will also be detailed to cover the R.E. working party which will be brought up to consolidate.

2. Packs will be stacked under Coy arrangements. Iron rations, filled water bottles, and damp respirators will be taken by each party.

3. Reports will be sent to Bn. Head Qrs which will be near the stable on the right of 'B' Coy's position.

4. The remainder of "A" Coy will be relieved by R.Fus. 'C' Coy will act as carrying party to take up "Redip" Solution, sprayers and rations to 'B' and 'D' Coys and bring away wounded.
  'B' and 'D' Coys will send guides for ration parties.

5. Companies will be ready to fall in at 8 p.m. by which time R.Fus will have relieved 'A' Coy's two platoons in support trench.

6. A block will be made 40 yards down the cmc trench running from the earthwork to German lines, loopholes slanting will be made at one end of block and a supply of bombs will be placed near.

7. 'B' Coy will be prepared to provide a garrison of 1 sgt and 10 men for the earthwork by day. The earthwork will be strongly held by night.

(sd) A.Stapleton, 2/Lt and A/Adjt.
1st Lincolnshire Regt.

On receipt of further orders that 'C' Coy could be at my disposal. 'C' Coy who were already parading and being told off into parties, were relieved by Yeomanry and (given) verbal instructions were given to O.C. to follow in rear ready to make a second attack should the 1st fail.
As all officers had attended when instructions were given for the attack, no further written orders were given out.

(sd) H.Boxer, Major.

O.C. R.E.
    The stables is being consolidated. The Germans turned machine guns on one Coy which attacked work. At present I do not know if I hold it or not but I should fancy not. The fire was too hot. Am about to send one company down as it will be daylight befo before I can get them back to wood.

1-50 a.m. 4/6/15   (sd) H.Boxer, Major, Comdg 1/Lincolns.

Shall retire the other company as soon as I can get them together as it will be no good attempting another attack tonight and if I have the work will hold it from the Coys here.

Reference ZILLEBEKE Sheet 1/10,000.

Redoubt — Germans
Lake
Annexe — Germans
Chateau
Germans (3 M.G.)
Germans — Trenches blown in thus +++++
I.12.d.
Stables
I.13.a.
HOOGE
Ivy
To MENIN
From YPRES
Subterranean Wet
Wet
Dry
Q.G.
I.18.a.
I.18.d
I.13.c.
Zouave Wood
I.18.c.

From L.E.S.
Capt. N.H. Simson R.E. 8/6/15

3rd Division

War Diaries

1st Batt. Lincolnshire Regt

August, To December

1914

9th Brigade
3rd Division.

Disembarked Havre 14.8.14.

1st BATTALION

LINCOLNSHIRE REGIMENT

AUGUST 1 9 1 4

Army Form C. 2118.

WAR DIARY
OF
INTELLIGENCE SUMMARY
(Erase heading not required.)

1st Bn. Bedfordshire Regt.

Instructions regarding War Diaries and Intelligence Summaries are contained in F. S. Regs., Part II. and the Staff Manual respectively. Title pages will be prepared in manuscript.

Hour, Date, Place	Summary of Events and Information	Remarks and References to Appendices
6 P.M. 4.8.1914 Portsmouth	Order to mobilize received from G.O.C. 9th Infantry Brigade.	
5.8.1914 Portsmouth	First day of mobilization.	
6.8.1914 Portsmouth	Second day of mobilization.	
7.8.1914 Portsmouth	Third day of mobilization. Three hundred and three Reservists joined the Battalion from Depôt, under Captain Dawson, about 5 a.m.	
8.8.1914 Portsmouth	Fourth day of mobilization. Two hundred and forty Reservists joined the Battalion from Lincoln under Lieut. MacGrath about 5 a.m.	
9.+10.8.1914 Portsmouth	Bn. standing by ready to move.	
11.8.1914 Portsmouth	15 Reservists N.C.O.s joined the Battalion from Grimsby about 9.30 p.m.	
12.8.1914 Portsmouth	The 105.0. & 79 officers & men under Lieut Bransbury proceeded to Plymouth to join the 2nd Battalion, the party formed up at 5.30 p.m. and entrained at Portsmouth Town Station.	

# Army Form C. 2118.

WAR DIARY
or
INTELLIGENCE SUMMARY
(Erase heading not required.)

Hour, Date, Place	Summary of Events and Information	Remarks and References to Appendices
6.45 A.m. 13.8.1914 PORTSMOUTH	2nd C.B. Bonfannies arrived at 6.45 a.m. and C.O. D. Bonfannies proceeded at 6 am. Arrived at Portsmouth Town Station and proceeded to Southampton. Arriving about 11 a.m.	
8 a.m. 13.8.1914 PORTSMOUTH	C.O.D. Bonfannies arrived at 8am and arrived at Portsmouth Town Station and ceased to Southampton arriving about 12 m.d.	
4 p.m. 14.8.1914 HAVRE	The whole Battalion embarked on the known Booth Liner "NORMAN" and sailed for HAVRE in FRANCE about 4.10pm and disembarked at HAVRE about 10am and marched to the Rest Camp at HARFLEUR FARM. The following officers accompanied the Battalion. Lt. Col. W.E.R. SMITH Commanding Major TOOGOOD 2nd in Command, Major D.H.F. GRANT, Captain F.W. GREATWOOD, HOSKYNS, H.M. DAWSON, F.C. ROSE Captain & Adjutant R.E. DRAKE Captain & MARRATT, G.N. BUTT, G.M. ELLISON, G.A. KEMPTHORNE, Paine, Lieuts E.L. WELCHMAN G.W. P. TEDDIE, L.M. BULLER, C.C. HOLMES, B.T. THRUSTON, A.E.C. BAINES, A.T.E. WYATT (2nd Bn) H.E. PESCOTT (2nd Bn) 2 Lieuts R.W. CAVEORNE, E.10 ARNES, E.W. WALES, C. HUTCHINSON, R.D. ROBERTSON, L.R. TRIST (SR) & Q. But. F.W. MASTERS. 2 Lieut E.W. WALES horses transport embarkment on … on the ITALIAN PRINCE.	

Army Form C. 2118.

WAR DIARY
or
INTELLIGENCE SUMMARY
(Erase heading not required.)

Instructions regarding War Diaries and Intelligence Summaries are contained in F.S. Regs., Part II. and the Staff Manual respectively. Title pages will be prepared in manuscript.

Hour, Date, Place	Summary of Events and Information	Remarks and References to Appendices
14.8.14. HAVRE	Weather very hot. Casualties about 40% men fell out, 90% only being inoculated on the 13th instant, all found within an hour of the Battalion arriving in Camp. Distance about 7 miles, mostly uphill, running to loose stones.	
15.8.14. HARFLEUR FARM Rest Camp	The Battalion regret all day in Camp. Rain falling heavily from about 1 p.m. The Battalion marched out of Camp at 9 p.m. and entrained at 11.45 p.m. at HAVRE.	
16.8.14. HAVRE.	The Battalion left HAVRE by train about 3.15 a.m. and arrived at LANDRECIES at 8 p.m. and went into billets at DUPLEIX BARRACKS.	
9.45am 17.8.14. LANDRECIES	The Battalion left LANDRECIES at 9.45 a.m. and marched to billets at NOYELLES arriving about 12.50 p.m. Weather Fine. Casualties - Nil. Distance about 6 miles. Roads good.	
18.8.14. NOYELLES	The Battalion remained in billets but Coys. organised 2/4 endeavoured to arrange Coy. Mess.	

Army Form C. 2118.

WAR DIARY
or
INTELLIGENCE SUMMARY
(Erase heading not required.)

Hour, Date, Place	Summary of Events and Information	Remarks and References to Appendices
21.8.1914 Noyelles 6.30 a.m.	Left Noyelles at 6.30 am to went into Billets at Longueville.	
22.8.1914 Longueville 6 a.m.	Left Longueville at 6 am & marched to Quesmes taking shelter in the same from a billeting for the night, to move at once on to Mons. to dig out the approaches at Mons. Trenches were erected by the Battalion which were held for a short time only, when the order to retire was received. The Bn retired to Nouvelles. Casualties at Mons 2 Lieut Cave-Orme & very slightly wounded in R. hand and 1 Pte wounded in the back. Retraced the same way returning to Frameries in manner at Frameries after dark and took over the posts of the Royal Scots Fusiliers.	
23.8.1914 MONS		

WAR DIARY
or
INTELLIGENCE SUMMARY
(Erase heading not required.)

Army Form C. 2118.

Hour, Date, Place	Summary of Events and Information	Remarks and References to Appendices
3.30 a.m. 24.8.14. FRAMERIES	The Battalion were in position in trenches two Coys of 5th Fusiliers on flanks. Germans gave starts shelling position at daybreak and the order to so empty eyes arm. when the order to retire was given. Germans Infantry advanced singing and shouting but our fire forced their attack. Casualties:- Captain F. O. ROSE, Lieutenants L.M. BULLER, O.C. HOLMES, E.L. WELOHMAN wounded. Captain J.M. CARTER Killed. 13 wounded 88, missing 29. Total 134. Retired from Frameries via EUGIES and BAVIA to BERNERIES.	
4 a.m. 25.8.14. INCHEY	Bn. formed up at 4 am and marched to INCHEY a distance of about 25 miles via Gommegnies. Bivouacked for night. The march was very hot in morning & part of afternoon. Heavy Thunderstorm late in afternoon then rained. INCHEY met about 2 pm. & went into billets at about 6 p.m.	
3.45 a.m. 26.8.14 INCHEY	Bn. paraded at 3.45 am. and entrenched about 1 mile South of INCHEY. Germans advanced and opened fire at 5am. In trenches all day. Our own Artillery keeping heavy fire on Germans. Towards the evening retired. Casualties Officers MAJOR C. Adjutant H.P.m. TOOGOOD. D.S.O. Wounded and left in trenches	

Army Form C. 2118.

WAR DIARY
or
INTELLIGENCE SUMMARY
(Erase heading not required.)

Instructions regarding War Diaries and Intelligence Summaries are contained in F. S. Regs, Part II. and the Staff Manual respectively. Title pages will be prepared in manuscript.

Hour, Date, Place	Summary of Events and Information	Remarks and References to Appendices
26th & 27th-8-1914	Other Ranks. Killed 3. Wounded 40. Prisoners 50. Total 93. Prisoners to the Corps via road of INCHEY & onwards when and killed at NOYAN.	
28.8.14 NOYAN	Bivouacked all night and up to 1 p.m. when orders to move to front and man guns. Enemy advanced with cavalry left at outpost to cover rest of Brigade retirement at 6 p.m. 13 m. who did not know why. On Brigade about 2 am after blockading roads etc by felling trees etc marched all night & following day the 30th until about 6pm & then billeted at RESSONS a distance of about 23 miles. Weather very hot. Rhode good. No reinforcements.	
29.8.14		
30.8.14 RESSONS		
31-8-14 RESSONS	Left RESSONS 5 am. REBATH & BERNEUIL. HERAPATH & LUCIEN NIES. Weather very hot. Roads good.	

1. See Sketch Map.   1st Lines 9/3

2. At about 3 p.m.
The advanced troops of the Brigade had retired from the Outpost Line before we withdrew.

3. I cannot show this on the map sketch. We marched towards NOUVELLES & on reaching the railway N.E. of CIPLY the road was blocked with troops of other Brigades retiring from East of MONS, & we remained halted for some considerable time in a field close to the railway. Soon after we resumed our march towards NOUVELLES it became dark, & as I was not leading the column I cannot tell what route we took, but it was a circuitous one as we did not reach FRAMERIES till about 11 p.m. [Lt.Genl.Shaw] The Battalion took up a position in a wood North of FRAMERIES, but as it is not marked on the sketch I cannot show it. The position was a right angled one facing North & West. We relieved the Scots Fusiliers who were very tired, the enemy had followed them up almost to FRAMERIES. We held this position throughout the night & dug ourselves in along the edge of the wood.

4. Some of our patrols came into contact with enemy's patrols during the night & the latter withdrew. There was no enemy pressure during the night from the time we took over from the Scots Fusiliers. There was a little shelling from the enemy who set a small house on fire, which was close in front of centre of N. edge of wood.

5. Nothing of importance happened beyond what is stated in 4. Patrols were out the whole night.

6. This is correct. The shelling was considerable from daylight onwards.

7. The ground was open & level as far as I remember & covered with corn stooks which enabled the enemy to creep up & snipe. The targets were therefore poor, as the enemy showed caution, except on our left front where along a road in the dip of the ground he advanced in fours & we did considerable execution with rifle & machine gun fire at about 400 yards range. Our expenditure of ammunition was not heavy.

8. The Battalion had no difficulty about extricating itself. As we retired through the outskirts of the town we were sniped by the enemy from our right as we retired. A few men had evidently succeeded in working round the flank. The position was not at all a satisfactory one, we were cramped for room, & we took up a right angle position along the edge of the wood. We were handicapped by taking up this position in the dark. There was a thick wood about 200 yards to our left front which had to be constantly patrolled during the night.

[app'ly of XXIII. R.F.A]

9. We had I think a section of a field Battery close on our right. This was quickly located & put out of action early in the morning, & so was one of our two machine guns.

10. This is correct.

11. If this was the night before the Le Cateau – Cambrai fight we had piquets on the roads before INCHY, but my Company was in billets at INCHY that night & I cannot give the dispositions. The men were not particularly tired at this period of the retreat, but they were short of food owing to commissariat arrangements failing us in some way.

12. Yes, the markings on the sketch appear correct.

For three Companies each Company had 2 platoons in Firing Line & two in Support. I am not sure about the 4th Company.
One Machine Gun was knocked out at FRAMERIES. I do not know where the other one was placed.

13. Field of fire excellent, the ground sloping down to INCHY. View extensive. We were well dug in, soil easy for digging. Parapet concealed with grass, corn etc.

14. Not much opportunity for fire. Enemy adopted cautious tactics, taking full advantage of cover in woods, behind hedges & corn stooks. We were considerably troubled by snipers who were difficult to locate. Not much S.A.A. used; Plenty in reserve. As we were well dug in, with traverses, it was easy to exercise control.

15. We were not at all pressed, in fact we could not understand why we were suddenly ordered to retire. The Brigade Major appeared on horseback, & shouted out to us to retire at once. He was mortally wounded whilst carrying out these orders. Enemy's snipers were 400 yards or more away.

16. The retirement was not at all pressed.

17. We did not take up a second position. The Brigade formed up on the main road somewhere South of BERTRY & retired in fours in a South Westerly direction.

18. No, but the enemy's horse artillery kept in touch with us & we were shelled at intervals.

The putting out of action of the enemy Battery was our next engagement.

19.
a. The value of our training in musketry, i.e. accuracy in shooting, rapid fire, and care of the rifle and ammunition.

b. The importance of direction & control of fire.

c. The difficulty, if not impossibility, of carrying out a retirement in face of the enemy & under fire, over open country, in accordance with the principles laid down in our training manuals.

$\frac{11}{\frac{2}{18}}$ F.W.Preatwood.

9th Brigade.
3rd Division

1st BATTALION

THE LINCOLNSHIRE REGIMENT

SEPTEMBER 1914

This diary continues until 2.10.14.

WAR DIARY or INTELLIGENCE SUMMARY

Army Form C. 2118.

(Erase heading not required.)

Hour, Date, Place	Summary of Events and Information	Remarks and References to Appendices

9.30 a.m.
1 . 9 . 1914.
VAUCIENNES

Left VAUCIENNES at 9.30 am and halted about 1 mile from GONDREVILLE from 11.30 am to 2 p.m. finishing in rear & right flank militia the night at BOUILLANCIES about 7 pm.

2 . 9 . 1914.

Bn. paraded at 9.30 am, proceeded about 4 miles then halted at 11.30 am will go to support 4th Division of reserve support not needed, march resumed and billeted at PENCHARD. Very hot day, bad roads & bridges, but company has stood it well, feet giving trouble, marching happened.

~~3 . 9 . 1914~~

3 . 9 . 1914.

Bn. paraded at 4.15 am and marched about 10 miles, forming the advance guard from 11 to 9 miles to the march halt and bivouacked at MAS BLANCHE near BAYOUVATOIS arriving about 2 p.m. weather very hot, made good.

4 . 9 . 1914.

Spent the 4th enduring to advance by rear to advance at about midday the Germans about 11.30 am forward about 1 mile halted in a field about 5 pm.

WAR DIARY
or
INTELLIGENCE SUMMARY
(Erase heading not required.)

Army Form C. 2118.

Hour, Date, Place	Summary of Events and Information	Remarks and References to Appendices
5-9-14 ~~6-9-14~~	and then marched all night to LIVERDY a distance of about 22 miles arriving at 7.45 am. the situation not being the same.	
6-9-14	The Bn. paraded at 6 am marched 3 miles & then billeted in an orchard until further orders from own Bgd. the march was then resumed and billeted the night at LA HOUSSAYE.	
7-9-14	The Bn. paraded at 12.30 pm marked about 6 miles & then halted until further orders at about 4.30 pm & while awaiting orders from & then marched to billets at MOULIN-DE-BOISSY.	
8-9-14	Bn. paraded at 6 am rear guard action 6 miles were kept in support until 5.30 pm, then like on the enemy advance being general for the German proceeding about 6 miles & the villages at LA BREDONNIERAE the Bn. kicked up the 2nd Reinforcements of 1 Officer Lieut. J.H. BLACKWOOD & 99 men	

WAR DIARY or INTELLIGENCE SUMMARY

Army Form C. 2118.

Instructions regarding War Diaries and Intelligence Summaries are contained in F. S. Regs., Part II. and the Staff Manual respectively. Title pages will be prepared in manuscript.

(Erase heading not required.)

Hour, Date, Place	Summary of Events and Information	Remarks and References to Appendices

9-9-14
o 8/9/14

Bn. advanced at 6 am. Bn. progressed about 6 miles & were kept in support (to the 7th & 8th Brigades) until 5.30 pm, & then took over Advance pickets to the Division when proceeding about 7 miles and billets at VILLARE for the night. The Bn formed outposts for the Brigade & Billeted in 3 & Coy & the others to Coy billets. The Bn started at 0700.

10-9-14
Casualty 9/9/14

Started about 4 am. and marched forward until 5 am. and proceeded about a mile and were into action at BEZU and were within 150 yards of German lines which were approached of the Enemy turning their shrapnel on our own Artillery who fire into Shrapnel causing C.O. Company to retire & preventing the withdrawal of the Bn. They were in action until 6.30 pm. Casualties Captain & Adjutant T.E. DRANE killed. Captain H.C.W. HOSKYNS & G.M. ELLISON & Lieut B.T. THRUSTON wounded. Other ranks 2 killed, 93 wounded. Summary. The Bn entrenched the night but nothing further happened.

11-9-14

The Bn marched about 6 am. and moved to CHEZY where the remnants of the Brigade went into action. The Bn were kept in Reserve and though skirmishing from 3 pm did not fire a shot. Several Germans went into a thicket. The Bn. went into billets

WAR DIARY or INTELLIGENCE SUMMARY

Army Form C. 2118.

Hour, Date, Place	Summary of Events and Information	Remarks and References to Appendices
12-9-14.	In the night at DAMMARD	
	The Bn. paraded at 6 a.m. & marched 12 miles & went into billets at 1.30 p.m. at OULCHY en VILLE. Weather fine. Roads good.	
13-9-14.	Bn. paraded at 5 a.m. and moved as advance guard to the Division and marched to BRAINE. Leaving the town under the Divisional artillery cover, though the wood North of BRAINE. About 2 Coys. of enemy were taken & a Machine Gun with horses & General Capt with horses. No casualties. Weather raining all day & roads bad. Went into billets at BRENELLE.	
14-9-14.	Bn. bivouacked at 5 a.m. & marched when 1 mile and then halting for about ½ hour, until 2.30 p.m. then marched about 2 miles going into action near the River Bank (RIVER AISNE) until dark & then crossed river and marched through the town of VAILLY & marched to the top of the hill WEST of VAILLY. MAISON FARM and bivouacked for the night. Raining heavily all night.	
15-9-14.	Bn. still entrenched. Twice attacked. The enemy & twice were taken by assault, about 5.30 p.m. On made a counter attack on the night of the "Royal Fusiliers" but subsequently retired. During the heavy fire & enfiladed by Artillery & machine Guns. The Bn again advanced and opened fire at night on the flank of the German of VAILLY. The Bn. has been fighting	

WAR DIARY or INTELLIGENCE SUMMARY

Army Form C. 2118.

Hour, Date, Place	Summary of Events and Information	Remarks and References to Appendices
15.9.14	Casualties:- Col. WEBSMITH 2/Lieut CHUTCHINSON & 2/Lieut H.L. TRIST were slightly wounded. Capt. F.W. GREATWOOD severely wounded. Lieut. Orr & Lieut. PEDDIE & Lieut WYATT wounded & missing. Capt. Q.A.K. REMPTHORNE R.A.M.C. missing. The Rank & Killed 102 wounded, 74 missing.	
16.9.14	The Bn. stood to arms and marched to the top of the hill again. Some kept in support till whole of the Bty. at dusk lay alongside the road. The Bn. then were all night. Found picquets from each Coy. and The Germans attacked my outer advance but were repulsed. The Bn. still remained in Reserve under heavy shell fire, but owing to the steepness of the ravine sheltering no suffered only 5 Casualties 8 Killed 3 wounded. We were anticipating an attack that night but none took place.	
17.9.14	As on 17th instant. Casualties 1 Killed 1 wounded. Captain Tolin's son joined Bn with 40 stragglers.	
18.9.14	As 16th instant. Casualties 1 Killed & 8 wounded. Heavy Artillery fire was opened about 8 a.m. under which the enemy (Infantry) attacked but were repulsed. The Bn. again moved up & A Company were sent to support the Royal Fusiliers.	

WAR DIARY or INTELLIGENCE SUMMARY

Army Form C. 2118.

Hour, Date, Place	Summary of Events and Information	Remarks and References to Appendices
19.00. 9.14	Through the 19-20th reinforcements other [than] 6th DCLI & 9 [?] marched [?] near the Reu [?]	
20.9.14	At dawn on the 20th. The enemy opened heavy Rifle & artillery fire, keeping up a very stiff fire mainly Infantry & the Jr [?] Royal Fusiliers were very hard hit. The two other Battalions of 5th Bgy. being sent to support the 7th Inf Bde. soon became involved. The attack was repulsed with considerable loss [?] but it was the turn by our Eleventh [?] Battery [?] to show 5-30pm [?] when we were able to receive the 17th [?] Bruelie [?] on the Ry [?] up [?] near Bruielesme [?]. The relief was effected without loss. The fire around us on [?] Rgt. We were relieved by the York & Lanc. Rgt. They [?] were wanted to support no engineer attack [?] was going somewhere about the Reu [?] we remained in what trenches except with they remained until 7pm in the evening of the 21st abt about.	
21.9.14	7pm. today, orders were received by the Reu. to move to COURCELLES to night, moving off under cover of the relief [?]. Regiments [?] the Reu. was heavily engaged. There were 2 men wounded during this withdrawal. The Reu reached COURCELLES at 11pm where went into billets.	

WAR DIARY
or
INTELLIGENCE SUMMARY
(Erase heading not required.)

Army Form C. 2118.

Hour, Date, Place	Summary of Events and Information	Remarks and References to Appendices
Courcelles 22.9.14	The Bn. remained in Billets at Courcelles where the work of re-fitting was carried on. A Re-inforcement Draft of about 6 p.m. of 2 POTTER arrived. 100 other ranks.	
23.9.14 24.9.14	The Bn. remained in Billets at Courcelles where the work of re-fitting was still carried on.	
25.9.14	Bn. remained in COURCELLES till 4.30 p.m. finding working parties. Bn. left Courcelles & took VAILLY & relieved the R. Scots in the trenches. This relief was completed without incident.	
26.9.14	The Bn. remained uneventful dull fine in the morning. Later in the afternoon this became very heavy. A German patrol being thrown into our lines about 750 yards but was driven by a few picked shots. Further news from the Commanding Officer Wondering two new. The Casualties for this day amounted to 3 men wounded by shell fire	

WAR DIARY or INTELLIGENCE SUMMARY

Army Form C. 2118.

Hour, Date, Place	Summary of Events and Information	Remarks and References to Appendices
27.9.14 VAILLY	"C" Company of the R. Scots Fusiliers was relieved by "A" Company in the night. The enemy shelled the Ridge periodically during the morning, fire in the evening. There were no attempts for about 1 hour. Casualties for the day killed 2 wounded 6. No disturbance occurred during the night.	
28.9.14	Reconnaissance over the line was made during the morning. The became very heavy during from 5 to 7 pm hill much as about 6 pm. The enemy spent in and out a shell Pomits Thurman's trench and killed 6 wounded. Others were seen retired. However, during this time of... The enemy this however the whole firing & 12 shells were fired mainly employing shrapnel. Some of these fell inside trenches. Casualties amounted to (6 wounds?) Two German aeroplanes however were seen the enemy the observing for the direction to keep two of their batteries...	
29.9.14	...	

WAR DIARY
or
INTELLIGENCE SUMMARY
(Erase heading not required.)

Army Form C. 2118.

Hour, Date, Place	Summary of Events and Information	Remarks and References to Appendices
30.9.14.	Shell short by our Artillery three batteries at one time to which the Germans certainly did not reply. Crowborough Hill.	
31.9.14.	No shelling at all. Br Crowsleer.	
2.10.14	Rifle & Artillery scarcer firing at our trenches, although continuing on our flanks. Br Chevalier during this service. During the whole of this remain service at Vailly, the Bn. was lying in trenches dug out of the side of the hill and well constructed, police were the whole time. The service fortunately was few casualties even appeared. The enemy shelling the approaches to the gun behind of the men.	
2.10.14	On the night of this day we were relieved about 7pm never again to enter the trenches, in the following day we marched by the Wynghuisne Fagne to Longueval, however there were no [...]	

9th Infantry Bde.
3rd Division

1st BATTALION

THE LINCOLNSHIRE REGIMENT

OCTOBER, 1914

Army Form C. 2118.

WAR DIARY
or
INTELLIGENCE SUMMARY

(Erase heading not required.)

Instructions regarding War Diaries and Intelligence Summaries are contained in F. S. Regs., Part II. and the Staff Manual respectively. Title pages will be prepared in manuscript.

Hour, Date, Place	Summary of Events and Information	Remarks and References to Appendices
2.10.14	officers until 6.30 pm on the evening of the 9th. No firing from the enemy, but on my ride to Fay, heard of that Germans still in the Chapelle there. In the afternoon rode over to visit Bn. was to attack and easily to a return from Missy-sur-Aisne 7km till Regt followed by the 7th Zouaves relieved the Aisne marching via CHAVENY, BRAINE, CERSEUIL, CUIRY-HOUSSE, SERVENAY where they put into billets SERVENAY at 3 am in the morning of the 3rd. The Regiment being temporarily billeted in available houses & other buildings	
3.10.14	Bn formed at 5.15 pm in the evening and marched to TROESNES via BEUGNEUX – PLESSIER – HULEU – BILLY-SUR-OURCQ, CHOUY, NOROY, a distance of 18 miles. Road very cold.	
4.10.14	Bn. Marched via 15 km - VAILDIS through Crepy-en-Valois enroute VAUCIENNES & rest of Retz	

WAR DIARY
or
INTELLIGENCE SUMMARY

(Erase heading not required.)

Army Form C. 2118.

Hour, Date, Place	Summary of Events and Information	Remarks and References to Appendices
4-10-14	Carrying out old bombing scheme of the advance at BIEFVILLE distance of about 88 miles at 2.30 am. been very stringent, riven into billets.	
5"&6-10-14	Reg. furnished at 6.45am and marched to the village of RHUIS where we halted for 2½ hours, the men have turned into stables & barns & after great however we managed to show what the Regt. should have between to LA CROIX St. OUEN for the further ? entertainment which they received as thoroughly deserved / as men were in a very exhausted condition, 7 days in the trenches & the trenches with no time to rest, yet they could not have only 1 day in which they could take their boots off. Men were attached for in a very kind manner & shown that in made & come materials have afforded something amounting to this equipment for the night however sufficient one horse cart to carry & Mechn [illegible]	

WAR DIARY or INTELLIGENCE SUMMARY

Army Form C. 2118.

Hour, Date, Place	Summary of Events and Information	Remarks and References to Appendices
6-10-14	Hot tea for the men. The Bn. were entrained for station near AMIENS to LONGRÉ where we arrived about 8 p.m. and after detraining there till 11 a.m. the following day we marched to ABBEVILLE where we debussed. We then moved to BUIGNY going into billets at 7 pm halting the miles then we marched twice by their own journey the following night next, and remained until 1. ostain the 9th inst.	
9-10-14	Bn. paraded at 1.30 a.m. and marched to CAUMONT arriving there about 7.30 a.m. Weather very bad. Distance about 15 miles.	
10-10-14	The Bn. again fell in at 12.45 a.m. and after having marched about 6 miles went into billets up to 3 A.M. where we went into billets again. Here we were joined by reinforcements. 3 the officers MAJOR BARCLAY, Captains FENWICK, TORR, INGOLDBY, WILLIS, TOLLEMACHE, Lieuts. BROMHEAD, KING, LYALL, PEASE and HARDY. Bn. paraded at 7.30 pm marched to BUISNES and we went into billets for the night. Weather dry.	

WAR DIARY or INTELLIGENCE SUMMARY

Army Form C. 2118.

Hour, Date, Place	Summary of Events and Information	Remarks and References to Appendices
12-10-14	Regt. being in support to the 2nd Bde, we bivouacked at 6 a.m. and after turning in about 8 a.m. before VIELLE CHAPELLE. Heavy fire increased upon church & steeple of the church. Fire then was continued & we eventually got in fire trenches. At dusk the men were given to relieve the Gurkhas but on our way there we met - & while to but on our way the 1st Brigade which was pleasantly we went to another informed we were expected to go COUTEAU engaged. We then entrenched ourselves in expectation of attack, which however did not materialise. Quiet night.	
13-10-14	On the early morning of the 13th, the Germans driven with shell fire. A chance to advance to the attack was at 5 am this did not materialise until 7 am which on the rear which was consequently up behind, moved on in the support of the 2nd Brigade, but owing to maps and newly drawn faulty nightfall were not caught up. Here we had a cross stream by a single plank bridge under infantry & rifle fire. The Regt. was however to bits the building but not till 2 pm. Bn. were now on the position still by small dark unseen lay, little damage however. During which men exchange comments to retire in the evening in order to received what was considered help lines. It was, however, quite dark before we got back to VIELLE CHAPELLE again. On this or back march were ordered to move on our own to Pontgoude & TOURET to reinforce the 14th Brigade.	

WAR DIARY or INTELLIGENCE SUMMARY

Army Form C. 2118.

Hour, Date, Place	Summary of Events and Information	Remarks and References to Appendices
14-10-14	If possible have all the play at the men rendered their toilet much inflamed owing to the heavy going want of sleep.	
d	The Bn bivouacked in a large barn. Some all day at 8pm by motor from the Brigade "D" Company were sent to support the Manchester Regt. Went to form the reserve move to reinforce bivouac for the Bn. Remained out about 4 hrs.	
15-10-14	Case A Coy was very much in support the D.C.L. Infantry with one machine gun. There were moved up on arriving to billets but were turned out again shortly afterwards owing to the engagement having resumed During this move to reinforce to attack to billets. We remained still under arms. At 10 Coys. Having returned marched back to VIEILLE CHAPELLE	
16-10-14	The Bn turned out at 2.30am reported by the 9th Brigade to the relief of the Coys. trenches along & under heavy rifle fire from their right at 7am. Learnt of the outpost line & West Regt Infantry when we entrenched. The Coys march past ROUGE CROIX was moved to the Bn Quarters from 3pm a further advance we entrenched on the new billets for the night. At about 7am the Bn advanced towards the attack	
17-10-14	having been ordered to seize the railway and tramway at the top of a ridge near LA CLIQUETERIE there was opposition with a sufficient suddenness at HERLIES an easy going to rush the village of HERLIES A&B Companies forming the firing line of fact C&D Companies the village of HERLIES looking at it what remained the fire from our attack was strenuous	

WAR DIARY or INTELLIGENCE SUMMARY

Army Form C. 2118.

(Erase heading not required.)

Hour, Date, Place	Summary of Events and Information	Remarks and References to Appendices

At the foot of a long gentle slope, fitfully shelled that time though withal effect, to our side [of the] village was reputed by strong entrenchments, further protected by before [?] prime entanglements. The enemy made no immediate effort to supplement by further troops or a holding artillery. The [?] advances were 1450 to within 1000 yrds of junction, whilst we quite to [?] ability of the [?] [?] front junction [?] was awaiting tion within 500 yrds [?] [?] of every [?] [?] [?] of [?] came [?] [?] [?] was ammunition that the village must at [?] [?] before what [?] was prepared along with upon before [?] SMITH gave the order of advance [?] rose as he saw another just in front of the battery to [?] [?] every time between on and 5th [?] quickly [?] [?] [?] [?] (the enemy connected to [?] [?] [?] many were seen to leave their trenches. But there were no [?] [?] the enemies [?] ? through crossing the entanglement [?] chapel. The [?] [?] [?] At this moment, unfortunately our artillery fired up and, top Change supposed no such firing was recommenced to shell the [?] a complete surprise to [?] [?] [?] the Regt. we entered the village, but they stopped when the firing after a short time out through it to [?] [?] to them most of the [?] came up shaking over [?] with (but [?] men command into [?] we went through into [?] the village also my platoon his 10th [?] Rifles. Lancashire [?] dead B [?] Ave. [?]

by Lieut PEACE

WAR DIARY or INTELLIGENCE SUMMARY

Army Form C. 2118.

Hour, Date, Place	Summary of Events and Information	Remarks and References to Appendices
18-10-14	(Contd) Wds received that Parks killed 10 wounded 65 missing 6. At 11:30 p.m. C/O of 9th Brigade "Rept 3rd Division congratulates us and so do I."	
19-10-14. H. Bayonwer 3.	Bn remained in reserve and received orders about 9 p.m. to support a night attack. This attack was unsuccessful in its attempt to retake the CLIQUETERIE FARM. Cavalier Supt. Yale killed by a stray bullet. Bn. relieved Royal Scots Lancers in the trenches at 3:45 am until daybreak. Cavalier wounded, wound slight & rifle fire all day. Cavaliers wounded officers 2 men 3.	
20-10-14.	Germans attacked on our left, were however kept by our Artillery fire. Germans attacked again on our position, were made all day with no great loss. Enemy's artillery kept up shell fire, we did nothing in reply, they relied to retire. About 9pm. Cpl. ? wounded it ? from a howitzer ? reserves ? stood Cover Pte Ham & Pte ? killed. Officers killed? men ? wounded ?men 1.	
21-10-14 & 22-10-14	Ditto as on the previous, stayed the 5th Brigade on our left were ? to ? situation remained ? the day before, at dusk we were ordered to retire & take up a position ? to allow 6000 yards in front before dawn owing to unity accomplished with ? fears ? army to	

WAR DIARY or INTELLIGENCE SUMMARY

Army Form C. 2118

Hour, Date, Place	Summary of Events and Information	Remarks and References to Appendices

23.10.14 — NEUVE CHAPELLE

Two other Regts. keeping late in morning. Bn. had only just got into position when the enemy fire with difficulty, few of the men of the line could be induced to do anything. Jake our Cmdrs. & killed 2g. wounded 2d.

Bde. was moreover subject to a heavy fire in rear in about 3 miles to rear, the 1st to 8th Rear Guards. Retirement commenced by the enemy. German snipers came up about 10 am & entrenched themselves at about 700 yds to our front. Their Artillery were commanding themselves by taking our line & commanding themselves filling in the Transport 3 miles in rear.

24.10.14 — The enemy attacked firing was kept up for about 12 hours heavy but we kept in the field, all about 3 rounds. The Bn. to the rear, at direct, but many of the enemy attacking heavily on the right. Lower line this location was unable to be carried out. The relieving Bn. having been sent in supports.

25.10.14 — About 3.30 a.m. Germans again attacked but without success. Sufficient continued throughout the day, a heavy rifle masked from the henry prosent on our trenches.

Casualties two Officers killed Capt Amphlett Lieut Willis, 16 Officers killed Capt Amphlett & the ranks 9 killed Weather very wet

WAR DIARY
INTELLIGENCE SUMMARY
(Erase heading not required.)

Army Form C. 2118.

Hour, Date, Place	Summary of Events and Information	Remarks and References to Appendices
26-10-14.	The Bn. were relieved in the trenches at about 3.30 a.m. by the 8th Northumberland Fusiliers & marched back to billets which were about 3 miles in rear of the village of ROUGE CROIX, in rear to redo's, however at about 3.30 p.m. that were received to move at once. The Regt. was formed up again to support the 1st Irish Guards & were sent to support at the village of NEUVE CHAPELLE. "A" and D Coy's the West Kents (that before dawn "B" Coy. had been sent up to "C": at about 11 am. another were received to attack up to the line on the village. The two two guides from the two Companies marched by A+D, midway between the West Kent. at about 3 p.m. The Bn. advanced to the attack (sic) in the firing line and supports & our own rifle municipal fire was brought to bear on us as the Germans held positions more advanced than our own, and as the position of the Germans, interfered for our support, & our own line, could not being the increase of which infers were scarcely extended in advanced, empty in Coy's approximated, but soon as it was dark before the 9 hours later after an attempt by continuous fighting the and of supply were reinforcing was excessively. In trying and another with to rifle the regiments on attack of the enemy. Casualties Officers Killed: Lieut. F. Henry Ridden. Major Camel, Capt. Waterson, Lt. K. Kep, all slightly wounded, Lieut. Rennie Killed. 13 rank & file	
27-10-14.		

WAR DIARY or INTELLIGENCE SUMMARY

Army Form C. 2118

Hour, Date, Place	Summary of Events and Information	Remarks and References to Appendices
28.10.14	[Battalion?] remained in their trenches subjected to intermittent sniping [and] occasional shell fire from the enemies heavy trench mortar batteries. Casualties 1 killed & 9 wounded.	
29.10.14	Battalion subjected to occasional rifle fire from the enemies snipers. About 7 p.m. orders were received from the 11th Bde that the Batt. was to be relieved during the coming night by the 2/9th Gurkhas, moving off at 11 p.m. by the 9th [Jullunder?] [Infantry?] & were not to take part in the relief but was to effect a concentration at a certain point behind the firing line — this point was afterwards named as [illegible].	
30.10.14	At [about] daylight the firing line reported that the Regt. Reserves [did not?] turn up, as a result our attention in the [illegible] [illegible] with the enemy arose actual [illegible] the occupation of a [illegible] [illegible] of the [illegible] [illegible] comparative [illegible] afforded us in the [illegible] normally taken in [illegible] to NEUVE CHAPELLE. At 10 a.m. the news came that we were in reserve to NEUVE CHAPELLE. At 3 p.m. moved into ESTAIRES as Army Reserve and were ordered to billet in the town. The men were very [fatigued?] [by reason of their] duties.	
31.10.14	At 6 a.m. [marched through?] NEUVE-EGLISE to LINDENHOEK to KEMMEL Hill and were [ordered?] to [illegible] the enemy advancing along the whole allied communication lay [illegible] was [illegible] [illegible] [illegible] [illegible] [illegible] [illegible] Division [illegible] was sent into KEMMEL to Millat. Whole day [illegible] [illegible]

9th Infantry Bde.
3rd Division.

1st BATTALION

THE LINCOLNSHIRE REGIMENT

NOVEMBER, 1914.

WAR DIARY
or
INTELLIGENCE SUMMARY

Army Form C 2118

Hour, Date, Place

1-11-1914.

Summary of Events and Information

At about 1.30 a.m. a runner who reported that the 1st Cavalry Bde. was to attack to WYTSCHAETE to retake it. The message was too indefinite & General Drummond could make nothing of it. Tried to communicate with K. to find out further. Rode off myself to the Cavalry Bde. near WYTSCHAETE Road and was unable in the darkness to reach the Railway Station which had been mentioned. S.W. of the village of K. & then were reported to have been held by British. Rode out through they could not defend themselves efficiently from interference we must be on the track of the Cavalry & return to find the D. General, who gave orders. They were other units which were needed — the right group stood for the R. Station. Office to some of our staff. We were heavily shelled by snipers Drummond I the Cav. Bde. & went to SHAW to fetch up further reinforcements. Glorious manner in which the trenches were held by some. The Germans must have suffered heavily & we nothing to fear in our front. A few rounds of artillery did much to keep our men from coming back. I made the retirement as full as I possibly could by carrying ammunition up & keeping the ...

Remarks and References to Appendices

1/10 E1

AR 9.26.

Instructions regarding War Diaries and Intelligence Summaries are contained in F. S. Regs., Part II. and the Staff Manual respectively. Title pages will be prepared in manuscript.

WAR DIARY
or
INTELLIGENCE SUMMARY
(Erase heading not required.)

Army Form C. 2118

Hour, Date, Place	Summary of Events and Information	Remarks and References to Appendices
	separating a fallow field from one of turnips and about 100 yards from the position so strongly held by the enemy behind us at a distance of about 150 yards. From a hedge row behind which a fold in the ground promised a certain amount of cover. To our left rear the country was absolutely open except for a thin wire fence. This position was to prove a death trap. ~~[illegible]~~ Until about 6.45 am we lay behind this ridge. As dawn broke we saw the people on our left retiring and in order to cover them the remnants of the London Scottish on our right we hung on. Germans worked round our left flank (we were fired at by our own Artillery in rear, by their guns in front by riflemen on both flanks. The place became absolutely untenable and our only chance was to make a bolt for it on Colonel Smith giving the word we got up & ran for our lives towards the dip. The enemy opening a murderous fire but probably owing to surprise & excitement a great many of their shots went high and many of us succeeded in reaching shelter. In the dip the men were roughly formed up into line as we now had to form up along a glacis like slope. On emerging from cover we again came under enemy fire but suffered very few casualties.	1/10

(9 26 6) W 257—976 100,000 4/12 H W V 79/3298

WAR DIARY or INTELLIGENCE SUMMARY

Army Form C. 2118

Hour, Date, Place | **Summary of Events and Information** | **Remarks and References to Appendices**

2-11-1914

The remnants of the Regt. were formed up by Colonel the Adjutant in the sunken lane to the village of LINDENHOEK. The withdrawing of about a Reserve Officers & 150 men enabled us to receive & cook the hot "Our Number" which is engaged was approximately 200, which must have suffered severely as the enemy mass of the German were killed before the guns say nothing of those men Evans and wounded & the enemy were repulsed by artillery and what small arm fire we had. Later on the Regt was withdrawn to MONT KEMMEL where the remnants bivouacked with some few transport near to LA CLYTTE. Here we got to. About 91 men under Major SHAW to re-join the remnants.

Casualties: Officers — Captain KING, 2/Lt BARNES, 2nd Lieut LEE, 3 Sergeants Captain HYTHE, JOHNSON (killed) Colonel SMITH, Captain TOLLEMACHE (wounded), Capt. BARLOW (missing)

Rank & File — Killed and Wounded in the three Coys. about 550 remained killed in the three Coys all day

WAR DIARY or INTELLIGENCE SUMMARY

Army Form C. 2118

Hour, Date, Place	Summary of Events and Information	Remarks and References to Appendices
3-11-1914 4-11-1914	Bn. moved to billets at BAILLEUL. Bn. was inspected by Sir HORACE SMITH-DORRIEN who complimented them on their appearance & on their behaviour during his Campaign. The General complimented Genl SMITH for the bravery & the way he handled his regiment in the action on the previous Sunday. The following General order was issued from Army Hd Qrs 4th Nov 1914. The Cps Comdr. has received a letter from General Sir E.H. ALLENBY, C.B. 5th Cavalry Corps which he desires me will make public. "My Dear Sir Horace, I must thank you for the help given me during the first six hours of my attack on Oct 31st. You were kindly sent by Gen. Snow and the LINCOLNS, K.O.S.B. 10/H the NORTHUMBERLAND Fusiliers. They arrived at a very critical time & their arrival saved the situation. They have suffered some too few very severely & I am deeply indebted to them to Bngd. General SHAW. Yours sincerely E.H. ALLENBY."	1/10.01 AR 2.12
5-11-1914	Bn. remained in Billets all day the work of fitting & reorganisation was carried on. Bn. still remained in billets but were ready to turn out at five minutes notice.	

WAR DIARY or INTELLIGENCE SUMMARY

Army Form C. 2118.

Hour, Date, Place	Summary of Events and Information	Remarks and References to Appendices
6-11-1914	Bn. left bivouacs at 10 a.m. & marched to the relief of the country East of YPRES covered with small fields, belts of willows and thick hedges. Halted near DICKEBUSCH.	
7-11-1914	At about 11 p.m. the Regt. reached the neighbourhood of HERONTHAGE, about 1½ miles East of HOOGE & relieved the 9th Regl. at about 11 p.m. in the following way. The 5th Fusiliers having been drawn from their trenches the Regt. was moved forward by companies to retake them. This movement owing to the darkness & fire & presence of the enemy was very difficult & in fact was impossible and we very only completed about 1 a.m. in front of the original tranches. The Coy. referred to in this Corridor was Cape in the firing line. A. & D. Coys were Bu. was subjected to shell rifle fire all day. Cavalcade to shell rifle fire all day.	7/10 a
8-11-1914	Two attacks were made during the night both were repulsed. 2nd Lieut A. Ricketts joined the Bn.	
9-11-1914	Bombardment continued unceasingly. A Coy trench in particular suffered. The chief fighting men suffered after attack. The enemy advanced to with in 20 yds. of our trench, were repulsed. Casualties Lieut. TOPP severely wounded 2/Lt. BLACK & other ranks to men wounded 30 men. Reinforcements joined.	

OR.4.

WAR DIARY / INTELLIGENCE SUMMARY

Army Form C. 2118.

Hour, Date, Place	Summary of Events and Information	Remarks and References to Appendices
10-11-1914	Situation unchanged.	
11-11-1914	The enemy opened heavy Artillery fire at daybreak, under cover of which they made an infantry attack which was again repulsed. The weather now turned very cold & there was much rain, some of the trenches becoming partially flooded. Enemy Trenches. 5 killed & 15 wounded by the Ranks.	
12-11-1914	Very heavy bombardment all day. Casualties 6 killed & 23 wounded of other Ranks.	
13-11-1914	Rn. was a very heavy shell fire all day at the time the Germans managed to get a small French mortar which threw an oval shell into the trenches caused considerable casualties at about 3 from they again attacked in and were repulsed. Casualties this field numbered seventeen rifles Captains Killam & G.B. Munro severely wounded all day men with being unable keep to need shelter. It was decided to take up a new line at the farm owing to the enemy having worked with both trenches on our left. Shortly a new left farm however established on about it was about 15 to 15. The withdrawal was carried out by the service Coy. & occupied a remainder all down position and & out by the Engineers. Casualties 5 killed & wounded by the wet weather still continues	CR2b.

WAR DIARY or INTELLIGENCE SUMMARY

Army Form C. 2118.

Hour, Date, Place	Summary of Events and Information	Remarks and References to Appendices
15-11-1914	Bn subjected to overnight shell fire but enemy in the trenches not reported as making any serious attempt, there were only a few snipers firing on us. The Regt was to have been relieved on this day by the Yorkshire Light Infantry but some hitch occurred and as D. Company only were relieved B. Co. remaining in the firing line but watch and ammunition & C. Co. in reserve.	
16-11-1914	R. Co remained. Various attempts by still rifle fire by snipers who could not be dislodged from the trench. We stopped on the trenches. Casualties 3 were relieved about 7 p.m. by the Yorkshire Light Infantry. Reserve and the village of HOOGE. We were supplied in intermittent shell fire. 8 men being wounded.	
17-11-1914	Bn was sent to relieve the R. Scots Fusiliers at Hooge. Relief carried out without mishap. Snowstorm. 1 wounded.	
18-11-1914		
19-11-1914	2 Coys were sent to support Northumberland Fusiliers in the trenches in support of the Cavalry, snow fell all day on these 2 Coys and were a very severe experience. The WEST KENTS relieved the 2 Coys at night. The Bn took part in the move S.E. ZILLEBEKE. This relief was carried out with great difficulty owing to the deep snow, heavy rain & gale in which the Germans had retreated from the firing line.	

WAR DIARY or INTELLIGENCE SUMMARY

Army Form C. 2118.

(Erase heading not required.)

Hour, Date, Place	Summary of Events and Information	Remarks and References to Appendices

20-11-1914

On arrival at [?] this day only 300 men of the [?] were collected this motion. Shortly afterwards the traffic was resumed on this line. Took the way to the relieved by the Dorsets at about 10 a.m. The 13[?] Reg[t] of Infantry came up later & were the pride of the Reg[t] to whom we are indebted to. Ce[?] to WESTOUTRE some 12 miles distance. This was a very difficult march owing to a several [?] of army cattle [?] on the roads & [?] impossible for some drawn transport. We all got [?] of us for some 6 miles only by falling trees & [?] on [?] traffic. Thus to Reg[t] was able to proceed at all. On arrival at WESTOUTRE at [?] reg[t] found no billets had been prepared for it the inhabitants [?] [?] [?] had been warned by the [?] to take all possible precautions to find some [?] while the country [?] a [?] was [?] before [?] men were eventually a [?] in some private houses farms & Ch[?]

Reinforcements arrived in the evening Capt [?] TATCHELL, Captain R.C.H., & Lieut JAMES with 215 other ranks. LIEUT & ADJT. F.H.R.LOCKWOOD proceeded to England on leave.

21-11-1914

d[itt]o Remained in Billets in farms in the village of WESTOUTRE where the [?] of refitting was carried out with the C.O. on the 23rd. The men were inspected by the C.O. and PRIVATE 6704.G.E.R.[?] was presented with the [?] [?]. [?] for [?] under orders in the field.

22-11- & 23-11-1914

N.B. 3998. [?] for his [?] act was given by the 2nd Army Corps Commander General SIR H. HORACE SMITH-DORRIEN, who spoke very highly

WAR DIARY or INTELLIGENCE SUMMARY

Army Form C. 2118

Hour, Date, Place	Summary of Events and Information	Remarks and References to Appendices
24-11-1914	of the work done by the Battalion while station- ed to the 1st. ARMY CORPS. Bn. still in billets. Captain SWORD of the DORSETS Refers returned to join the Battalion from leave to England.	
25-11-1914. 26-11-1914.	Bn. still in billets. Bn. still in billets. At 2pm. the Bn. were arranged for inspection by the Commander- in-Chief General SIR JOHN FRENCH who complimented all ranks on their achievements in the field during the campaign.	
27-11-1914	Bn. left their billets at 2.30pm & proceeded via WESTOUTRE and LOCRE to KEMMEL arriving at their peace about 6pm returning the Regiments billets. Infantry on this trench did the advance was very long & without mishap, although a very bright moonlight night. The relief was completed by midnight.	
28-11-1914	2 C & D Companies formed the firing line with B. Coy. in support. A. Coy in reserve. 600 yards on left of the firing line shout all day, only occasional shots from snipers. At night working parties from Engineers were strongly occupied. Casualties other ranks 1 Killed, 1 Wounded.	
29-11-1914	The day was fairly quiet. There was an artillery Duel fired off until 6pm which subsided after our batteries ceased firing. 1 killed & 3 wounded.	
30-11-1914	The FRENCH on our left attempted an attack. At 6.15 am which ended without any ground being gained. Rifle fire was kept up by the Bn. to support the attack Heavy Germans from our front, in reply the ene- my at Place The remainder of the day was quiet. The Bn. was relieved between 6 & 7.30pm by the 1st Wiltshire Reg-	

WAR DIARY
or
INTELLIGENCE SUMMARY

(Erase heading not required.)

Army Form C. 2118.

Instructions regarding War Diaries and Intelligence Summaries are contained in F. S. Regs., Part II. and the Staff Manual respectively. Title pages will be prepared in manuscript.

Hour, Date, Place	Summary of Events and Information	Remarks and References to Appendices
20-11-14	Battalion marched into Billets at WESTOUTRE. Casualties 9 killed 24 wounded	AR 94.

9th Infantry Bde.
3rd Division.

1st BATTALION

THE LINCOLNSHIRE REGIMENT

DECEMBER, 1914

Army Form C. 2118.

WAR DIARY
or
INTELLIGENCE SUMMARY.
(Erase heading not required.)

1st Bat'n Inniskilling Rgt.

Hour, Date, Place	Summary of Events and Information	Remarks and references to Appendices
	December 1914	
1-12-1914.	The Bn remained in billets and the work of re-organizing & refitting was proceeded with. Major F.R. BAKER joined from the 2nd. Bn: also Captain Wm. SAURIN & Lt & 2nd Lt Corkyhue Regt: transferred to 1st Bn Inniskilling Regt.	
2-12-1914.	Still in billets, a draft of two military Captain R.A.M. FORTE 3rd Bat'n Inniskilling Regt. and Lieut T.G. NEWBURY and 170 other ranks arrived from England.	1/0
3-12-1914.	Still in billets. His Majesty the KING came through Inspection West PUTRE on his Journey up on the roadside with guns lines of the Brigade and were drawn up Infantry of His Majesty proper being keep clear in an automobile accompanied by the Commander-in-Chief & the specimen army. Everything it the afternoon received in which the majesty expressed great pleasure at left afterwards upon appearance of the Troops.	N.B.

Form./C. 2118/10

Army Form C. 2118.

WAR DIARY
or
INTELLIGENCE SUMMARY.
(Erase heading not required.)

Instructions regarding War Diaries and Intelligence Summaries are contained in F.S. Regs., Part II. and the Staff Manual respectively. Title pages will be prepared in manuscript.

Hour, Date, Place	Summary of Events and Information	Remarks and references to Appendices
4-12-1914	A party of 50 N.C.O's men under the orders of Captain E. TATCHELL went to D.C.R.E. Euston from where his Majesty a Guard of honour where his Majesty presented medals for distinguished conduct to the N.C.O.'s men of the Brigade and PRIVATE STRUDGER being the only representative sent to see the other N.C.O's men who had been awarded the medal being killed or wounded. The On December at 3.30 pm they returned to their billets in the morning line. Sent on fatigue at D.C.R.E. ready to hand to on support.	
5-12-1914	To the HR instant.	
6-12-1914	As HR & 5th instant. Captain R.S.M. FORTE admitted to Hospital with Rheumatism. Pte. marched out of billets into 9.30 pm. Proceeded to KEMMEL to relieve the 1st Royal Scots Regt. in the trenches. Owing to the Recent heavy rains the trenches were in a very bad state, some places 4/13

WAR DIARY or INTELLIGENCE SUMMARY.

(Erase heading not required.)

Army Form C. 2118.

Hour, Date, Place	Summary of Events and Information	Remarks and references to Appendices
	being knee deep in mud spoilt it. B.O.T. Companies formed the firing line. A Company in support in a support line to the Rr. Headquarters. We obtained several hundreds of Jackets, planks & boards& plenty of straw from the rear. There also managed to stand up the new wraps to make rounded roof to keep the mud from & help the walls. They were also spread over little coverings over the trenches. day. I managed to interview the Brigadier into holes at the right of the line today being passed by the Brigadier officer in the trenches who told me after being shown to the Company officers post by me that the Company of Infantry found it absolutely necessary to keep relieve them by the Company of Supports. The men being in such a state of exhaustion. 2/Lieut. A.S.S. WADE & 2/Lieut. A.B.L. PARISH joined the battalion. Casualties. 1 Killed & 1 wounded.	
7.12.1914.	Rain was falling almost continually for the last 24 hours covering the trenches to become pure like manure canals. The firing all day except for an occasional shot from snipers.	6/13

WAR DIARY
or
INTELLIGENCE SUMMARY

(Erase heading not required.)

Army Form C. 2118.

Hour, Date, Place	Summary of Events and Information	Remarks and references to Appendices
8.12.1914	Crawlies / Killies (?) 10 parked. The day passed very quietly, until about 10 am when a message was received from the G.O.C. of the Division that the 10th Battalion were to prepare to make an attack at 3 p.m. against the enemy trenches in front of the Right of that position held by the Battalion. Reconnoitring parties were immediately sent out to ascertain if the trenches were strongly held by the enemy & were received by a fairly hot fire but the information they brought made that it was difficult to determine a fairly long extent of the field by the enemy a fairly long extent of the trench in front of the enemies trenches. Orders were then sent forward to the O.C. No. 2 Coy to the effect that work being done by Officer Williams & the Royal Engineers two Companies need to go off the attack. No. 3 Coy forming the front line strengthened by a detachment of F Coy in support about 10 fm the attack was to have been carrying line morning forward which little opposition was encountered at the German front trench, which was gained to the full extent of wanted, the new work to the trench to march to the trench to march to the trench was joined to the trench to march to... A/B	1/10 61

WAR DIARY

INTELLIGENCE SUMMARY

Hour, Date, Place	Summary of Events and Information	Remarks and references to Appendices
8.12.14.	Apparently got to the other side of their trench when were then supported by A Coy. They were then met by a heavy rifle fire & machine gun fire left was left exposed, that the Company Commander of "A" & "B" were wounded. Captain TATCHELL re ceiving a bullet wound in knee and Sergt JAMES a wound in arm & Sergt JAMES a wound in knee back. The fire became so heavy it was absolutely necessary for the men to fall back out to their own trenches, which was carried in very good order. This attack was a very fine achievement considering the difficulties under which it was carried out. The men were very much fatigued by being in the trenches which were full of water, and the effect of heavy ground fire which they then had to advance over and save the men having to advance each other out if they trenched, having to shift to get out without aid. Casualties 4 Officers 19 wounded & 18 missing. The ranks Captain SAURIN who commanded C Coy was wounded early in the day.	1/10
9.	Remained 19/13 struck in there places by shrapnel.	

WAR DIARY
or
INTELLIGENCE SUMMARY.
(Erase heading not required.)

Hour, Date, Place	Summary of Events and Information	Remarks and references to Appendices
9-12-1914	receiving a severe wound in the left hand & a wound in each thigh. After the attack about 40 men were relieved from the trenches by the Company at the viewpoint destined. The two Companies made no attempt to do more. Went and lay anything which it was also together with 2nd Lieut. WADE who had been severed to a hospital, no trenches were to be found not been seen by stragglers from any part of the Regiment. At about noon the Officer Surgeons met at our medical Officer & it was found that Lt. Col. Bn. left the trench, but remained with two Company & gone forward with the attack and had not returned. The Officers cap was brought in yesterday belonging to Officer WADE. The cap had a bullet hole right through it. The Officer was reported as missing. The Bn. was believed in the evening by the Wiltshire Regt. to whom which the Bn. handed themselves to their trenches, having over those three killed, they then previously held before going to the trenches. Casualties about Killed	1/10 4/13

Army Form C. 2118.

WAR DIARY
or
INTELLIGENCE SUMMARY.

(Erase heading not required.)

Army Form C. 2118.

Hour, Date, Place	Summary of Events and Information	Remarks and references to Appendices
10-12-1914.	Buring billeted, Reporting (who carried out from Colonel W.E.B. SMITH) Gone to England.	
11-12-1914.	Bn. remained in billets & draft of 1 Officer (Lieut.) MORRIS & 27 NCOs and fifteen to Bn.	
12.12.1914.	Bn. still in billets at LOCRE	
13.12.1914.	Bn. still in billets at LOCRE.	1/10
14.12.1914.	An order came for the Bn. to parade at 6.30 am to proceed to a point ½ mile WEST of KEMMEL to take up a position in Reserve to the 9th Infantry Brigade who were at the time in the trenches. An attack was to made by the 9th Bde. who were going to advance through the gr. Rd. The attack was remanded. At 7.45 am the Bn. remained in their position until dusk (?) firing remaining quiet. Our Artillery kept up a very heavy bombardment on the enemies lines. Advance WYSCHEATE about 4 pm. An order came for the Bn. to move forward & billet in KEMMEL 8/13	

WAR DIARY or INTELLIGENCE SUMMARY.

Army Form C. 2118.

(Erase heading not required.)

Hour, Date, Place	Summary of Events and Information	Remarks and references to Appendices

15.12.14.

for the night.

At 5 a.m. an order was received for the Bn. to move to the position they had occupied the previous day. On their arrival at Forum Farmwell in their position about 6 a.m. About 9 a.m. rain started to fall & continued to do so for about 9 hours. An order was received that if we wished the Bn. could move into the billets they had occupied the previous night, just to the rear of the enemy shells about shelling the village. The Bn. moved into KEMMEL arriving in there about 10.30 a.m. Nothing happened but was under shell fire when the Bn. was ordered about 3.0 p.m. to march to WESTOUTRE, being relieved by the 7th Brigade.

16.12.14. Bn. returned to billets at WESTOUTRE
17.12.14. Do Do
18.12.14. Do Do

WAR DIARY
or
INTELLIGENCE SUMMARY.
(Erase heading not required.)

Army Form C. 2118.

Hour, Date, Place	Summary of Events and Information	Remarks and references to Appendices
19-12-14	A draft consisting of 1 Officer 2/Lieut H.C. DISBROWE & 15 R.F. when joined the Bn.	
20-12-14	Bn. still in billets	
21-12-14	Do. Lieut BRYN RAMé attached to the Bn. Received orders to engage on service. Received by Lieut F.S. WILSON. RAMé The Bn. Battalion at KEMMEL marched via LOCRE and KEMMEL to the trenches, relieving the 1st Royal Scots, the relief being carried out between 6 & 9pm. Bn. "D" Companies occupied the front line & "B" Cy in support. "C" Cy in Brigade Reserve at KEMMEL & "A" Cy at KEMMEL Shelters. HOULTON joined the Bn. at KEMMEL Capt WESTOUTRE a party consisting of D & R.F.R.'s men have left behind to proceed to MONTNOIR to form a guard for the Corps Commander.	
22-12-14	The day passed very quietly. Colonel NEID SMITH rejoined the Battalion at 8pm in the evening. Colonel relieved "B" Company from the firing line	A/13

Army Form C. 2118.

WAR DIARY
or
INTELLIGENCE SUMMARY.
(Erase heading not required.)

Instructions regarding War Diaries and Intelligence Summaries are contained in F.S. Regs., Part II. and the Staff Manual respectively. Title pages will be prepared in manuscript.

Hour, Date, Place	Summary of Events and Information	Remarks and references to Appendices
23-12-14	B.Coy going into support. C Coy into reserve in the infantry lines. The day however very quietly in the evening strong 6th Bn C Coy relieved 'A' Coy from the firing line. 'A' Coy going into reserve at the LATERIE.	
24-12-14	The morning was quiet, about 2 p.m. the enemy shelled round Rue Kband. Quarters without doing any damage. During seven shells from the R.H.A. coming the Rue was returned but the 1R Rn. Royal Irish Rifles suffered which one jun/seven men & to LOURE to killed.	
25-12-14	Christmas Day a very seasonable, all ranks shifted themselves, the Commanders to celebrate the Great anniversary in an impossible way to the conditions permit. Christmas Greetings were received from Field Marshal SIR JOHN FRENCH GCB, RCVO, KCMG, Commander-in-Chief of the British Army in the field, as follows:- "In offering to the Army my sincere wishes and earnest Goodwill hopes for X-mas & the New Year, each anspeare	A/13

Hour, Date, Place	Summary of Events and Information	Remarks and references to Appendices
26-12-14.	tries made to express the admiration I feel for the valour & endurance & the hope displayed throughout the campaign to wounded & dying & the devoted & such magnificent troops in the field will be too hard to remember. & my wife & I wish to be remembered." All ranks of the Bn. received Xmas cards from the KING & QUEEN & a present from H.R.H. Princess MARY, containing a Pipe (containing Tobacco), Xmas Card, & Cigarettes. Also entertaining Games which was greatly admired by all ranks of the Battalion. Presents were also received from the MAYOR & Citizens of LINCOLN showing they interested in the welfare of the Regiment.	1/10
27-12-14	Bn. remained in Billets at LOCRE.	AB
	— do —	

Hour, Date, Place	Summary of Events and Information	Remarks and References to Appendices
28-12-14	Remained in Billets at LOCRE. LIEUT. PAYN reported off leave from England.	
29-12-14	Remained in Billets at LOCRE. During the repairs of Battalion in billets a party of NCO's and men under 2nd LIEUT T.G. NEWBURY were exercised in the use of hand and rifle grenades. Company QMS Duncan and Acty Sergt T. Hubbard awarded Distinguished Conduct Medal for gallantry on 14th November.	
30-12-14	Remained in Billets at LOCRE. 2nd Lieut. H. INGOLDBY and 2nd Lieut M.D. WILSON reported off leave from England.	
31-12-14	The Battalion relieved the 1st Royal Scots in the trenches during the evening. There was a heavy burst of fire from the enemies lines about 11-0pm (receiving time 1/2-0 mn (human time)) and ringing was heard from German trenches. The French batteries also opened fire in reply. Casualties Nil	

3rd Division
9th Infantry Brigade
1st Lincolnshires

From 1 July To October 1915
To 62nd Bde 13 November 1915

To 21 DIV. 62 BDE

9th Bde.
3rd Div.

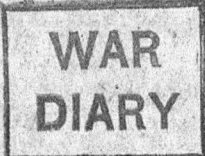

1st LINCOLNSHIRES

July

1915

On His Majesty's Service.

Army Form C. 2118

1st Battn Lincolnshire Regt.

WAR DIARY
or
INTELLIGENCE SUMMARY.
(Erase heading not required.)

Instructions regarding War Diaries and Intelligence Summaries are contained in F.S. Regs., Part II. and the Staff Manual respectively. Title pages will be prepared in manuscript.

Hour, Date, Place		Summary of Events and Information	Remarks and references to Appendices
1.	15	The Battn. remained in Bivouac and rested.	
2.	15	Parades were held during the day. Physical Drill, Rifle Exercises & Field training were carried out. The Grenadier Section received special instruction. The Bermuda V.R. Contingent was inspected by the Commanding Officer. A draft of 128 other Ranks joined.	
3.	15	The Battn. paraded at 9.30 am and was inspected by the Brigadier. Other parades were held as on previous day.	
4.	15	The Battn. was On Duty from reveille until reveille 5th. Parades carried out as usual. Lincolnshire Territorial Band played in our camp during the evening.	
5.	15	Parades carried out as usual. 2nd Lt G.M.S. BRUCE & 2 Lieut A.T. HARRIS joined.	

Forms/C. 2118/10

Army Form C. 2118.

WAR DIARY
or
INTELLIGENCE SUMMARY.
(Erase heading not required.)

1st Bn Lincolnshire Regt

Hour, Date, Place	Summary of Events and Information	Remarks and references to Appendices
6. 7. 15.	Lieut H. T de la MOTTE joined. Parade as usual were carried out.	
7. 7. 15.	Usual parades were held.	
8. 7. 15.	Usual parades were held. The enemy fired six shells into BUSSEROOM, no damage resulted. D.C. Medals were awarded to No 7970 Cpl DAVIS F. and No 7113 A/Cpl BREEZE E for Gallantry on 24. 8. 15. at FRAMERIES.	
9. 7. 15.	The Batt" was on "Duty" from reveille until reveille 10th. Parade were held as usual. A draft of 30 O.R. joined.	
10. 7. 15.	The usual parades were held. A reinforcement of 6 Machine Gunners joined.	
11. 7. 15.	Divine service parade at 10.30 am. Capt W L FENWICK joined.	

Army Form C. 2118

WAR DIARY
or
INTELLIGENCE SUMMARY.
(Erase heading not required.)

1st Batt: Lincolnshire Regt

Instructions regarding War Diaries and Intelligence
Summaries are contained in F.S. Regs., Part II.
and the Staff Manual respectively. Title pages
will be prepared in manuscript.

Hour, Date, Place	Summary of Events and Information	Remarks and references to Appendices
12. 7. 15.	Parades were held as usual. 2nd Lieut M CHURCHOUSE and 2nd Lieut J EDES joined.	
13. 7. 15.	Parades were carried out as usual. Fine summer weather has prevailed from the beginning of the month. The Baths was on Duty from Reveille. C. O. Inspection parade held at 9am.	
14. 7. 15.	The Batt: paraded at 8-0pm and proceeded via MILLE CHAPELLE and DICKEBUSCH to relieve dug-outs in RIDGE WOOD, with Headquarters in GORDON FARM (N5a. 4ca) relieving the 1st Middlesex Regt. The relief was carried out in a heavy rain and was completed at 12 midnight. Casualties, nil.	
15. 7. 15.	Working parties were employed on redoubt at the Brasserie (N6a 2.2) making fire & communiks. Reinforcements of 20 O.R. joined at DUSSEROOM. Weather fine. Casualties nil.	

Army Form C. 2118.

WAR DIARY
or
INTELLIGENCE SUMMARY.

(Erase heading not required.)

1st Batln Lincolnshire Regt.

Hour, Date, Place	Summary of Events and Information	Remarks and references to Appendices
16. 7. 15.	Working parties were employed as yesterday. Draft with other details joined from BUSSEBOOM. Two whom guns on our front during day. Burst of rapid rifle fire occurred between 10 p.m & 10-30 p.m. Weather showery during day. Heavy rain at night. 2nd Lieut. G.M. ROWLAND and 2nd Lieut. W.B. DUNCAN joined.	
17. 7. 15.	Working parties continued as yesterday. The day passed quietly. Strong west wind. Heavy Rain. Weather.	
18. 7. 15.	Working parties were employed as yesterday. Ridge Wood was occasionally shelled during the day. Casualties 1 O. of wd. 1 wounded Weather fine. Strong westerly winds.	
19. 7. 15.	The work at Ridgewood and vicinity was continued. Ridgewood was shelled by enemy. Casualties O.R. 1 wounded.	

Army Form C. 2118.

WAR DIARY
or
INTELLIGENCE SUMMARY.

(Erase heading not required.)

1st Bn Lanarkshire Regt

Instructions regarding War Diaries and Intelligence Summaries are contained in F.S. Regs., Part II. and the Staff Manual respectively. Title pages will be prepared in manuscript.

Hour, Date, Place	Summary of Events and Information	Remarks and references to Appendices
20. 7. 15.	The work on the Defences was continued. Enemy shelled our position in reach of our Batteries. Enemy aeroplane also much in evidence during the day. Casualties Nil Weather fine. Strong West wind.	
21. 7. 15	Working parties were employed as previously. Infantry on our front engaged with heavy bursts of rifle fire towards midnight. Weather fine. S.W. wind. Casualties nil	
22. 7. 15	Work was continued on Reserve Defences vicinity. Enemy shelled vicinity of our position at intervals several shrapnel shell bursting on our right. Weather fine during day, showers at night. Moderate S.W. wind. Casualties Nil	2nd Lieut F W CLIFTON & R R WATT joined

Forms/C. 2118/10

Army Form C. 2118.

WAR DIARY
or
INTELLIGENCE SUMMARY.
(Erase heading not required.)

1st Roth Lincolnshire Regt.

Instructions regarding War Diaries and Intelligence Summaries are contained in F.S. Regs., Part II. and the Staff Manual respectively. Title pages will be prepared in manuscript.

Hour, Date, Place	Summary of Events and Information	Remarks and references to Appendices
23.7.15.	Work on defences carried on as yesterday. One company of Manchester Regt. (32nd Bde) this a'noon was attached to the Batn. for instruction. Weather cool & showery. Strong S.E. wind. Casualties nil.	
24.7.15.	Work was continued on Reserve defences. Parties of Manchester Regt. were attached to our working parties. Artillery fire was exchanged occasionally during the day. Enemy's shrapnel fired over our own dug-outs near Neuvegaten. Towards evening enemy aeroplane were much in evidence, 1 were shelled by our anti aircraft guns. Weather Cool. Occasional showers. Strong S.E. wind. Casualties nil. The Transport moved from RUSSEROOM to a position between OUDERDOM and REMINGHELST G 35 a 8.8. 27 O.Rank Reinforcements joined.	

Army Form C. 2118.

WAR DIARY
or
INTELLIGENCE SUMMARY.
(Erase heading not required.)

1st Bn Lincolnshire Regt.

Hour, Date, Place	Summary of Events and Information	Remarks and references to Appendices
25. 7. 15.	The Working Parties were employed as yesterday. All was quiet on our front. Weather cool & showery. Casualties nil.	
26. 7. 15.	Working Parties continued their work on defences. Conditions quiet during day. About 6 p.m. the enemy heavily bombarded the area to our right with large high explosive shell. Several fragments fell on Headquarters farm & vicinity. Our Artillery replied & the shell continued intermittently until midnight. Several bursts of rapid rifle fire occurred on our front and the Bn stood to Arms. Casualties O.R. 1 wounded. Weather fine & cool. No. 13985 Pte CRESSWELL A, awarded D.C. Medal for gallantry & devotion to duty during the action at HOOGE 16. 6. 15. [signature]	

WAR DIARY or INTELLIGENCE SUMMARY.

(Erase heading not required.)

Army Form C. 2118.

1st Bn Lincolnshire Regt.

Hour, Date, Place	Summary of Events and Information	Remarks and references to Appendices
27. 7. 15.	Work was continued on the defences. All was quiet on our front until midnight when a mine was exploded by our engineer. The Bathe standing to arms. Weather cool & showery. Casualties, nil.	
28. 7. 15.	Work continued on defence. Condition quiet on our front. Weather cool. Slight showers.	
29. 7. 15.	Work continued on defence. Conditions on our front remain quiet. Weather fine. Strong S.W. wind.	
30. 7. 15.	About 3 P.M. heavy rifle & whilling fire was heard on our left. The Battn stood to arms. The firing died out again during the afternoon & again toward midnight. Work was continued, the whole Battn being employed by day or night. Casualties, Nil. Weather fine. Strong S.W. wind.	

Form C. 2118/10

Army Form C. 2118

WAR DIARY
or
INTELLIGENCE SUMMARY.

(Erase heading not required.)

1. Enclosure Reg.

Instructions regarding War Diaries and Intelligence
Summaries are contained in F. S. Regs., Part II.
and the Staff Manual respectively. Title pages
will be prepared in manuscript.

Hour, Date, Place		Summary of Events and Information	Remarks and references to Appendices
31.	15	Work was continued on the Reserve Defences. On our front all was quiet. On the left artillery on both sides were very active. Enemy aeroplanes flew over our position in the evening & were shelled by anti-aircraft guns. Weather fine. Courcelles Vole. WP.	

9th Bde.
3rd Div.

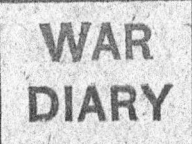

1st LINCOLNSHIRES

August

1 9 1 5

On His Majesty's Service.

Army Form C. 2118.

WAR DIARY
or
INTELLIGENCE SUMMARY.
(Erase heading not required.)

1st Battn Lancashire Regt

Hour, Date, Place	Summary of Events and Information	Remarks and references to Appendices
1. 8. 15	An order having been received that the Battn would be relieved at night, the work on the defences was not carried on further. The relieving unit was the 12th Battn Manchester Regt (52nd Bde) Casualties Nil	
2. 8. 15	The relief was completed at 1-0 am. The Battn marched via Dickebush to bivouac at G.35.a.8.8. arriving about 2-30 am. The Battn had been relieved in order to take up a position of the firing line in the YPRES Salient where the enemy had been making a big new turning liquid on the British. After resting and refitting the Battn paraded at 3-25 pm and marched through OUDERDOM by road to H.14.f. thence across country to H.16.c, then by road through H.10.c. H.11 central to YPRES skirting round the north of the city and crossing on the POTIJZE ROAD and continuing to the trenches at C.29 a central.	

Army Form C. 2118.

1st Battn Lincolnshire Regt

WAR DIARY
or
INTELLIGENCE SUMMARY.
(Erase heading not required.)

Instructions regarding War Diaries and Intelligence Summaries are contained in F. S. Regs., Part II. and the Staff Manual respectively. Title pages will be prepared in manuscript.

Hour, Date, Place	Summary of Events and Information	Remarks and references to Appendices
2. 8. 15 (continued).	During the march a heavy thunderstorm came on making marching conditions very unpleasant.	
3. 8. 15	The Battn relieved the 2nd Durham L.I. The relief being completed about 1-0 a.m. Headquarters in dug-out near POTIJZE CHATEAU. A Coy in A8 fire trench, D Coy & BHQ in A7 fire trench. B Coy in X4 and C Coy in X5 support trenches. Condition normal on our front. At about 7-0 a.m. our artillery bombarded the enemy trenches to our right for 1 hour. An intermittent exchange of artillery fire ensued during the day. Several "whiz bangs" burst near Headquarters. Casualties: Other Ranks, 1 wounded. Weather — showery. SM wound.	
4. 8. 15	Condition normal on our front. Working parties from Companies in support carried on improving	M

WAR DIARY or **INTELLIGENCE SUMMARY.**
(Erase heading not required.)

Army Form C. 2118.

1st Battn Lincolnshire Regt

Hour, Date, Place		Summary of Events and Information	Remarks and references to Appendices
4.	15. (Continued)	Communication trenches etc during the day. Went on fire trench was carried out at night. Artillery duel occurred at intervals during the day. Intermittent artillery fire at night. Casualties other Ranks 16 wounded. Weather showery. SW wind.	
5.	15.	The day passed quietly. Improvements to trenches continued. Hostile aeroplane were very active all day & were shelled by our a/a aircraft guns. Casualties other Ranks wounded. Weather dull.	
6.	15.	Conditions normal on our front. Artillery on both sides very active all day. Several "whiz bang" shells over headquarter dug-out. Sent twenty large High Explosive shells burst on the road in our right. Casualties OR 3 wounded. Weather dull.	

Form/C. 2118/10

Army Form C. 2118.

WAR DIARY
or
INTELLIGENCE SUMMARY.
(Erase heading not required.)

1st Batt^n Lincolnshire Regt

Instructions regarding War Diaries and Intelligence Summaries are contained in F. S. Regs., Part II. and the Staff Manual respectively. Title pages will be prepared in manuscript.

Hour, Date, Place	Summary of Events and Information	Remarks and references to Appendices
7. 15.	The enemy shelled our front line of trenches between 4-5 am and 6-8 am causing several casualties. Artillery on both sides were active all day. Several enemy shells burst among Headquarters dug-outs but no damage was caused. Improvements to trenches were continued. Casualties Other Ranks 14 wounded.	
8. 15.	Situation normal on our front in the morning. The work of strengthening our position was continued by the enemy. In the afternoon the enemy shelled our trenches with "whizz bangs" and LIEUT H.C. DISBROWE was severely wounded. Enemy aeroplane were much in evidence. Owing to recent rain the trenches became very wet in places, necessitating further flooring and revetting. Casualties Officer 1 wounded, Other R. Killed 9 wounded. Weather dull & showery all day. M.	

WAR DIARY or INTELLIGENCE SUMMARY.

(Erase heading not required.) 1st Batt. Lincolnshire Regt.

Army Form C. 2118.

Hour, Date, Place	Summary of Events and Information	Remarks and references to Appendices
8.-15.	Tondition normal in the morning, about 2-0 pm the enemy shelled the village of ST JEAN with large shells. The trenches in our right were also shelled. The enemy kept moving along to our position, inflicting casualties on our working party. The enemy snipers were busy in the evening. Snipers' posts had been established in our position and our snipers succeeded in keeping down the enemy's. The transport conveying rations for the Batt. was caught by the enemy's shell fire during the night on the YPRES — POTIJZE ROAD wounding Trans: Corp. Gr. Sergt and a driver. Lieut R P NASH R.A.M.C. the Battalion Medical Officer was wounded by a splinter from a "whiz bang". Capt. C. JACOBS R.A.M.C. (Gunner) I took over duties of Medical Officer to the Batt. Casualties. 1 Killed 12 Wounded (other Ranks) 1 Officer wd. Weather. Mild & cloudy. Wind S.W. Reinforcements joined 11 O Rank. (6 Machine Gunners & 5 Signallers)	

Army Form C. 2118.

WAR DIARY
or
INTELLIGENCE SUMMARY.
(Erase heading not required.)

1st The Lincolnshire Regt.

Hour, Date, Place	Summary of Events and Information	Remarks and references to Appendices
10. 8. 15.	Conditions normal on our front. Intermittent exchange of artillery fire on our right all day. Reinforcement of 11 other Ranks (6 Machine Gunners & 5 signallers) joined the Battalion at OUDERDOM. Casualties O.R. 2 wounded. Weather fine. S.W. wind.	
11. 8. 15.	There was a heavy mist at dawn, but the atmosphere cleared rapidly about 10·0 a.m. when the weather became high[?] warm. At midday the enemy commenced shelling the village of P.071372E with light shells, and gradually shortened the range until reaching our trenches which were heavily shelled. Damage was done to dug-outs and several large hits were directed down two communication trenches and fire trenches were being banged and a working party suffered casualties. The shelling continued intermittently until dusk. B & C Coy relieved A & D Coy from the fire trenches at night. Casualties O.R. 3 killed 8 wounded.	

WAR DIARY
INTELLIGENCE SUMMARY.
(Erase heading not required.)

1st Batn Lincolnshire Regt.

Army Form C. 2118.

Hour, Date, Place	Summary of Events and Information	Remarks and references to Appendices
8. 12. 15.	Conditions on our front normal. About midday enemy's artillery shelled the wood in rear of our H.Q. Our artillery were active all day. During the afternoon enemy shelled road to Brigade Dump. Drawing of tanks was carried out by Companies in support. Our Machine Gun detachments were relieved by the M.G Detachments of 7th The Rifle Bde in the evening. Casualties. O.R. 1 killed 4 wounded. Wire dummies weaker. Light S.W. Breeze.	
8. 13. 15.	All quiet during the morning. Weather brighter, warmer light S.W. Breeze. At about 2.20 pm the enemy commenced shelling the wood between support trenches and N.Q. and also shelled the gas dug-outs with light charges. A report came from D Company in the support trenches that the enemy were using gas-shell. Anti-Shells were quickly adjusted and were effective in preventing the fumes from doing any harm other than a slight irritation of the eyes. Conditions became quiet about 4-15 pm. O.K.	

Forms/C. 2118/10

WAR DIARY
or
INTELLIGENCE SUMMARY.
(Erase heading not required.)

1st Bn. Lincolnshire Regt.

Army Form C. 2118.

Hour, Date, Place	Summary of Events and Information	Remarks and references to Appendices
13. 8.15 (continued)	The Bn. was relieved towards midnight by the 7th Battn Rifle Bde. Casualties 1 killed 2 wounded.	
Summary.	The extension of front held by the Battn was about 350 yards. The distance between our fire - trench and the enemy varied from 400 yds to 600 yds. Communication trenches connected the fire trench and support trenches, and support trenches were about 150 yds in rear of fire trench. The support trenches were about 500 yds in rear of fire trench, Head Quarters were in a wood 250 yds in rear of support trenches. Headquarters could be approached during daylight without exposure to the enemy. The enemy systematically shell our position during the period with high-shells, otherwise conditions were normal.	

WAR DIARY or INTELLIGENCE SUMMARY.

(Erase heading not required.)

Army Form C. 2118.

1st Batt. Leicestershire Regt.

Hour, Date, Place	Summary of Events and Information	Remarks and references to Appendices
14. 8. 15	The Battn. marched back to OUDERDOM bivouac arriving about 3.30 am, and rested the remainder of the day.	
15. 8. 15	Companies were occupied in physical training from 7am to 9 am. No parade was held. Divine service for R.C.s in Reninghelst Church at 11.0 am; Church of England in 4th R.F. us Camp at 10.30 am. Dickebusch was shelled and two of our men attached to 2nd Divisional Salvage Company were severely wounded, afterwards both dying of their wounds.	
16. 8. 15	Companies were occupied in physical training from 7am to 7.45am. The remainder of the day inspections were carried out under Company etc Officers Arrangements. Weather dull & close.	

Army Form C. 2118.

WAR DIARY or INTELLIGENCE SUMMARY.

(Erase heading not required.)

1st Batt. Leicestershire Regt.

Hour, Date, Place	Summary of Events and Information	Remarks and references to Appendices
17. 8. 15.	The Baths were "on duty" from reveille until reveille 18.8.15. Parades were held as on previous day. Lieut. E.J. du C. Bagge proceeded to Base for temporary duty. 9 other ranks proceeded to be attached to 17th Tunnelling Coy. R.E. Weather dull & close in the morning, heavy rain from noon to 1 p.m., afterwards showery.	
18. 8. 15.	Parades were held as in previous day. Weather fine.	
19. 8. 15.	The Commanding Officer inspected the Baths by companies during the morning. The Baths paraded at 4:45 p.m. and marched via OUDERDOM to Road junction H14 & hence to KRUISTRAAT. Having the bivouacs of the 4th Battn. & 5th Battn. Leicestershire Regt. the march continued via bridge 14 and through communication trenches, which attain ZILLEBEKE LAKE, to SANCTUARY WOOD, where the Baths arrived about midnight. 1 casualtie, 1 wounded. Weather fine.	

(3 29 6) W4141—493 100,099 9/14 H W V   Forms/C. 2118/10

Army Form C. 2118.

WAR DIARY
or
INTELLIGENCE SUMMARY.
(Erase heading not required.)

1st Batt: Lincolnshire Regt

Hour, Date, Place	Summary of Events and Information	Remarks and references to Appendices
20. 8. 15.	The Batt: relieved the 1st Shropshires & occupied at about 2 am. B Coy occupied B4 fire trench. C Coy - B3 fire trench and D Coy B6 fire trench. A Coy, B7RC took up a position in B7 support trench. Headquarters in dug-outs in Sanctuary Wood. The 1st Bn R Berks Regt were on our right and 1st Batt: Royal Fus. (17th Bde) on our left. Between 6-30 & 7 am an enemy aeroplane appeared to be making a prolonged examination of our position. Other enemy aeroplanes were noted in evidence during the morning and were dealt with by our anti-aircraft guns. At 1-20 pm our guns opened a bombardment of the enemy's position about HOOGE & the MENIN RD. The enemy's guns replied to our fire; the duel continued until about 3-0 pm. Shell burst well from our guns dropped short pitching within 15 yds of B8 trench. The Brigadier visited the trenches held by the Bn during the afternoon. About 3 pm R Coy fired on a German working party & observed fire from B4 trench. M.	

Form/C. 2118/10

Army Form C. 2118.

WAR DIARY
or
INTELLIGENCE SUMMARY.
(Erase heading not required.)

1st Batln Inniskilling Regt

Instructions regarding War Diaries and Intelligence Summaries are contained in F.S. Regs., Part II. and the Staff Manual respectively. Title pages will be prepared in manuscript.

Hour, Date, Place	Summary of Events and Information	Remarks and references to Appendices
20. 8. 15.	The Machine Guns Detachment took over position from the Sherwood Foresters. Detachment about 40 officers. Two gun teams in Tpt and two in Tpt. Casualties 1 wounded. Weather fair.	
21. 8. 15.	Enemy aeroplane active all day, keeping the anti-aircraft guns busy. The enemy threw bombs into a listening post held by D Coy. Our bombers replied with a greater number and quietened the enemy. The day was rather quiet. Worked on trenches and entanglements carried out at night. Casualties 2 killed 1 wounded. Weather showery. Reinforcements 30 other ranks joined at OVERDOM.	
22. 8. 15.	Enemy aeroplane again very active. Conditions very quiet except upon shelling by anti aircraft guns. Officer of 1st Royal Scots Fusiliers visited the trenches in the afternoon. Casualties 1 OR wounded. Weather fine. (A)	

(9 29 6) W 4141—463 100,000 9/14 H W V Forms/C. 2118/10

WAR DIARY
or
INTELLIGENCE SUMMARY.

(Erase heading not required.)

Army Form C. 2118.

9th Batt. Hampshire Regt.

Hour, Date, Place	Summary of Events and Information	Remarks and references to Appendices
22. 8. 15.	The day passed very quietly, at night prior to relief the enemy threw bombs into B Coy trench, causing casualties. The Batt. was relieved about midnight by 1/4th East Yorkshire, and marched back to bivouac at OUDERDOM. Casualties. O.R. 3 killed 6 wounded.	
24 5. 15 Summary.	During the period 20th to 23rd August the Batt. occupied the trenches East of Sanctuary Wood with a frontage of about 350 yds. The distance between our fire trench and the enemy varies from 50 yds at one point to 100 – 400 yds. General condition generally. The close proximity of portion of the enemy line to 34 trench was responsible for occasional bombing on both sides. The support trench was covered by communication of fire trench and could be approached in daylight thence. The trenches could be approached in daylight from Headquarters without being seen by enemy. W.	

Army Form C. 2118.

WAR DIARY
or
INTELLIGENCE SUMMARY.
(Erase heading not required.)

1/4th Lincolnshire Regt.

Hour, Date, Place	Summary of Events and Information	Remarks and references to Appendices
24.8.15	The Baths renewed in Reserve at Dickebusch resting.	
25.8.15	Reinforcement of 6 Officers & 6 Machine Gunners joined. Companies were exercised in physical drill in the morning, and musketry parades were carried out under Company etc Officers arrangement.	
26.8.15	Parade as previous day. The Commanding Officer inspected the troops at 10.0 am. Lieut. J.E. IMPEY and Capt. M. FENWICK to Field Amb: sick. 2 Lieut F.W. CLIFTON takes up appointment of Machine Gun Officer. The Machine Gun Detachment and Reserve Machine Gunners paraded at 5-0 pm and proceeded to SANCTUARY WOOD in order to relieve Machine Gunners & Reserve of 1/4 Leicestershire during the following day. The Commanding Officer inspected the Baths by Companies etc, commencing at 9-0 am.	
27.8.15		

Army Form C. 2118.

1st Batt. Lincolnshire Regt.

WAR DIARY
INTELLIGENCE SUMMARY.
(Erase heading not required.)

Hour, Date, Place	Summary of Events and Information	Remarks and references to Appendices
27. 8. 15 (continued)	Lspr. J. W. G. HOPPER to Field Ambulance sick. The Batt. paraded at 5 pm and marched via OUDERDOM, KRUINSTRAAT, BRIDGE 14 and ZILLEBEKE to SANCTUARY WOOD relieving the 1st Royal West Surreys or about midnight. Casualties Nil.	
28. 8. 15	A Company occupied trenches B2 & B3 Fire trench. B Coy. B1 and B2 Fire trenches. D & RC manned redoubts. C company 24 and D company R5 in support. The frontage held by the Batn. was about 400yds and the distance to the enemy's front line was from 700 yards = to 250 yards. The shelling on both sides very active toward noon. Quiet in afternoon, but renewed about 6pm until 8 pm. Casualties, 1 killed 2 wounded. Weather fine.	
29. 8. 15	Condition quiet until noon when enemy shelled our front, no damage occurring. Artillery exchanged fire during afternoon.	

WAR DIARY
INTELLIGENCE SUMMARY
(Erase heading not required.)

Army Form C. 2118.

1st Battn Herefordshire Regt.

Hour, Date, Place	Summary of Events and Information	Remarks and references to Appendices
29. 8. 15. (continued)	Weather fine in morning. Heavy rain fell during the evening. Casualties. Nil	
30. 8. 15	Work on making communication trenches carried out before daylight. Day passed quietly. At 6-0 p.m enemy shelled a dummy trench to our left with high explosives. Casualties 3 wounded. Weather dull & cool	
31. 8. 15	The morning passed quietly. About 3-45 p.m. our anti aircraft and machine guns succeeded in bringing down an enemy aeroplane. The pilot however guided his machine down behind his own line. Another enemy aeroplane made a prolonged examination of our lines, although subjected to heavy fire from our anti aircraft machine guns. At 11.30 p.m. the Regt was relieved by the Border Regt (7th Rile) A. Company remaining in the trenches. The Regt marched back to bivouac in OUDERDOM & bivouac. Nil. N-	

9th Bde.
3rd Div.

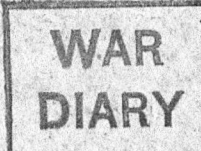

1st LINCOLNSHIRES

September

1915

On His Majesty's Service.

Army Form C. 2118.

WAR DIARY
or
INTELLIGENCE SUMMARY.
(Erase heading not required.)

1st Battn Lincolnshire Regt

Hour, Date, Place	Summary of Events and Information	Remarks and references to Appendices
1.9.15	The Battn arrived in bivouac schedule 2 am and not 7am and rested remainder of the day. Heavy rain fell during the whole of afternoon. Lieut A.E.C BAINES joined 31.8.15. 2nd Lieut S.S BANISTER joined 1.9.15.	
2.9.15	At 7.0 am preparations were commenced for moving into new bivouac in G17c 2.3 (28 map). The Battn paraded at 10 am and marched to new bivouac arriving about 11 am. Heavy rain commenced to fall at 7.0 pm and continued almost incessantly throughout the day, causing great inconvenience to all ranks, but the adverse weather conditions were endured cheerfully by all ranks. Lieut A STAPLETON left the Battn by order of 2nd Army Commander (70A/1000(C)) on medical grounds. He having served continuously with the Battn since it arrived with the Expeditionary Force in France on 13/8/14. Lieut J.E. IMPEY rejoined the Battn from Convalescent Depot. Capt H MARSHAL assumed duties of Actg Adjutant. A Company were relieved by a Company of 1st Northumberland Fusiliers and arrived at Battn bivouac about 7am 3rd Sept. Casualties. 1 killed, 1 wounded.	JM.

WAR DIARY
or
INTELLIGENCE SUMMARY

(Erase heading not required.)

Army Form C. 2118.

1st Battn Lincolnshire Regt

Hour, Date, Place	Summary of Events and Information	Remarks and references to Appendices
3. 9. 15	Heavy rain fell during the whole of the day causing the usual parades to be abandoned.	
4. 9. 15	Inspection parades held under Company arrangement. Machine Gunners and Grenadiers under their respective Officers and N.C.O.s paraded for instruction. Two working parties of 400 and 150 respectively were detailed for work during the night on defences and communication trenches in ZILLEBEKE area. They marched off in parties of 50 under an Officer at about intervals commencing at 5.0 p.m. and proceeded via KRUISSTRAAT, BRIDGE 14, and through one tunnel to MAPLE COPSE. Work was commenced under the direction of an R.E. Officer. Rain fell heavily greatly hampering the men in their work. Weather conditions necessitated that word should cease shortly after midnight and the parties marched back to bivouac. Casualties O.R. 2 wounded. Reinforcements 20 O.R. joined.	L.M.

Army Form C. 2118.

WAR DIARY
or
INTELLIGENCE SUMMARY.
(Erase heading not required.) 1/4th Berkshire Regt.

Hour, Date, Place	Summary of Events and Information	Remarks and references to Appendices
5.9.15	Showers fell during the day. The men, who were much fatigued owing to the adverse weather condition of the previous night remained in bivouac resting. Similar working parties were ordered for work on the ZILLEBEKE SWITCH to continue work commenced last night. These parties paraded about 5 p.m. and moved off at short intervals. The roads were in a very bad condition and marching was indeed very difficult. The men were kept on their work by rain and mud. The parties returned to bivouac early next morning, arriving about 5 am in a much fatigued condition. Casualties, OR 1 wounded. Lieut T.E. DES who was attached to 9th Brigade Machine Company was admitted to field ambulance severely wounded.	L.M.

Instructions regarding War Diaries and Intelligence Summaries are contained in F. S. Regs., Part II. and the Staff Manual respectively. Title pages will be prepared in manuscript.

(9 29 6) W 4141-463 100,000 9/14 HWV Forms/C. 2118/10

Army Form C. 2118.

WAR DIARY
or
INTELLIGENCE SUMMARY.
(Erase heading not required.)

1st Batn Lincolnshire Regt.

Instructions regarding War Diaries and Intelligence Summaries are contained in F.S. Regs., Part II. and the Staff Manual respectively. Title pages will be prepared in manuscript.

Hour, Date, Place	Summary of Events and Information	Remarks and references to Appendices
6. 9. 15.	The weather cleared up during the morning and remained fine during the rest of the day. A working party of 5.50 was ordered for work on ZILLEBEKE SWITCH where they previous worked. 150 at short intervals, commencing at 5.0 pm. Work was carried on throughout the night, weather conditions being greatly improved. The parties returned to bivouac during the early hours of the following morning. Casualties O.R. 1 wounded.	
7. 9. 15.	Fine summer weather all day. Two working parties of 150 and 100 were ordered for continuance of the work at ZILLEBEKE SWITCH. Parties marched off on 5's commencing at 5.0 pm at intervals. The men were carriage by train from the cross roads at F24.c to KRUISSTRAAT and marched from there to MAPLE COPSE. Work was continued on YEOMANRY POST and ZILLEBEKE defences. Casualties O.R. 1 wounded. Lieut H.T. de la MOTTE left for England.	F.M.

Army Form C. 2118.

1st Battn Lincolnshire Regt.

WAR DIARY or INTELLIGENCE SUMMARY
(Erase heading not required.)

Instructions regarding War Diaries and Intelligence Summaries are contained in F.S. Regs., Part II. and the Staff Manual respectively. Title pages will be prepared in manuscript.

Hour, Date, Place	Summary of Events and Information	Remarks and references to Appendices
8.9.15.	The Battn paraded at 3.0 pm and was inspected by Maj Genl Wallace (2nd Divisional Commander) who presented to Pte A CRESSWELL with a D.C.M ribbon. At 3.30 pm the Battn was inspected by the Army Commander - Lieut General Plumer. The Battn marched off at 3.45 p.m. (less A Coy & R.I.R.C. who returned to bivouac) and proceeded to the trenches in SANCTUARY WOOD, relieving the H.A.C. C Coy occupied C1 Fire Trench. B " " B8S D " " C1S & C1R R.S.1 " by 6 men of C Coy & 7 men of B Coy. Headquarters in dug-outs in MAPLE COPSE The relief was complete about midnight; 1st Worcesters on our left. Royal S. on our right. Casualties nil. Weather fine.	J.M.

Army Form C. 2118.

WAR DIARY
or
INTELLIGENCE SUMMARY.
(Erase heading not required.)

1st Bn Inniskilling Rgt:

Hour, Date, Place	Summary of Events and Information	Remarks and references to Appendices
9. 9. 15.	Day passed quietly. A Company provided working party of 50 for work on YEOMANRY POST during the night. Reinforcements of 25 O.R. joined in bivouac. Casualties O.R. 1 wounded. Weather fine.	
10. 9. 15.	Our artillery bombarded the enemy's trenches on our right front between 1-30 pm and 2-30 pm, demolishing about 20 yards of parapet. Enemy aeroplanes were active over our position during the afternoon. A Coy & DVRC found similar working party on Turneur night. Casualties O.R. 2 wounded. Capt: M. FENWICK rejoined from 2nd Lieut. Weather cool. Wind east. fine.	
11. 9. 15.	Quiet until 4-0 pm when the enemy bombarded the unoccupied area to left rear of C1 trench. Machine Gunners and Grenadiers returned during day by those of 4th Londons. Casualties Nil. Weather fine. Wind S.E. mod.	F.M.

Army Form C. 2118.

WAR DIARY
or
INTELLIGENCE SUMMARY.
(Erase heading not required.)

1st Battn Lincolnshire Regt.

Hour, Date, Place	Summary of Events and Information	Remarks and references to Appendices
12. 9. 15.	In the morning our artillery bombarded the enemy's trenches on our front. C Company relieved the R.I.F during this operation which lasted about 15 mins. Casualties if any, quite Casualties nil. The Batt. were relieved about 10-0 p.m. by 4th Bn Gordon Highlanders. A Company paraded at bivouac about 4 p.m. and proceeded to the trenches, occupying B3 trench.	
Progress summary	The Battn. spent in bivouac about 3 days and respecting the day. The frontage occupied by the Battn. during the period 8th-12th depth was about 200 yards. Distance to enemy fire trenche from 200yds to 300yds. Our support trench were connected to fire trench by communication trench, 0 fire trench were approached in daylight. On the night of 9th + 11th covering parties were formed by the Battn. for working parties of R.I.R. Worcester.	J.W.

Forms/C. 2118/10

Army Form C. 2118.

WAR DIARY
or
INTELLIGENCE SUMMARY.
(Erase heading not required.)

1st Batt. Lincolnshire Regt.

Hour, Date, Place	Summary of Events and Information	Remarks and references to Appendices
13. 9. 15.	The Battn arrived in bivouac about 3-0 am, and rested during the day. Cleaning & refitting also proceeded with.	
14. 9. 15.	Company Officers held usual inspections. A working party of 150 proceeded to ZILLEBEKE to continue work on defences at night. Casualties O.R. 1 killed 5 wounded. Capt R.J. TUCKER died of 2d Amb.	
15. 9. 15.	Battn remained in bivouac reorganising & refitting. Similar fatigue party found as on previous day. A Company relieved from trenches by a company of 3rd K.R. Rifles, and occupied dug outs in SANCTUARY WOOD. Casualties O.R. 1 killed 1 wounded. Reinforcements 20 O.R. joined. Weather fine.	
16. 9. 15.	Reorganising and refitting continued. Similar working party found as previously. Casualties Nil. Weather fine.	J.W.

WAR DIARY
or
INTELLIGENCE SUMMARY.
(Erase heading not required.)

1st Batt: Lincolnshire Regt

Army Form C. 2118.

Hour, Date, Place	Summary of Events and Information	Remarks and references to Appendices
17. 9. 15.	Baths still in trenches, working parties found as previously. 9014113 Cpl KING E. awarded D.C.M. Weather cloudy. Casualties nil.	
18. 9. 15.	The Baths paraded at 4-30pm to proceed to the trenches. D & B Companies were conveyed by buses to the chateau at Vlamertinghe, the remainder marching via usual route joined up with D & B Coys, and proceeded to the trenches previously held by the Batt, in SANCTUARY WOOD. D Coy occupied C1 fire trench and C1S. C Coy & TMRC occupied B8S. B Coy " " " " " RS1 A " " " " " Dug-out. Headquarters in dug-out at MAPLE COPSE. The relief was completed about midnight. Casualties nil. Weather dull, cool. Lieut A.N. T PERKINS admitted to Fd Amb. G.M.S. TRUCE " " " " " 2nd Lieut C.B SIPPE joined.	J.M.

WAR DIARY
or
INTELLIGENCE SUMMARY.
(Erase heading not required.)

1st Batt. Warwickshire Regt.

Army Form C. 2118.

Hour, Date, Place		Summary of Events and Information	Remarks and references to Appendices
19.	9.	15	Our artillery bombarded the enemy's trenches on our front from 9.40 am until 10-30 am. During the morning a bomb was dropped from an enemy aeroplane into Sanctuary Wood causing a casualty in the 4th R.F. From 5 pm to 5-70 pm the enemy bombarded our position with both high explosive shells and shrapnel which caused a few casualties and slight damage to trenches. Casualties O.R. 8 wounded. Weather fine but cool.	
20.	9.	15	At 11 am two enemy aeroplanes began shelling over Sanctuary Wood but were driven off by our anti-aircraft gun. C1 and C15 were clear during the morning to allow our artillery to range on enemy trenches on our front. During the afternoon our artillery heavily bombarded the enemy's position on our left front. All day the enemy's snipers were constantly shooting along the road near the dressing Station in Sanctuary Wood. Casualties Nil. Weather cool SE wind	F.W.

WAR DIARY or INTELLIGENCE SUMMARY.

Army Form C. 2118.

1 st Batt Lincolnshire Regt.

Hour, Date, Place		Summary of Events and Information	Remarks and references to Appendices
21.	9. 15.	An artillery duel occurred on our immediate left between 4 am & 6 am. At 6 am a British Biplane was observed engaging a German monoplane, but neither was brought down. Four bombs dropped in and near Kemmel Wood during the skirmish. 108th and 109th Field Batteries bombarded the enemy's lines 9.23 — 9.25 from 3.45 pm until 4.30 pm. To allow for this C.I. trench was evacuated during the bombardment. 6 Siege Battery bombarded enemy supports and one trench west of Khilog Castle during the same period. Casualties O.R. 1 killed 1 wounded. Weather Dull. Wind SE moist.	
22.	9. 15.	During the morning our artillery bombarded the enemy's trench on our front. The enemy's front line has been found on two or three occasions during the day to be almost evacuated, and containing only a few men on look-out. A working party at C.15 was seen by the enemy and shelled causing the party to endeavour L.M.	

Army Form C. 21

WAR DIARY
or
INTELLIGENCE SUMMARY.
(Erase heading not required.)

1st Roy Berkshire Regt

Hour, Date, Place	Summary of Events and Information	Remarks and references to Appendices
	into the trenches.	
	2.1 Trench evacuated at 3.50pm to allow our artillery to bombard the enemy line, on our front. The bombardment ceased about 4.45pm after which the enemy trench appeared to be very badly damaged. Casualties OR 2 wounded. Weather fine. Light S.E. winds.	
23. 9. 15.	Heavy bombardment of German line on our front from 4 am to 5 am, and from 12-0 noon to 1-30 pm. The enemy replied to our batteries ineffectively, his shells bursting mostly on unoccupied ground. Battn Headquarters moved to Sanctuary Wood in view of pending operations. The Suffolk (7th Bn) N.g. overlying the dug-out in Maple Copse. The Companies were relieved from the trenches and occupied support dug-outs in Sanctuary Wood. Casualties 1 killed 1 wounded. Light showers in the evening	F.M.

Army Form C. 2118.

WAR DIARY
or
INTELLIGENCE SUMMARY.
(Erase heading not required.)   1st Batt. Lancashire Regt.

Instructions regarding War Diaries and Intelligence Summaries are contained in F.S. Regs., Part II. and the Staff Manual respectively. Title pages will be prepared in manuscript.

Hour, Date, Place	Summary of Events and Information	Remarks and references to Appendices
24. 9. 15.	From 4 am to 5 am the enemy trenches were heavily bombarded. The Batt. remained in dug-outs in Sanctuary Wood. Heavy rain fell all day. Casualties Nil.	
25. 9. 15.	The bombardment of the enemy's lines by our artillery commenced at 3.40 am and was continued until 10.30 am. The enemy's artillery replied immediately and kept up a heavy fire all morning. Two mines at B4 and B1 were fired at 5.5 am after which the 4th Gordons & 1st R.S.F. rushed the first two enemy lines which were taken with little resistance. Our bombers reinforced the R.S.F. and took part in the hand to hand fighting which occurred while taking the enemy's 3rd line trenche. The captured trenche became unteneable owing to the heavy bombardment by the enemy's artillery. F.M.

WAR DIARY or INTELLIGENCE SUMMARY

Army Form C. 2118

1st Batt. Lincolnshire Regt.

Hour, Date, Place	Summary of Events and Information	Remarks and references to Appendices
26.	and were abandoned as unnecessary. 'C' Company reinforced the R.S.F. at 4-30 pm in our original front line. At 8.15 pm the Bn H.Q. took over the H.Q. dug-out from the R.S.F. and our Companies commenced the relief of R.S.F. Companies in the trenches. 'A' Company occupies F.3 line trench, 'B' Coy F.3 redoubt, 'C' Coy in reserve trench, 'D' Coy & R.P.C. in R (reserve) trench. Heavy rain fell all day & added to the difficulties of the operation. Casualties O.R. 1 killed, 18 wounded. 2nd Lieut. A.J. RAHLES-RAHBULA joined.	
9. 15.	Condition very quiet during the day. The Batt. was employed in repairing parapet & trenches, and on salvage work. Relieved at night by 4th Bn South Lancs Regt. H.Qrs, C & D Coys & R.V.R.C. billeted in ramparts at YPRES. A & B Coys proceeded to bivouac at G.17.c. Casualties O.R. 2 wounded. Weather. Morning cloudy, afternoon sunshine.	F.M.

Army Form C. 2118.

WAR DIARY
or
INTELLIGENCE SUMMARY.
(Erase heading not required.)

1st Batt. Lincolnshire Regt.

Hour, Date, Place	Summary of Events and Information	Remarks and references to Appendices
27. 10. 15. (?)	Nothing noteworthy occurred during the day. Headquarters and Europeans at Romford left Nr. about 9-30 p.m. and marched to bivouac at -F19C. Casualties Nil.	
28. 10. 15. (?)	The Batt. remained in bivouac. Weather showery.	
29. 10. 15. (?)	Rain fell almost continually throughout the day. No parade were held.	
30. 10. 15. (?)	At 1.45 p.m. a message arrived ordering the Batt. to proceed at once into reserve at NEUSTRAAT. The whole Batt. had marched off by 2-0 p.m. and occupied dug-outs at the abovementioned place. Casualties Nil. Weather showery.	L.M.

9th Bde.
3rd Div.

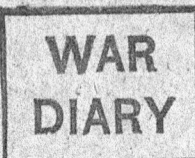

Battalion went to 63rd Bde., 21st Div 13.11.15.

1st LINCOLNSHIRES

OCTOBER 1915

On His Majesty's Service.

Army Form C.

WAR DIARY
or
INTELLIGENCE SUMMARY.

(Erase heading not required.)

1st Batt: Lincolnshire Regt.

Hour, Date, Place	Summary of Events and Information	Remarks and references to Appendices
1. 10. 15.	The Batt: remained in dug-outs at TRANSPORT acting as Divisional reserve until 1.45 pm when orders were received to move back to bivouac at G.17.c. The Batt: arrived in bivouac about 4.0 pm Weather Dull. Road muddy.	
2. 10. 15.	No parade held. The men bathed and attended to their arms, clothing & equipment.	
3. 10. 15.	Commanding Officers' inspection parade held at 9.15 am. Companies paraded independently to march to the trenches, at five minutes' intervals, 'A' company marching off at 4.0pm. The Batt: relieved the 9th Royal Fusiliers in the trenches most forward. A Coy occupied C4 and C5. and D Coy C6 and C7 fire trenches. B Coy occupied R55. BYPC-C7R support trench and B Coy in reserve dug-outs. Headquarters in dug-out at half way house. Carnoy Pit Weather Dull & Cool.	

Forms/C. 2118/10

WAR DIARY
or
INTELLIGENCE SUMMARY.
(Erase heading not required.)

Army Form C. 2118.

1st Bn Lincolnshire Regt.

Instructions regarding War Diaries and Intelligence Summaries are contained in F.S. Regs., Part II. and the Staff Manual respectively. Title pages will be prepared in manuscript.

Hour, Date, Place	Summary of Events and Information	Remarks and references to Appendices
4. 10. 15.	Quiet during morning. About noon C Company were shelled without casualties, being enemy's aeroplane of both sides active towards 4-5pm. Casualties, 1 OR wounded by sniper. Weather stormy in morning, during an afternoon.	
5. 10. 15.	A Company were bombarded by enemy's trench mortars & light field guns during the morning. Our artillery replied; the enemy cease fire. Fires from enemy's trenches heard, apparently caused by driving stakes. In the afternoon the enemy shelled in vicinity of Bellewaarde farm — three of the aeroplanes could be seen thereover. Casualties, O.R. 1 wounded. Weather cold. slight showers.	
6. 10. 15.	At 4-30 am enemy sent about 20 shells into neighbourhood of N of C.T. During the night A Coy were employed improving parapet of which had been destroyed by our own mines, and shells during the engagement of Sept 25th. Working parties commenced thinning of	

Army Form C. 2118.

WAR DIARY
or
INTELLIGENCE SUMMARY.
(Erase heading not required.)

1st Batt. Lincolnshire Regt.

Instructions regarding War Diaries and Intelligence Summaries are contained in F.S. Regs., Part II. and the Staff Manual respectively. Title pages will be prepared in manuscript.

Hour, Date, Place		Summary of Events and Information	Remarks and references to Appendices
6.	10.15.	Communication Trench "Regent St" which was one to two feet deep in mud and water. 3 platoons of B Company returned to trenches during the night. Casualties OR 1 wounded	
7.	10.15.	Considerable shelling of Zouave Wood by enemy in the afternoon. C Company relieved A Company in fire trench in the evening. One company of N. Staffs Regt attached to Batn for instruction in trench warfare. Weather fine. Light N.W. wind. Casualties OR 1 killed, 2 wounded. Lieut Engs PRICE reported from Base with 13 O.Ranks.	
8.	10.15.	The enemy shelled the Menin Road about 9 am. During the early morning a heavy artillery bombardment was heard to be in progress on our right. During the day the enemy on our front were heard working on their trench increasingly. Condition on our front remained quiet. Heavy engagement in progress all day on our right in direction of Kemmel. Weather fine. Casualties OR 2 wounded, 2nd Lieut H.T.A. SIMPSON joined.	

WAR DIARY
or
INTELLIGENCE SUMMARY.
(Erase heading not required.)

Army Form C. 2118.

1st Batln Lincolnshire Regt.

Hour, Date, Place	Summary of Events and Information	Remarks and references to Appendices
9. 10. 15.	Condition quiet on our front all day. Between 7.30 p.m. and 8.30 p.m. the enemy shelled the Menin Road and round our vicinity which we were by hayshoot. The company of Essex Regt which was relieved by another company of the same unit during the evening. Casualties O.R. 1 wounded. Weather cool and cloudy.	
10. 10. 15.	Quiet on our front all day. Heavy engagement heard to be in progress in the direction of Hanover from 12.30 p.m. until about 6.30 p.m. Enemy aircraft particularly active over our position during afternoon. A platoon of B company reinforced C company on fire trench in the evening. Casualties O.R. 1 killed, 2 wounded. Weather fine and very clear.	
11. 10. 15.	Menin Rd. shelled by enemy from 9 am to 9.30 am. Enemy aeroplane much in evidence during the morning, one being hit by our antiaircraft. The machine turned completely over, but made a	D.M.

Army Form C. 2118.

WAR DIARY
or
INTELLIGENCE SUMMARY.
(Erase heading not required.)

1st Batt: Lincolnshire Regt:

Hour, Date, Place	Summary of Events and Information	Remarks and references to Appendices
11. 10. 15.	wonderful recovery and escaped behind the enemy's lines. The engagement to the right still tend to be in progress during the day. The Batt: was relieved at night by 1st Northumberland Fusiliers, and proceeded to dug-outs at KRUISSTRAAT to act as Brigade Reserve. Casualties Nil. 2nd Lt: E. G. W. HANNING joined. Weather Fine & Clear.	
12. 10. 15.	Batt: remained in dug-outs at KRUISSTRAAT. Fatigues and Machine Gunners proceeded to Transport Line for bath and change. Weather cloudy. Slight showers during evening	
13. 10. 15.	Position as previous day. B and D Companies proceeded to Transport Line for bath and change. Slight showers.	
14. 10. 15.	Position as previous day. A and C companies proceeded for bath and change. Good Machine Gunners Weather dull. Batt: Guardian proceeded to trenches in relief of Grenadiers Hand Machine Gunners of 4th Bn: R.Fs	RFA

Army Form C. 2118.

WAR DIARY
or
INTELLIGENCE SUMMARY.
(Erase heading not required.)

1st Bn Lincolnshire Regt

Hour, Date, Place	Summary of Events and Information	Remarks and references to Appendices
15. 10. 15.	The Battn 2 Platoons of B Coy who returns to Turcoe to Marchant Wood, paraded at 5-15 pm. and proceeded to Marchant Wood, relieving 1/4 R.F. Relief completed about 11-30 p.m. A Company occupies C1 fire trench and C.1.S. B " " C3 " " " D " (2 Platoons) " C2 " " and R.S.3. C " " R.T., R.S.1, and R.S.2. B.v.R.C. " C.I.R. Headquarters in dug-outs at Zouave wood. Snipers, Grenadiers, and Sketcher Reserve at Tromency Road. Roads approaching position in very muddy condition. Weather showery. Casualties. O.R. 1 wounded. Reinforcements joined :- 47 other Ranks.	
16. 10. 15.	The enemy shelled C.I.R. trench from 5-0 a.m. until 5-20 a.m. with heavy mortars and light guns, no damage was occasioned. Remainder of day quiet. A mist caused observation impossible until 10 a.m. when the air became clear. One company of 8 K.R.O. R Lancaster Regt attached for instruction. Reinforced R.S.3 Casualties O.R. 1 wounded.	

Army Form C. 2118.

WAR DIARY
or
INTELLIGENCE SUMMARY.
(Erase heading not required.)

1st Battn Lincolnshire Regt.

Hour, Date, Place	Summary of Events and Information	Remarks and references to Appendices
17. 10. 15.	The enemy shelled C.3 trench from 12-45 p.m until 1-30 p.m causing considerable damage and several casualties. Our artillery retaliated and shell were seen to burst directly on the enemy trenches on our front. Casualties O.R. 1 killed, 7 wounded, also 3 O.R. of 8th York Regt killed.	
18. 10. 15.	Quiet in the morning. Between 3-30 p.m and 4 p.m enemy shelled area in vicinity of R.S.1., R.S.2., and R.S.3., with heavy howitzers at 2 second intervals. The projectiles coming from direction of Hill 60. No damage was incurred. About 6 p.m heavy artillery engagement heard from direction beyond Potinge. Enemy aeroplanes active over our position. Air very clear. 2 casualties nil.	
19. 10. 15.	Enemy aeroplanes very active at 7.0 a.m and our own aircraft much in evidence at daylight. At 4-30 p.m about 12 heavy howitzer shells coming from direction of Hill 60, exploded about C.1 trench. A company in C.1 were relieved by portion of D Company at night, and B Coy in C.3 relieved by rem of A Coy on R.S.3. Casualties O.R. 4 wounded, also 1 York Regt. killed.	

WAR DIARY
or
INTELLIGENCE SUMMARY.
(Erase heading not required.)

Army Form C. 2118.

1st Bn Loyalshire Regt

Hour, Date, Place	Summary of Events and Information	Remarks and references to Appendices
20. 10. 15.	During the night the enemy had apparently opened water flood down the beck to Cutroad. The enemy's BELLEWAARDE LAKE water gates, a large volume of objective being undoubtedly to flood the Menin Road Culvert and ZOUAVE WOOD. A message from 42nd Brigade (on left of gr Rifle) reported large volume of water coming into Canal near there H.E. Just N. of YPRES, which is the proper outlet. A 2nd report stated that there was no danger as the waters were taking the natural outlet and flowing into the Canal. Enemy shelled C.1 with light shells at 10-20 a.m. one bursting in an old M.G emplacement causing casualties. Conditions quiet remainder of day. Weather fine, air clear. Casualties. O.R. 4 wounded.	
21. 10. 15.	Quiet on our front. Enemy shelled portion of Sanctuary Wood on our right during morning. Reinforcement 20 O.R. joined. Many dug-outs were damaged. Casualties to Rathe & til. Weather fine.	

Army Form C. 2118.

WAR DIARY
or
INTELLIGENCE SUMMARY.
(Erase heading not required.)

1st Batt: Lincolnshire Regt:

Hour, Date, Place		Summary of Events and Information	Remarks and references to Appendices
22.	10. 15.	4th Bn Royal Fusiliers on our Left, 7th Bn Lincoln R on our right. At 3-30 pm Enemy shelled Menin Rd and in rear of C.1 from direction of Hill 60. Casualties O.R. 1 killed, 2 wounded. The Battn was relieved by 7th Yorkshire Regt at night and returned to bivouac. Roads dry and good condition. Weather fine.	
23.	10. 15.	After resting in bivouac during the day the Battn paraded at 5-30 pm. and marched to GODEWAERSVELDE via RENINGHELST and ROESCHERE, a distance of about 9 miles, arriving at 10 pm and billeted. Roads in good condition. Weather fine.	
24.	10. 15.	The Battn remained in billets resting. Rain fell at intervals during day and in the evening.	
25.	10. 15.	During the day the command met weather no parades could be held. Capt. W.L. FENWICK and 2nd Lieut A.J. RAHLES-RAHTULA sick to Field Ambulance.	

WAR DIARY
or
INTELLIGENCE SUMMARY.
(Erase heading not required.)

1st Battn Lincolnshire Regt

Army Form C. 2118

Hour, Date, Place	Summary of Events and Information	Remarks and references to Appendices
26. 10. 15.	The Battn was on duty from reveille until reveille 27th. Alarm Post at 9.17. to 10.5. (27 map). Companies baths at Divisional bath house. Platoon Drill and having canvas out by companies.	
27. 10. 15.	Parades for physical drill, platoon drill, instruction for N.C.Os and junior officers, were held. A section of 20 N.C.Os men under Lieut. R.M.S.TRYCE proceeded to STEENVOORDE and formed part of a Brigade Company which attended a Ceremonial Parade held before His Majesty the King. Weather showery. Reinforcement 5 O.R. joining.	
28. 10. 15.	A 10 miles route march for the Battn was ordered but was postponed owing to wet weather.	
29. 10. 15.	Battn paraded at 9.15 am and proceeded on route march going towards STEENVOORDE through CAESTRE and ECKE returning to billets about 1.45 pm. Weather fine. Roads rather muddy.	
30. 10. 15.	Parades for physical drill, platoon drill and company drill were held. Bombing, Machine Gunners & signallers instructed as usual. Lieut. J.W. CLIFTON sick to F. Amb.	
31. 10. 15.	Battn on duty from reveille until reveille 1/11/15. Devine Service by C of E, R.C. and Presbyterian	RM

www.ingramcontent.com/pod-product-compliance
Lightning Source LLC
Chambersburg PA
CBHW080824010526
44111CB00015B/2605